D0969582

158 CLE 2001

Cleland, Jane K.
Putting first what matter
most : proven strategies

PUTTING FIRST WHAT MATTERS MOST

PROVEN STRATEGIES FOR SUCCESS IN WORK AND IN LIFE

Jane K. Cleland

NEW AMERICAN LIBRARY

NAL Books

Published by New American Library, a division of

Penguin Putnam Inc., 375 Hudson Street, New York, New York 10014, U.S.A.

Penguin Books Ltd, 27 Wrights Lane, London W8 5TZ, England

Penguin Books Australia Ltd, Ringwood, Victoria, Australia

Penguin Books Canada Ltd, 10 Alcorn Avenue, Toronto, Ontario, Canada M4V 3B2

Penguin Books (N.Z.) Ltd, 182–190 Wairau Road, Auckland 10, New Zealand

Penguin Books Ltd, Registered Offices: Harmondsworth, Middlesex, England

First published by New American Library, a division of Penguin Putnam Inc.

First New American Library Printing, February 2001

10 9 8 7 6 5 4 3 2 1

 REGISTERED TRADEMARK—MARCA REGISTRADA

LIBRARY OF CONGRESS CATALOGING-IN-PUBLICATION DATA:

Cleland, Jane K.

Putting first what matters most : proven strategies for success in work
and in life / Jane K. Cleland.

p. cm.

ISBN 0-451-20248-1 (pbk. : alk. paper)

1. Success—Psychological aspects. I. Title.

BF637.S8 C5224 2001

158—dc21

00-060088

Printed in the United States of America

Set in Garamond Light

This book is printed on acid-free paper. ∞

CONTENTS

✦

Chapter Six. *Know Your* Unspoken Expectations   172

Chapter Seven. *Evaluate Priorities—Time and Significance*   209

INTRODUCTION

✦

Success Starts with a Dream

What You Want Is Clearly in Sight

Wouldn't it be great if you could move confidently through each day, in control of your time and energy? Picture yourself walking with a bounce in your step and a smile on your face. Imagine what it would be like to know you're accomplishing all that *you* want to do.

Does it ever seem as if your every move is dictated by other people? Do you sometimes feel as if each waking moment is consumed by the minutia of day-to-day life, that your actions are prescribed by events beyond your control? It doesn't have to be that way. Long ago Henry David Thoreau wrote, "The mass of men lead lives of quiet desperation." If those words ring true for you, this book can help.

Using the techniques described here, which have been tested and proven to work by thousands of people just like you, you can achieve success in all aspects of your life. This book won't help you become the fastest rat in the rat race. It will help you to accomplish what really matters to you, to live a life that's full and satisfying. No longer will you feel as if you're floating rudderless down the stream of life. Instead, you'll be in control, making

decisions with confidence, secure in the knowledge that your actions are moving you ever closer to realizing your dreams.

It's hard to find the time and energy to pursue our dreams.
Many people report that they face tougher workplace expectations than ever before, and family obligations that seem unend-
ing. But by using the step-by-step approach in this book you can
join the men and women who enjoy their jobs and have satisfying relationships. It's true! You can be among the people who
wake up eager to begin each day.

Overwhelmed? You're Not Alone

Most people report that they're working longer and harder
than ever before. You know who you are. Haven't some of you
been downsized, reengineered, reorganized, or right-sized to
within an inch of your lives? Aren't some of you doing jobs that
used to be done by two or even three people? Given the reality
of American business and culture in the twenty-first century, the
pressures are going to get even worse.

- Consolidation within many industries means that employees can no longer expect cradle-to-grave job security. Paternalism has given way to impersonal profit-driven
  decision-making.
- Organizations value productivity, efficiency, and systemization over individual needs or desires. It's hard to feel part
  of a team when success is defined by the bottom line.
- Technological advances contribute to the problem. Sometimes it seems impossible to keep current. It's as if new
  products and software are obsolete as soon as you learn to
  use them. And with every reorganization come new systems and procedures. The pressure to keep up is constant.
- Expectations are higher than ever. With streamlined processes and cutting-edge technology, corporate standards
  have risen. You're expected to produce more output of
  higher quality while using fewer resources.
- More and more information is more and more readily avail-

able. Maybe you feel you *ought* to take advantage of the abundance, and feel guilty when you don't. And it's all happening faster than ever.

- Flexible schedules, telecommuting, and job-sharing arrangements require employees to change long-familiar habits.
- Longer hours are the norm. According to the United States Department of Labor, we're working eleven percent longer than we were ten years ago.

In addition to business issues, complex family relationships force people to make choices in no-win situations.

- Blended families often require logistical juggling acts. Co-ordinating parent-to-parent visits is tricky enough. The fact that kids are participating in more and more activities can create scheduling nightmares.
- Frequent relocations require that we travel farther and more often to visit relatives and friends. Even suburban sprawl becomes an issue as longer commutes become the norm.
- More frequent relocations translate into less support. Long-term friends are the exception, not the rule. Trusted family members may be far away. More and more people report feeling on their own.
- Volunteerism is up. You want to participate in community activities, and many of you are doing so—another demand on your time and energy.
- Opportunities for leisure activities seem boundless, especially in an age of prosperity. You're expected to take advantage of the options, and you may feel deprived if you don't. Leisure time has not been cut. Sleep has.
- Sleep deprivation makes concentration harder. People are more vulnerable to stress and accidents.

As you scan the points above, do you recognize yourself or your situation? Between social pressures and professional and personal responsibilities, you may be convinced that there's no escape. None of us wants to become a better robot, working ever more efficiently on tasks that have no meaning for us. But if you're like most people you would like to:

- take your dreams and turn them into reality
- figure out your big-picture goals and learn how to achieve them
- juggle priorities, especially when yours seem to conflict with other people's
- manage your time and energy effectively so that you can pursue several priorities simultaneously

This book provides the answers you seek. You'll learn how to regain control of your life and refocus your efforts so that everything you do contributes to outcomes that *you* desire.

You *Can* Achieve Your Goals

Chances are that you have a good work ethic. People with a good work ethic tend to be competent and uncomplaining. They work hard. They work efficiently. They get a lot done. Is this you?

Have you ever noticed what happens to people with a good work ethic? They get more work! Some of you are reading this book hoping to pick up some ideas on how to become more productive, organized, or efficient. The truth is that you may not need help doing your job more productively—you just need help! For you, this book offers a tried-and-true method for acquiring the resources you need, whether it's approval for a larger staff at the office or a car pool arrangement that works better with your schedule.

Only you can define what you want to accomplish. Think about it. It's up to you—each of you—to determine your own priorities. No book can do that for you. But what it can do is to provide you with:

- strategies to convert your dreams into specific and achievable goals
- tactics to convert your goals into action steps

- shortcuts to manage your time and energy efficiently
- tips to help you motivate yourself

You'll meet people in these pages who are just like you, people who work and have families and who are struggling to give their best efforts to both. Like you, they're working longer hours, and many report that they're feeling overwhelmed, even out of control. Whether you are considering a major life change or a small readjustment, you'll learn approaches here that will make the change manageable.

This book will help you no matter what your circumstances. Do you seek funds for your Internet start-up company, or are you trying to justify adding new equipment at work? Are you considering a new career, one that requires going back to school, and you're wondering how you'll support your family during the transition? Or have you been a stay-at-home mom who's now ready to reenter the work force? Whatever it is that you wish were true in your life, the strategies in this book will help you identify it and make it happen. By using the systematic approach to defining, communicating, and accomplishing tasks that is detailed in this book, you'll achieve success—however you define it.

Maybe you have long known what you want, but have no idea how to get it. That was Tina's dilemma. "My problem is frustration," she explained. "I'm incredibly frustrated. Not frustrated with my job. I like what I do. It's just that I have a dream. I want to see the world. Yeah, right. On a hairdresser's salary? I don't think so."

Or maybe you're recently divorced and want to begin a new social life. Or have become disabled and must find a new career, one that doesn't require physical labor. Perhaps you're in a relationship—at home or, like Glenna, at work—that unexpectedly ends. "I certainly didn't plan on quitting my job," Glenna said. "It happened because of an issue on which I felt I had to stand firm. But it sure turned my world topsy-turvy."

Maybe you need to address a smaller or more specific issue. "My problem is my boss," explained Helene. "He's a great guy, and terrific at what he does, but he's so disorganized, he's driving me crazy and making me look bad in the office, as if I'm the one who's disorganized. In order to manage my priorities, I have to help him become more efficient. How can I do that? What system works best for someone like him?"

"I get myself in trouble," Carlos said, "because I have so much trouble saying no. I'm spread so thin, I'm surprised you can't see through me."

"I hate to write," explained Hal. "I have this huge project on my desk—to write a procedure manual. I've become completely inert, and I don't know how to deal with it. I know what my priority is: writing the manual. But knowing the priority and acting on it are two separate things. What can I do to motivate myself?"

What are the problems you face? Do you hate your work and wish you could find a new career? Do you need to jump-start your social life? Do you have a dream that seems unattainable, like Tina? Are you facing an untenable situation, and thinking about quitting your job or leaving a relationship, like Glenna? Is there someone with whom you work who's making your job harder, like Helene? Do you have trouble saying no, like Carlos? Is there an aspect of your job that you hate so much that you procrastinate, like Hal?

Or do you have to deal with multiple bosses, conflicting priorities, demands from both home and work that are pulling you in many directions? Do you have impossible deadlines? Whatever your particular concerns are, you'll meet people in these pages who have faced the same dilemmas, and who have successfully met the challenges. You'll meet Tina, Glenna, Helene, Carlos, Hal, and more than a hundred other people in this book, people who succeeded in dealing with issues big and small. You'll learn from their experiences. You'll celebrate their accomplishments.

Each of you reading this book is doing so for a different set of reasons. While your specific situation may vary, the underlying issues are universal. Using the techniques, or "tools," detailed in this book will help you achieve your goals. You'll refer to the book over and over again as you integrate the tools into your daily living.

Success isn't an accident. Achievement is the natural outcome of doing things sequentially, one task after another. The tools presented here will help you avoid traps that commonly inhibit success. Applying the principles you'll learn is guaranteed to lead you to a more fulfilling and satisfying life, both personally and professionally.

An Easy-to-Use Step-by-Step Approach

The book is divided into two parts. In Part One you'll discover how to communicate effectively with people of varying personality styles. As you become skillful at recognizing other people's types, you'll know how to "speak their language," and thus secure their cooperation and support quickly and efficiently. You'll learn techniques to ensure that others pay attention to your priorities.

Part Two addresses the actual priority-setting process. Various tools will help you sort through competing, even conflicting priorities. Perhaps, for example, you're walking through the office with two pieces of paper in your hand. Both pieces of paper relate to projects that are critical to your own and your company's success. How do you decide which one to work on first? What if you have many projects, all competing for your time and energy? How do you sort through them? What if your priorities change from day to day—or even from hour to hour? The strategies and techniques explained in the book provide the answers.

Taken together, the two parts of this book offer a step-by-step system. Using the system will enable you to take advantage of your strengths and avoid problems that spring from your weaknesses. The practical decision-making tools equip you with working models and safety nets. Your decisions won't be based on who's complaining the loudest, your gut instinct, or whimsy. You'll make decisions more quickly, and with confidence, and you'll be able to defend your decisions should you be challenged. You'll be perceived as efficient, organized, and productive. You will not simply *feel* more in control, you'll *be* more in control.

Change What You Do, Not Who You Are

Robert Crandall, retired chief executive officer of American Airlines, agreed with me that the importance of effective communication cannot be overemphasized. "The wisdom of changing what you say—and the ability to do so—comes with experience," he said in a recent conversation. "It works, so you do it. You can modify your words, change your vocabulary, shift your phrasing, all without affecting your core message."

Notice the emphasis placed on doing *what works*. Throughout the book you'll be reminded not to do things that don't work. To repeat an activity that didn't work the first time doesn't make any sense. Don't do things that aren't getting the results you want. Yes, persevere. Yes, give new behaviors a fair shot. But don't keep doing things that aren't working simply because this book says they will work, or because you think they *ought* to be done that way, or because you've *always* done them that way, or because you hope that if you *keep trying*, they will finally work. Be realistic.

Likewise, if something you're doing does work, keep doing it. Most adults find that it takes three to five weeks for any new behavior to become a habit. That's a long time to do something that doesn't *feel* right. Demonstrate this to yourself. On a blank sheet of paper, sign your name. Done? Now take the pen or pencil in *your other hand* and sign your name again.

Didn't it feel awkward? Does it look less polished than your regular signature? Is it even legible? What do you think would happen if you signed your name with your *wrong* hand several times a day for the next month or so? If nothing else, wouldn't it become a more familiar activity? That's the point. Applying the principles discussed in the book is going to feel awkward and strange at first.

As you'll see from the examples in every chapter, there is very little discussion of how people feel about what they're doing. This is not to denigrate your emotions, nor is it to suggest that feelings are irrelevant or inconsequential. Rather, it is to suggest that you maintain a proper perspective. Emotions should be viewed as one of many factors—not as the central point.

"That I didn't give in to my frustration is one of the things I'm most proud of," says Tina, the hairdresser who dreamed of travel. "As my frustration and hopelessness built up, depression became my constant companion. What I did was ignore it as best I could.

If I'd focused on my feelings, I never would have found the answer to my dilemma. All that would have changed is that I would have become bitter. In my case, my depression was situational, not chronic. As soon as my situation improved, the depression disappeared. And the proof is in the pudding, as they say. By focusing on behavior, not feelings, I was able to land a dream job." When you meet Tina again later in this book, you'll see how she did it. And you'll discover that the methodical, logical approach she used to achieve her dream will work for you too.

Here's the bottom line: this book is not about changing who you are or how you feel. It's about changing what you do. Not all flaws need to be fixed. Not all weaknesses need to be overcome. Armed with information about your abilities—good or bad—you can strive to optimize your strengths and compensate for your weaknesses.

In our society, we're told to face problems squarely, but that is not necessarily a good idea. For instance, if you're in a dark alley and someone comes running at you brandishing a lead pipe, do you want to face that problem? Most of us would turn and run in the other direction.

Let's say that you hate your boss and have been considering your options. You've thought of talking to someone in Human Resources, confronting your boss directly, requesting a transfer, or quitting. You decide to think about it over the weekend, come in on Monday, and act. You go to work on Monday, and your boss announces that he's just accepted a terrific new position and will be leaving in two weeks. Do you want to face the fact that you hate your boss and try to work it out? Most of us would keep our heads down and try to avoid him until he's gone.

Clearly, *some* problems need to be faced, but others need to be avoided, and from some problems you should run as fast as you can in the opposite direction.

An Opportunity to Pause and Assess Yourself

Throughout the book you'll be challenged to assess yourself and to evaluate the potential benefit of various strategies.

The assessments are intended to help you identify your strengths (so you can make the most of them) and your weaknesses (so you can avoid their potential to hurt you). They also give you a chance to try out the ideas offered.

When taking the assessments, follow the directions. Tell the truth. Answer the questions thoughtfully, but don't belabor any answer. There's never a right or wrong answer. In order to derive the most benefit, you need to avoid wishful thinking and a lack of focus. How can you identify what behaviors you want to change if you answer the assessments as you wish you were, not as you truly are? Given that the assessment is private, no one but you need ever know how you score yourself.

I urge you to participate actively as you read. When asked to think about something, pause in your reading and think. When invited to take an assessment, take it. When an exercise challenges you to use the tools, complete the exercise honestly. Take advantage of the opportunity to practice. You'll prove to yourself that you can use the tools presented. And you'll have fun!

Transformed Lives

Karen A. Polan, senior field specialist for First Energy in Ohio, wrote after attending my seminar, "I feel like I'm drowning at work, and through this material, the rescue boat is in sight and coming my way."

Your reward will be success—as you define it. Whether your dreams are big or small, you'll accomplish what you want to accomplish. People who have used the techniques presented in this book have transformed their lives, doubled their salaries, forged more meaningful relationships, found ways to better balance work and family, and changed jobs or started exciting new careers. They report that they're happier and more at peace than they ever would have believed possible. You'll meet many of them in the pages that follow. Join their ranks. Turn the page, and let's get started.

PART ONE

✦

Communicate Your Way to Peak Performance

CHAPTER ONE

Know Yourself

Communicate Well to Get Your Priorities Met

Managing priorities well requires that you get the best from others:

- the highest-quality work
- the most efficient and organized cooperation and support
- non-judgmental help

The cleverest time-management tools and organizational strategies won't help you manage priorities well unless you communicate them effectively to others so they'll help and not hinder your success. Let's say, for instance, that you want to:

- ✔ attend an optional, company-sponsored, three-week leadership training conference. Unless your neighbor agrees that she'll care for your children during your absence, attending would be impossible for you.
- ✔ join an expedition to climb Mt. Kilimanjaro. In order to take the leave of absence required, you need to win your boss's approval for the leave, inform your customers whom to contact in your absence in such a way as to retain their

loyalty, and receive your colleagues' assurance that they'll cover for you while you're gone.

✔ move to a new city after your divorce. Because you want to relocate right away, you need to receive expedited authorization from your company's personnel manager to transfer.

In all three examples, getting what you want requires cooperation and support from others. As you'll see, this is true in all aspects of our lives. Whatever your priorities are, managing them well requires that you interact effectively with other people. And effective interactions require the ability to make your points in a compelling manner. What one person finds compelling, however, is inevitably very different from what appeals to someone else. Furthermore, even with good intentions, people misunderstand one another all the time.

FAQ: *Do I have to change who I am to get along with my boss?*

A: No. Not at all. That's part of the beauty of my approach. You probably need to change some of what you *do*, but not who you *are*.

Simple adjustments to your message and delivery give you an enhanced chance of achieving success—however you're defining it. You will learn to modify:

● the words you choose
● when you deliver your message
● the emphasis you put on one issue or another
● your modes of communication

All of these factors and more play a role in whether people understand what you need from them and are motivated to help you.

Consider, for example, software analyst Edwina. "I needed to update Hillary, a vice president, about a meeting she had to miss. It was important for my work that she understood what was covered in the meeting, and expressed it to the client with enthusiasm.

"I told her that I wanted to 'share' what happened at the new client project meeting; I could see the impatience in Hillary's eyes. The look on her face said, 'Share? I don't think so.' I could tell she was wishing I'd get to the point. 'What was the bottom line?' that's what she wanted to know. Until I took Jane's seminar, I hadn't realized that she heard the word share as weak, unfocused, and touchy-feely. I had diminished myself in her eyes because she's work-oriented, forceful, and focused on the objective. I used that verb without thinking about it; to me, it just sounds right—it's how I talk. But now I understand that while it's my natural style and reflects the fact that I'm people-oriented, gentle, kind, and giving, it doesn't serve me well when I'm talking to people of different personality types."

Had Edwina simply changed her vocabulary, she would have had a much better chance of getting what she wanted. "Now I focus on the other person. I consciously adapt my communication style to fit what is most natural to them, not to me; it's amazing how much more cooperation I receive. If I had known and used this information with Hillary, I think it's likely that she would have enthusiastically supported my position to the client. Instead, she spoke the words, but she neither felt nor conveyed excitement." In other words, Edwina's priorities weren't served.

Sometimes the consequences are more severe. Stanley H. Kaplan, founder of the test-preparatory company that bears his name, built his company from a one-person operation to four thousand employees; he excelled at getting the best from others. But he hates to hear the word share.

"Of course it matters what words you use!" he told me in an interview. "When someone wants to 'share' something with me, I immediately suspect that they have an ulterior motive. I wonder to myself—if they're a smart person, why are they putting it that way? I hear the word share, and I feel as if it's a ploy. . . . I suspect that they're trying to grab me." Notice that Mr. Kaplan doesn't merely respond negatively to the language, he shuns the person.

Surprise! Take the Personality Profile and Identify Your Type

The first step in managing priorities is identifying your own personality style. Once you know what your style is, what others' styles are, and how your style affects your ability (or inability) to interact effectively with others, you'll be in a good position to get the best from yourself and from others. You'll no longer be swimming against the tide. You'll be treating other people the way *they* want to be treated—not the way *you* want to be treated.

There are four predictable personality categories that reflect the four basic personality types. I call them: the *Accommodator*, the *Optimist*, the *Producer*, and the *Data-Collector*.

- The *Accommodator* likes people but prefers small groups. *Accommodators* are kind, gentle, calm, methodical, and prudent.
- The *Optimist* is sunny in spirit, impulsive, dramatic, fun, articulate, emotional, and sensitive. *Optimists* are party animals.
- The *Producer* is impatient, focused, ambitious, goal-oriented, competitive, and intolerant of people's foibles. *Producers* are terrific problem-solvers.
- The *Data-Collector* is independent, self-reliant, rational, curious, systematic, and self-contained. *Data-Collectors* love research.

The Personality Profile below will give you a snapshot of your own personality. Try to complete the questions in one sitting, without interruptions. It will take you about ten minutes to complete.

Answer the forty questions by considering whether the statement is absolutely true about you (and therefore worth a ten), the statement is absolutely *not* true about you (and therefore worth a one), or the statement is sort of, kind of, maybe, or sometimes true about you (and therefore worth a five). There are no right or wrong answers, just as there is no one best way to be. Each of us is a mixture, to a greater or lesser extent, of all four of the personality types. Don't spend too much time thinking about any one question. If your answer feels true for you, it probably is true for you.

FAQ: *Is it realistic to think that a short assessment will give me an accurate understanding of my personality?*

A: Yes, it's realistic—for our purposes. If you're like most people, you'll be astonished at how you recognize yourself after taking the ten-minute Personality Profile. But think of the resulting profile as a quick sketch, not a finely textured oil painting. Remember that our goal isn't to identify nuances in your personality. Rather, we're looking for patterns and trends.

As you consider each of the forty questions, you may find yourself thinking that at work, you'd score it a ten, but at home, you'd score it a four. This is normal. Most people behave differently in different situations. For instance, hanging out at home with friends, you behave in a certain way and expect certain treatment in response. With your boss, however, your behavior and the responses you expect are likely to be different. Being aware of how you act in different environments provides important clues about what contributes to or detracts from your happiness and success. You will begin to identify your strengths, as well as your weaknesses, as you take the assessment. The explanations and examples that follow will enable you to make better use of your strengths and diminish your vulnerability from your weaknesses.

After the Personality Profile, each of the four personality types is explained. In each description, and in the explanations of various combinations, you'll recognize specific qualities in yourself and others. If you're strongly of only one personality type, when you read that section you're going to think it was written just for you. If your personality is a mixture of two, three, or all four types, you'll recognize some but not all of each personality type. Each of us is unique, with strengths we use to maximize our potential, and with weaknesses we must compensate for, in order to avoid frustration and failure. We can't begin the process of change until we learn who we are.

PERSONALITY PROFILE

Answer each question twice, once for work, once for your personal life. The tally of these two answers represents your score for the question. Use a scale of one to ten, with ten being most true and one being least true, and assign a number to each of the following statements as you rank each as true or false for how you are at work, and then for how you are at home. As you evaluate each, answer how you truly are, not how you wish you were, or how you used to be, or how you promise to be tomorrow. Tell the truth—how are you now, today, really. After you're done, tally your score using the instructions that follow the assessment.

Consider question two, for example. *"I hate wasting time. I'm always busy and productive."* At work, you might rank this a ten. At home, however, you might know you relish kicking back and relaxing. Time at home has an entirely different meaning for you than time at work. When you think of how you are at home, you'd score this question only as a four. Your work environment rates a ten, your home environment rates a four, and they're *both* true. Thus your score for question two would be fourteen.

FAQ: *I'm different at home than I am at work. How can that be?*

A: It's very common for people to act in different ways depending on the environment. You have only one personality, but you're likely to bring forth different aspects of it in response to different situations.

---

1. I love chattering away about everything under the sun.

- work_____
- home_____   Total_____

2. I hate wasting time. I'm always busy and productive.

- work_____
- home_____   Total_____

3. Rules were made to be bent, maybe even broken.

- work_____
- home_____   Total_____

4. All my life, people have told me that I'm a good listener.

- work_____
- home_____   Total_____

5. I hate it when people try to hurry me up. What's worth doing is worth doing right, no matter how long it takes. Quick work often equals sloppy work.

- work_____
- home_____   Total_____

6. To me, a crowd is a nightmare. I prefer to work on teams or to interact in small groups.

- work_____
- home_____   Total_____

7. I always see the glass as half full, and to me, lemons mean lemonade.

- work_____
- home_____   Total_____

8. It's all about the bottom line.

- work_____
- home_____   Total_____

9. I have a long fuse. I don't get angry easily or often, and when I do, people are surprised.

   - work_____
   - home_____   Total_____

10. I hate saying no, more than just about anything.

    - work_____
    - home_____   Total_____

11. A friend or coworker who calls me up and says, "Let's go out to lunch or dinner or a party," can be pretty certain I'll be answering, "Sure!"

    - work_____
    - home_____   Total_____

12. When people start giving me excuses about why they missed a deadline, every hair on my neck stands up.

    - work_____
    - home_____   Total_____

13. No problem is too complex to think through logically, or too minor to be worth full evaluation.

    - work_____
    - home_____   Total_____

14. Doing good for others makes me feel good, whether it's helping out an overwhelmed coworker or participating in a local charity.

    - work_____
    - home_____   Total_____

15. Most people waste time covering their butts. If they spent the same effort working as they do worrying, they'd get a whole lot more done.

- work_____
- home_____   Total_____

16. Team management and building consensus are the secrets to accomplishment, both personally and professionally.

- work_____
- home_____   Total_____

17. Save for retirement. Oh, please! We may all die tomorrow. Live for today—that's my motto.

- work_____
- home_____   Total_____

18. It's been said that Frank Lloyd Wright remarked, "God is in the details." I couldn't agree more.

- work_____
- home_____   Total_____

19. I love a deadline! I'm great under pressure.

- work_____
- home_____   Total_____

20. There's a lot of kindergarten fluff that goes on around me. People should stop whining.

- work_____
- home_____   Total_____

21. I tend to devalue emotion because I've seen how it interferes with productive thinking.

- work_____
- home_____   Total_____

22. The newest restaurant is the one I want to be at! The newest outfit is the one I like best. I love that the world is constantly changing. Things are so flat, so stagnant, so boring otherwise!

- work_____
- home_____   Total_____

23. I cry at sad endings, and empathize deeply with other people's difficulties.

- work_____
- home_____   Total_____

24. I analyze things carefully before I make a decision.

- work_____
- home_____   Total_____

25. When I have to speak in public, even at a team meeting or at a local community function, I'd just as soon die.

- work_____
- home_____   Total_____

26. I could go for days without talking to another human being with no problem.

- work_____
- home_____   Total_____

27. I'm easygoing and calm.

- work_____
- home_____   Total_____

28. I'm curious about everything.

- work_____
- home_____ Total_____

29. It's easy for me to tell people what I think directly and openly. I get to the point.

- work_____
- home_____ Total_____

30. People tell me I'm overly dramatic, but I really don't know what they mean. I just am who I am!

- work_____
- home_____ Total_____

31. I mind my own business. I don't want to make waves.

- work_____
- home_____ Total_____

32. I like to take my time as I think things through.

- work_____
- home_____ Total_____

33. I'm very focused and goal-oriented.

- work_____
- home_____ Total_____

34. Stop me in the middle of the corridor and ask for an idea then and there—you bet! Ask for me to think it out and write you a memo which is due next Wednesday—yuck.

- work_____
- home_____ Total_____

35. I'm impatient with other people.

   - work_____
   - home_____   Total_____

36. Sometimes the smallest-seeming facts are the ones that reveal the most important patterns. There is no detail too small to be of interest.

   - work_____
   - home_____   Total_____

37. I'm not good around anger. If someone is upset, I seem to lose my ability to explain my point of view. Their anger— even if not directed at me—upsets me.

   - work_____
   - home_____   Total_____

38. My approach to decisions is systematic. First I identify factors that matter, then I research alternatives. I'm not impulsive.

   - work_____
   - home_____   Total_____

39. People spend too much time daydreaming. They say they're getting ready to do things. If they'd focus more on the doing—not on the "getting ready"—they'd get more done.

   - work_____
   - home_____   Total_____

40. I love meeting new people and doing new things. I always feel that something wonderful is likely to happen.

   - work_____
   - home_____   Total_____

Total your scores for questions 4, 6, 9, 10, 14, 16, 25, 27, 31, and 37 and divide by two. This number is your *Accommodator* score.

Total your scores for questions 1, 7, 11, 17, 19, 22, 23, 30, 34, and 40 and divide by two. This number is your *Optimist* score.

Total your scores for questions 2, 3, 8, 12, 15, 20, 29, 33, 35, and 39 and divide by two. This number is your *Producer* score.

Total your scores for questions 5, 13, 18, 21, 24, 26, 28, 32, 36, and 38 and divide by two. This number is your *Data-Collector* score.

Your Personality Revealed

The most you could score in any one category is one hundred. The higher your score, the more of that personality type you have. If you scored over eighty in a category, you have a lot of that personality type in your mix, and when you read the description below, you'll think it was written just for you. Everyone is a blend of all four types; however, most people discover that they tend to display one of the personality types more often than the others.

FAQ: *What's the best personality type to have in order to achieve success?*

A: People of all personality types can be—and are—successful. The trick is to capitalize on your strengths and mitigate your weaknesses.

While most researchers believe that personality doesn't change in essential ways over time, neither is it static. Think of the big events in your life, the major challenges and stresses you've faced; consider how you act in the different environments of your life. For instance, many, perhaps most, people say that they act differently at home than at work. They *want* to be treated differently.

And yet we have only one personality. We bring forth different aspects of who we are at different times in different environments. Think of it as putting the accent on a different *syl-LAB-le*. Also think of how you've matured over time.

Maybe, for instance, you've learned the value of appearing calm under pressure, even though you're inclined to explode. That's exactly what happened to Mark. "For years," he explained, "if I felt angry, I'd yell. I remember moving into my first apartment out of school and the appliance company messed up the delivery of my refrigerator. I screamed at the dispatcher. Not only did I not think it was wrong to yell at her, I was convinced that if I hadn't yelled, I wouldn't have gotten the delivery rescheduled so quickly.

"A few years later, I overheard my boss telling his boss that he wasn't going to allow me to attend a conference because I had such a bad temper. I was, as he put it, 'a loose cannon.' I flipped out, and wanted to take my boss on then and there. Instead, I left the office and walked around the block; I forced myself to acknowledge that my quick temper was hurting me. But I didn't know what to do.

"It was around this time that I attended Jane's seminar. I learned that I was a *Producer*, and that one of the characteristics of the personality is an explosive temper. I also learned that just because I'm naturally explosive doesn't mean I have to act like a jerk. There are alternatives."

Mark added, "Things still infuriate me, and I still express my anger. I just don't yell like an out-of-control maniac. I remain calm. This was a major change in my life, and resulted from my perceiving a weakness in myself and determining how to fix it.

"Just the other day, I had an important presentation before senior executives at a convention site in town. Top location. At one point I grabbed a marker and began making notes on a flip chart. The marker was dry. I felt the familiar anger rising.

"When the A/V guy stopped in at the break to ask how it was going, I wanted to tell him, 'Your markers suck, you ass.' If I had, I know what would have happened: he would have fled. And I wouldn't have got new markers. So I didn't. Instead I said, 'Thanks so much for asking. To tell you the truth, the markers are kind of dry, and I'd love fresh ones.' I had new markers like that, in less than a minute!"

Mark identified a quality that wasn't serving him well and changed his behavior. We can't control who we *are*, or how we *feel*, but we certainly can control how we *act*.

Is Your Personality Mix the Best?

While it is very unusual to score more than eighty in any one area and less than twenty in the other three, it's important to realize that there is no one best way to be. Most people are more evenly balanced than that, but whatever your scores reveal, in the discussion of the personality types and various combinations that follows, you will learn your strengths and weaknesses. *This knowledge is the foundation of successfully managing priorities,* enabling you to build a solid structure as you work to profit by your strengths and compensate for your weaknesses.

Imagine, for example, that you scored eighty-six in the *Accommodator* type, thirty-two in the *Optimist* category, fifty as a *Producer*, and forty-three as a *Data-Collector*. That's pretty evenly mixed. While you're clearly stronger in the *Accommodator* category, you have qualities of the other three integrated into your personality. On the other hand, perhaps your scores are clustered in the mid-range, with no one category predominant. That implies that you're a balanced person who is likely to see others' points of view easily, and probably you're someone who's quite flexible. *Keep in mind that there is no one best way to be.*

The following descriptions are written as if someone was strongly in one category or another. If your score in that particular personality type is over eighty, you'll probably ask yourself, "How does she know these things about me?" If, on the other hand, you're pretty evenly divided among two categories, part of the description about each of those two categories will seem relevant and right on the mark, and part will seem to have been written about a stranger. If a quality in the following descriptions strikes a chord in you, you're saying it's probably true for you. If it doesn't speak to you, that characteristic is probably not part of your persona. Think of your personality as a tapestry. Each quality, attribute, and characteristic, whether a strength or a weakness, is a thread. Taken together, the threads form a tapestry of you.

Tell Yourself the Truth about Your Strengths and Weaknesses

Each of the four personality types reacts differently—*and predictably*—in different situations. Consider, for example, how a representative of each of the four personality types would return an office chair to the store.

Accommodators' strengths include:

- consensus building
- care taking
- relationship building

Accommodators' weaknesses include:

- delaying confrontation
- avoiding saying no
- freezing under pressure

Accommodators are friendly, warm, polite, pleasant, and unconfrontational. *Accommodators* would hesitate to return a purchase—even if they had the receipt and were within the proper time frame. It *feels* so uncomfortable to them, they may avoid it.

"The chair felt great in the store," Amanda, a self-employed public relations agent, told me. "When I got it home, it just didn't feel as good as I thought it would. I thought about returning it, but the thought of the questions the clerk would ask—the inconvenience I'd create for everyone, and I knew he'd think I was foolish—well, I decided to keep it as a guest chair instead of returning it."

Accommodators hate anger or anything that smacks of anger. They tend to avoid confrontation—and other personality types are sometimes surprised at what an *Accommodator* perceives as a confrontation. Simply disappointing someone feels like a confrontation to them, and so they tend to have trouble saying no. Saying no may start a confrontation, one that could result in anger, if the person they're saying no to yells at them.

Optimists' strengths include:

- creative thinking
- poise under pressure
- buoyant spirit even in the face of failure

Optimists' weaknesses include:

- neglecting details
- failing to follow up
- forgetting obligations they don't enjoy

Optimists, while gregarious, enthusiastic, charming, and articulate, are notoriously disorganized. "I'd lost the receipt for the chair. I couldn't believe it. How could I have lost the receipt?" asked Brenda. "The reason it was unbelievable was that I was always losing receipts, keys, phone numbers, business cards—you name it, I've lost it, so I remember making a conscious decision to put the receipt in a safe place. Heaven only knows where I'll find it. Once I found my glasses in the linen closet."

Brenda didn't just lose the receipt, she also missed the return deadline. "No biggie," she explained. "I figured I could convince the clerk to take the chair back anyway. My experience is that if you joke around a little, people want to help you."

Lighthearted and playful, *Optimists* would instinctively joke or flirt with the clerk. As *Optimists* tend to be utterly disorganized, they often depend on their charm and charisma to talk their way out of the consequences of their disorganization. "It worked," reported Brenda. "The clerk was a doll, very cooperative—a real sweetie."

Producers' strengths include:

- focusing on goals
- problem-solving
- assimilating complex information quickly

Producers' weaknesses include:

- alienating people with tactless or brusque behavior
- impatience
- ignoring rules and procedures

Millie, a *Producer*, had thrown the receipt away. "I'm not concerned," she said. Direct and forceful, *Producers* tend to be serious and competitive in all aspects of their lives. "To me," Millie explained, "it was a given they would accept the chair as a return. When they said no, I simply informed the clerk that that was not acceptable. I stood my ground, and of course they took it back. As it happened, I had to complain to the supervisor, but that's just par for the course."

Producers have tunnel vision when it comes to achieving their goals. They speak to the point. Their focus is absolute.

Data-Collectors' strengths include:

- rational and analytical thinking
- curiosity
- self-reliance

Data-Collectors' weaknesses include:

- distrust of emotional displays
- insensitivity
- being overly bureaucratic

Eliot, a *Data-Collector*, went to return the chair well prepared. "As I told the clerk, if she needed me to fill out any paperwork, I'd be happy to do so. I wasn't concerned about returning the chair because I knew I was well within the return period, I had the original receipt, plus a copy for my records, and the chair was undamaged. I was right—it wasn't a problem at all."

Data-Collectors are cautious, methodical, systematic, deliberate, polite, distant, and unemotional. They tend to be even-tempered, feeling neither euphoria nor despair. As Eliot explained, "It's a rational process. I'm very comfortable in those situations."

You Share Qualities with Others

The grid below is a visual display of the primary qualities of the four personality types. (Please see page 32.) Words written outside the box reflect qualities common to two personality types. Words written inside the box relate only to that one type.

Note that *Accommodators* and *Optimists* share two qualities. They both:

1. socialize a lot—they like people and they need people
2. avoid being alone—they get lonely easily

Optimists and *Producers* share two qualities as well. They both:

1. wear their hearts on their sleeves—you always know how they feel at any moment, because they'll tell you directly. Ask and they'll answer. Don't ask, they'll tell you anyway.
2. favor a swift pace—they move fast, assimilate information quickly, and get bored easily

Producers and *Data-Collectors* both:

1. prefer the task at hand to interacting with other people— they like being alone
2. show enormous self-reliance

Data-Collectors and *Accommodators* both:

1. value privacy—they're a little hard to get to know, and neither is naturally demonstrative

EASY-TO-USE SUMMARY CHART

Interactive—Social

	Accommodator	Optimist	
Private—Patient	• harmony • help • family	• new • chatty • fun	**Quick—Outspoken**
	Data Collector	Producer	
	• facts • rational • curious	• goals • bottom line • impatient	

Hands-on—Independent

2. demonstrate tolerance and patience—they don't lose their tempers easily

How You Process Information Differs from Others

Each of the four personality types receives, evaluates, and provides information in different ways. *Accommodators* and *Data-Collectors* are at their best when they have a little time to get their thoughts in order. They're not comfortable reacting off the top of their heads; they prefer a methodical, considered approach. *Optimists* and *Producers*, on the other hand, are at their best under pressure; they're most effective when reacting without preparation—right off the top of their heads.

Dixie, an *Accommodator*, was a senior office manager in a medium-sized city government office. She was stunned when she stepped into the elevator and the only other occupant was the mayor, an *Optimist*. "He's very nice, but I don't have a lot of one-on-one interaction with him. So when he said he was glad he ran into me, that he wanted to know what I thought of the new computer system, well, first I was flattered, second I froze, and third I said something—but to this day, I can't remember what. Then, of course, at three a.m. the next morning, I'm wide awake, saying to myself, '*I should have said . . .*'! That kind of delayed reaction happens to me all the time."

One of the major benefits of understanding this personality information is the dramatic impact it can have on your efforts to get the best from others. Dixie isn't shy or tongue-tied; whatever it is she said to the mayor probably sounded fine. But had the mayor applied the systems detailed in this book, he would have recognized Dixie as an *Accommodator* by her friendly attitude and conservative attire. (How to identify people's personalities by their appearance and other clues is discussed in Chapter 2.)

He would have known to say, "I'd love to know what you think about the new computer system. Take a few days, get your thoughts in order—send me a quick e-mail." *And he would have gotten a higher-quality response.*

Understand the power of this information: if the mayor had treated Dixie in a way that was likely to bring out her best work, not only would she have *done* better work, and not only would she have *felt* less uncomfortable and more valued, but the mayor would probably have received a higher-quality response. Treating Dixie as *she* wanted to be treated—not the way that felt most natural to the mayor—would have helped him get his own needs met—*he would have known what Dixie truly thought about the new computer system*.

If Dixie had been using this material, she would have been much more likely to have achieved *her* goal—*time in which to think*—before answering the mayor's question. She would have maintained control of her own time. Recognizing the mayor as an *Optimist* by his gregariousness and his cartoon-character tie, she would have understood that the mayor was naturally inclined to think on his feet, without preparation. Given her own goal— time to think—she would have known to smile warmly and say something like, "Thank you! I'm flattered! I'd like to take a quick survey and give you a short report in a couple of days. Is Wednesday all right? I could e-mail you." Notice that this is a no-risk approach. If the mayor insists, Dixie can answer. But there's a good chance that she will get the outcome she seeks.

Whereas *Accommodators* and *Data-Collectors* perform best

with time to prepare, *Optimists* and *Producers* are the opposite. The tighter the deadline, the higher the quality of their work is likely to be. If Dixie had been an *Optimist* or a *Producer*, the mayor's question, "What do you think of the new computer system?" would have been answered more articulately and completely on the spot. The instruction to think about it and write an e-mail—well, *that's work*.

Data-Collectors in Dixie's situation would have frozen. Since they know they are *not* good off the top of their head, it makes sense for them to have a prepared reply for when they're asked to respond immediately.

A *Data-Collector* who coaches his department's softball team, for example, might prepare the following response to the inevitable managerial question "So, how's Tom's (or Julie's or Carlos's) game going?" A *Data-Collector* who answers, "He's a great guy. (Or, "She's a great gal.) Why don't you come to one of our games and see for yourself?" buys himself some time to think while giving a tactful response.

Note that this approach doesn't challenge you to change who you are. Your challenge is twofold:

1. to know your strengths and use them, and to know your weaknesses and consistently compensate for them
2. to quickly identify others' personality types and modify what you do to suit (discussed further in Chapters 2, 3, and 4)

How You Handle Trouble Differs from Others

By looking at how four people, one representing each personality type, deal with adversity, you can see vividly the differences among them. If four employees, for example, have a flat tire on their way into work, consider how each would likely experience the same event.

Mandy, the *Accommodator*, comes rushing into work a little late, and very concerned about her tardiness. *Accommodators* take commitments to heart, and agreeing to arrive at work on time is a commitment. "I had a flat tire! But it could have been so much worse," Mandy explains calmly. "Luckily I was able to reach AAA on my cell phone, and the nicest fellow came and changed the tire."

Note that *Accommodators*:

- always have a cell phone (they believe that it's just not prudent to be on the road without one)
- make sure the cell phone's battery is always charged (they're organized)
- keep up their membership in AAA (another example of their prudence)
- always find people who come to help are very nice (genuinely nice themselves, *Accommodators* tend to see the best in others)

Kim, the *Optimist*, also comes rushing in to work a little late. Her gestures are bolder, her entire presentation is more dramatic. "You're not going to believe what happened to me!" she exclaims. "I had a flat tire. Why do these things always happen to me? I picked up the cell phone. My battery's dead. Why is my battery dead? Then it occurred to me that it didn't matter because I forgot to renew AAA anyway. I'd meant to renew—but the form is gone. Where's the form? It must have sprouted feet and run away! I had to stop traffic. The nicest man helped me. I kept the cars at bay while he changed my tire."

Notice that *Optimists*:

- tend to be terrible with details (losing forms is typical) and aren't organized (renewal dates are frequently missed and batteries are rarely charged)
- thrive on drama (if dramatic things don't happen to them, they put a dramatic spin on things that do)
- excel during a crisis (they rarely panic until *after* the crisis has passed)
- joke in the face of bad news (they maintain good spirits in all situations, even the bleakest)

Sam, a *Producer*, fixes the flat quickly, but may be careless about safety. When he arrives at work, he doesn't explain his lateness unless asked, and at no point does he apologize. "It wasn't my fault," he would say.

Note that *Producers*:

- work quickly (they tend to be impatient with interruptions, unexpected events, problems, and human foibles)
- don't ask for help (they're self-sufficient)
- focus on the primary goal (fix the flat without worrying much about safety)
- don't apologize (doing so doesn't occur to them)

Annie, a *Data-Collector*, fixes the flat tire herself, carefully ensuring every lug nut is tightened, and she does so only after placing the appropriate number of flares in the proper locations. When she arrives at work, late, she fills out an incident report, annotates her time sheet, or otherwise documents with meticulous accuracy her tardiness.

FAQ: *Can I use this approach in interviewing to predict a potential employee's success?*

A: Research is mixed about the value of using personality assessments as a predictor of hiring success. However, any objective measure, including personality assessments, is probably more reliable than gut instinct or rapport. But if you limit yourself by hiring only those people who match a profile, you may miss out on a terrific employee, one who happens not to fit the profile. Also, by hiring only people who share one personality type, you sacrifice the potential benefits of a different perspective.

Note that *Data-Collectors*:

- prefer to work alone (they think others might do sloppy work)

- pay painstaking attention to detail (they're methodical and cautious)
- take safety seriously (they adhere to rules, procedures, and policies religiously)
- report the facts unemotionally (they value the truth)

Are You a Planner or Are You Spontaneous?

As you read the following descriptions, consider how your views of the importance of planning and goal setting might help you succeed or inhibit your success.

Accommodators are methodical and careful planners. They defer gratification easily. They tend not to be impulsive or spontaneous; they're highly organized and systematic. They prefer participation from many people throughout the planning process.

Ken, an *Accommodator*, was in charge of planning his family's vacation. "We decided to go to California, so I went to the state's Department of Tourism Web site and found loads of info. I e-mailed them for the package of information they'd advertised on the Web. Also, I contacted the chambers of commerce in the cities we're interested in visiting. They were all very helpful at sending brochures. When everything arrived, I read it all, highlighting the parts I thought would be of interest. I created a spreadsheet and used it to set our agenda, and tracked different categories of information with color-coded files. Things like restaurant options and water sports, and so on. It worked well. We had a lot of fun, didn't forget anything we'd wanted to do, and we had no bad surprises."

Notice that *Accommodators*:

- prefer set schedules
- are uncomfortable with uncertainty
- happily take time to prepare
- use their organizational skills in both their personal and professional lives

Optimists, on the other hand, love spontaneous vacations. They tend to be creative. They love to brainstorm, think up new ideas and innovative approaches, and are unconcerned about the idea's value. *Optimists* value "art for art's sake."

Risk taking figures predominantly in many aspects of an *Optimist*'s life. *Optimists* hate planning for the future, for example. Investing for retirement is a bore, and they don't perceive the risk of running out of money. Delayed gratification is a foreign concept to an *Optimist*. Because they know how deft they are at dealing with whatever comes up, they're comfortable taking risks and adept at dealing with consequences.

Paula, an *Optimist*, recalled a vacation she'd organized a few years ago. "I was having a horrible time at work. We were in the middle of a merger, people were dripping anxiety, and it finally got to me. I called my husband and said, 'Let's get out of here.' He's a teacher and was on his summer break, so he said sure. That was a Thursday at three in the afternoon. At ten the next morning we were on a flight to Hawaii. That's what I call planning!"

Note that *Optimists* are:

- impulsive
- quick to act
- unconcerned about practical details such as cost
- focused on pleasure

Producers are creative too, but in a different way. *Producers* come up with ideas on an "as-needed" basis, and never lose sight of the bottom line. *Producers* are as direct, open, impatient, and focused as *Optimists*. But whether they admit it or not, they don't like people very much, and so they tend to bulldoze their way through, not concerned with alienating people. To a *Producer*, the only thing that matters is the ultimate outcome.

Adam, a *Producer*, explained, "A bunch of us go skiing every winter. Friends from college. I end up planning it, because if I didn't, no one would, or no one would do it right. I don't understand what the big deal is. You make a few calls to compare prices, book the condo with the best deal, call your travel agent to get the air tickets and rental car—what's so tough about it?

But I'm telling you, the one year I got fed up and told them it was someone else's turn—guess what? The guy who did it waited until the last minute and we were in a tiny condo a half hour's drive away from the mountain. It's just another example of if you want something done right, you'd better do it yourself."

Producers typically:

- define their goal clearly
- accomplish the goal efficiently
- become impatient with other people
- have high standards

Becky, a *Data-Collector*, prefers plenty of structure on a vacation. "I recently went on a theater tour in London. It was excellent. We were given a schedule with ample free time, interesting tour options, and sensible amounts of on-your-own time. It was perfect for me. I'd researched several competing tours on the Web, through my travel agent, through a coworker's travel agent, and by buying several travel magazines. The tour I selected offered less marketing hype and more down-to-earth details. For example, they didn't just provide the titles of the plays we were scheduled to see; they also provided a couple of paragraphs describing each plot. The explanations of the restaurants we were booked into didn't say 'a charming pub.' Instead it detailed the history of the pub in a few sentences. The attention to detail was very appealing to me. They also got me interested in things in advance. For example, one of the optional side trips was to the maze at Hampton Court. I remember reading in the brochure how people would be lost for hours, unable to penetrate the secret of the labyrinth."

Notice that *Data-Collectors*:

- conduct exhaustive research
- reward providers of detail
- choose a set schedule rather than unstructured time
- enjoy having their curiosity piqued

Get *Your* Needs Met by Doing It *Their* Way

Using the material in this book will effectively ensure that people are motivated to cooperate with you. When you treat people in a way that appeals to *them* rather than *you*, they're more likely to help you with your own priorities, and more likely to do so in a timely manner.

Because they feel valued, they put your priorities on top of the pile. You know the old saying, "You catch more flies with honey than you do with vinegar." It's true. But what's honey to one person is vinegar to another. In order to have your priorities dealt with expeditiously and effectively, you need to know what's honey to the people with whom you interact. By observing how the personality types naturally interact with others, we can discover clues to define honey to each.

Accommodators are:

- emotional but not demonstrative—they express their emotions privately, only to a few trusted friends or family members
- family-oriented, and likely to talk about leisure activities and hobbies, as well as their plans for family events or activities. They excel in small groups, such as teams.
- deeply invested in people getting along. They value relationships more than issues.
- available to you when you need them. They're flexible, ready to wedge you in to their schedule, no matter how busy they are.

Optimists are:

- sensitive, as if their nerve endings are closer to the surface than most other people. They're empathetic and good at accurately reading situations. They're intuitive and poised.
- easily bored; they relish new activities and become lethargic and depressed without nearly constant stimulation.

They're happiest when coming up with ideas, but hate the follow-through.

- passionate; they feel things intensely. They'll have nightmares for a week if they see a scary movie, for example, insist on the hotel room with the view, and wouldn't think of reading a romance novel without a box of tissues nearby
- fun-loving; they entertain frequently, are playful and outgoing

Producers are:

- demanding. If they ask a question, they want the answer then and there. They don't want guesses—they want definitive answers.
- dictatorial, believing "It's my way or the highway"
- doers, not talkers. They have trouble delegating because they think it's quicker to do it themselves than it is to teach someone else to do it. They expect as much or more from themselves as they do from others.
- brash, using sarcasm to express frustration or displeasure

Data-Collectors are:

- unemotional, as if their nerve endings are buried a little deeper than everyone else's. It's not that they bottle up their feelings; they simply view the world pragmatically, not emotionally.
- loners, preferring solitary work; there's no fact unworthy of being ferreted out, no detail too small to be of interest, and no analysis too minor to be run
- polite and pleasant; they tend to express their thoughts and feelings euphemistically, not directly
- procedural, needing and respecting clear policies and rules, preferring highly structured environments, such as bureaucracies, and disliking ambiguity

What matters to each person—and thus what is likely to motivate each person—varies and is related to personality. In summary:

- *Accommodators* value *being needed by others, people getting along well*, and *small groups*.
- *Optimists* value *having fun, brainstorming*, and *change*.
- *Producers* value *accomplishment, definite answers*, and *productivity*.
- *Data-Collectors* value the *truth, details*, and *proper procedures*.

Can You Recognize Personality Types?

Read the following scenarios and see if you can recognize the personality type based on the description.

Scenario One

Fred got caught sneaking out of the copy room. In his hand was a wad of crumpled, burned, browned, curled acetate transparency. There are two kinds of acetate transparencies: one goes through photocopiers, one does not. Fred had used the wrong kind and thus had broken the photocopier. When challenged by his boss, he said, "I'm really sorry. I was just sure that it was the right kind. I'm on my way right now to call the repair person." And he was gone.

What personality type is Fred?

Approach the analysis methodically: neither a *Data-Collector* nor an *Accommodator* would ever be in that position! *Data-Collectors* and *Accommodators* would have read the side of the transparency box or consulted the instruction manual. *Optimists* and *Producers* never, ever look at instruction manuals—unless it's to go to the back and look at the trouble-shooting guide after something's already broken! And the *Producer* wouldn't have apologized.

Did you identify Fred as an *Optimist*?

Scenario Two

Kya reported that the occupational therapist she had to see for a broken finger had a "mean streak." "One of my exercises was squeezing a sponge, and it hurt," she said. "One day I was in her office squeezing her sponge, and I said, 'Ow! It hurts!' You know what she said to me? I couldn't believe it. She wasn't even looking at me—she was looking at my hand, and she said, 'You can squeeze harder.'

"It sounded so harsh, but I realized that it wasn't personal. She wasn't thinking of me as a person; she was focused completely on my finger, as if it had been her own. She wasn't going to let me hurt myself. She just wasn't the sort of person to engage in chitchat. Over the months we worked together, I grew to appreciate her goal orientation, and I came to be very grateful to her. She helped me get better quicker."

What personality type is the occupational therapist?

Approach the analysis methodically: An *Accommodator* would have responded to Kya's pain with an outpouring of soothing attention. An *Optimist* would have joked with her to try to take her mind off the pain. If the therapist had been a *Data-Collector*, she would have explained the treatment procedures in detail, believing that knowledge would help diminish the pain.

Did you identify the occupational therapist as a *Producer*? *Producers* tend to have tunnel vision when it comes to achieving goals. They always see the shortest way to get from wherever they are to wherever they want to be. It may not be pretty—but it will happen. They don't talk about things—they *do* things.

Scenario Three

Sachiko had to select new office space for the small architectural firm for which she worked. She explained that her boss wanted to know which of the two locations under consideration was her favorite. "It was funny, but I simply couldn't tell him. Other people say, 'I haven't decided yet, but isn't that one place's view great?' or 'I haven't decided yet, but such and such a place is willing to give us a right of first refusal on the office next door,' but I can't say that. Until I finish my research and analysis, I simply don't have a preference. And for something as important as our new office space, I won't be hurried, even by my boss."

What personality type is Sachiko?

Approach the analysis methodically: An *Accommodator* might say, "I'm leaning toward space option one, but I want to talk to a few more people before I decide." An *Optimist* sets out to lease an office at ten on a Tuesday morning and is done by noon, having leased the jazziest place in town, and having already made friends with the folks next door. *Producers* don't consult anyone, but educate themselves sufficiently so they make the decision with confidence.

Did you recognize Sachiko as a *Data-Collector*? She values research more than instinct. Until her research was complete, she believes any opinion she gives would be premature and pointless to discuss. To Sachiko, as to most *Data-Collectors*, an opinion is not formed lightly, nor is it easily changed once it's set.

In general, *Accommodators* make decisions and manage by consensus, whereas *Data-Collectors* make decisions and manage by policy, *Optimists* by crisis, and *Producers* by fiat. *Accommodators* and *Optimists* are deeply invested in people getting along, *Data-Collectors* don't notice, and *Producers* don't care.

Scenario Four

Connie, a set designer for a regional opera company, needed a new vacuum cleaner. "Mine broke. It flat-out died. I needed a new vacuum cleaner. But there was a teeny little problem: I knew *nothing* about vacuum cleaners, and the last thing I wanted to know anything about was vacuum cleaners. So I put it off, and put it off, and put it off. The dust bunnies were growing, my cat's fur was ankle deep, but my attitude was, oh well!

"Except that this really cute guy asked me out and was picking me up for dinner in five hours. So off I went to the local discount store, determined to buy a vacuum. Oh, my God. There were a dozen options. Who knew? I started on one end of the row of vacuums and read the labels, comparing price, capacity, and so on. Boring! And then I remembered the time my dad took me to a Rotary meeting.

"The speaker was the owner of a famous vineyard. He told us his secret of choosing wines: if you're not looking for a specific wine, go to the category you want—California reds, for instance—and select the second from the least expensive; he guaranteed it would always be a good solid choice. I've used that tip countless times, and it has always been a winner. I get to look like I know what I'm doing, *sans* the work. So I applied the same principle to vacuum cleaners, and I've been happy with it ever since. But don't even talk to me about that date!"

What personality type is Connie?

Approach the analysis methodically: People collect and assimilate information in varying ways. *Data-Collectors* and *Accommodators* are methodical and cautious in their thinking. *Optimists* and *Producers* tend to be more impulsive. Only an *Optimist* would compare buying a vacuum cleaner to selecting wine! Also, there was a playful tone to her description of the dust and fur, and she didn't mind living in disarray.

Did you recognize Connie as an *Optimist*?

Capitalize on Your Innate Abilities

It's clear that each personality type features both strengths and weaknesses. The chart on page 47 highlights how the four personality types differ in key areas. The secret to effectively using this book is to identify your own and others' strengths and *then to capitalize on them*. You can't get other people to change. But by identifying others' strengths, and positioning your request in such a way that it appeals to how they're naturally programmed to react, you have the best chance of getting your own needs met.

In order to do so, you must sharpen your skills at reading other people. You don't need to delve into their psyches; you do need to know how to recognize the signals they send out about how they want to be treated. And as you'll discover in Chapter 2, there are additional easy-to-recognize clues.

Tips

- Changing simple things (the words you choose, the timing of delivering your message, and whether the message is in writing or not) based on other people's personality types helps you improve the likelihood that your priorities will be met.
- All personality types and combinations feature strengths and weaknesses. Don't pretend you're good at everything. No one is! Working within your limits, and maximizing your capabilities, is a key to living the life you really want.

EASY-TO-USE SUMMARY CHART

Attribute	Accommodator	Optimist	Producer	Data-Collector
Generally prefers to be alone	No	No	Yes	Yes
Methodical	Yes	No	No	Yes
Impulsive	No	Yes	Yes	No
Tends to look for and then adhere to rules	Yes	No	No	Yes
Impatient with details and background information	No	Yes	Yes	No
Tactful and indirect in presenting negative information	Yes	No	No	Yes
Kind and empathetic toward others	Yes	Yes	No	No

CHAPTER TWO

Know Others

How Others View You: Does It Match How You Think of Yourself?

As you recognized yourself from the descriptions in Chapter 1, it probably became more clear why you do what you do. The next step is to consider how others perceive you, and why you get the reactions from others that you get. For example:

> "As soon as I read that an *Accommodator* is family-oriented and non-confrontational, I recognized myself," explained Hank. "This comes up in my life all the time."

When asked for an example, Hank said, "One day last week my boss left me a late afternoon voice mail that he expected me to work late to update a report. I knew there wasn't a reason in the world that I couldn't update that report the next morning. He was just throwing his weight around. But he's the boss, so normally I would have stayed and done the report. I hate to rock the boat. But I was due to referee my daughter's soccer game.

"I had a choice: stay or leave. I decided to leave. Another choice: confront or not. I decided not to raise the issue. Instead of telling him no, I pretended that I didn't get the voice mail until the next morning.

"While it's clear to me that my daughter is my top priority, my work is important to me too. If I hadn't avoided the confrontation, I wouldn't have been able to balance both priorities. As it happened, it worked out all right, but after reading about the different personalities, I can see how bottom-line people—*Producers*—might perceive me as lazy or uncommitted. The opposite is true, so I really need to watch that I don't get misunderstood. The value of this information isn't only that I've gained a new understanding of myself, but also that I now understand how others perceive me."

Evvie, an *Optimist*, said, "It was a revelation to me that my impulsive nature and my devil-may-care spirit are qualities typical of the personality type and not unique to me."

When asked how her spontaneity manifested itself day-to-day, Evvie said, "I'm impulsive all the time. And I rarely think about consequences. Once, I missed a job interview because a friend had two free tickets to Las Vegas. She called up and said, 'Let's go!' And I went. It felt terrific at the time—very of the moment—but to this day, I can't remember any specifics of our Vegas holiday. I guess we had fun.

"Isn't that amazing? It felt critical to my happiness and terribly urgent back then that I go to Vegas, but then—poof—the memories are gone. I missed an important job interview, and I don't even have good memories to show for it. Who knows where I might be today if I hadn't been so impulsive?

"I've known for a long time that most other people aren't as spontaneous as I am. What I've never realized, and what's so useful to me to understand now, is that other people aren't necessarily amused by my antics. I used to think that their lack of spontaneity came from a lack of courage or imagination. Now I know they're just different from me, nothing else. And from their point of view, they probably think that I'm irresponsible."

"I know I'm goal-oriented," said Jackie, a *Producer*. "What I didn't know was how my ambition might be seen as a negative by other people."

Asked for an example, Jackie explained, "When I was in grade school, I wanted to be a crossing guard. I thought they looked so great, so important. I wanted the uniform. The first time I applied for the position I was in the first grade, and the principal explained that you had to be in at least fifth grade to apply. I was crushed, but all it did was increase my determination to make the cut some day. After a few years of unremitting envy, I decided that I couldn't wait any longer. I applied again when I was in fourth grade. I told Mrs. Myerson that the rule that you had to be at least a fifth-grader was wrong and that she should let me apply now. I will never forget the shocked look on her face when I walked into her office.

"Of course, she said no, but that isn't the point. The point is that I've seen that shocked look from a lot of different people over the years. It's only now, though, that I understand that it may well be my problem, not other people's.

"The thing is that I've always been proud of my direct approach. I'd thought that anyone who couldn't take it was a wuss. Now I see that, as a *Producer*, I have a responsibility to moderate my approach if I want other people to cooperate with me. It doesn't matter whether I'm right. If I want people to hear my message, I have to make sure they aren't turned off by harsh words or the tone of my voice. Period. End of discussion. If what I do makes them feel steamrollered, they're not going to be motivated to help me. Do you have any idea how important that information is to me?"

"When I read that *Data-Collectors* are introspective and detail-oriented, I immediately recognized myself," explained Cherie.

She put it this way: "I question everything. I assume nothing. I want independent verification of each fact. I've always been this way. I remember asking my mother how she knew milk was good for me when I was a kid.

"I'm chief operating officer for a major fashion designer. He's brilliant. His designs are innovative and figure-flattering. But you buy his fashions because of me. I don't mean to sound immodest, but it's clear to me that this is true. It's one thing to have wonderful ideas. It's an entirely different thing to bring those ideas to market. It's my job to take care of the details. I love it, and I'm good at it.

"I get called a lot of names. I'm called a 'bean counter,' a 'number hound,' and 'Miss Persnickety.' It's not a surprise that people think I'm into the details, but what is a surprise is my realization that while I perceive myself as careful, appropriate, and analytical, other people sometimes see me as nitpicky and over-the-top."

Whether your realizations are as startling as Hank's, Evvie's, Jackie's, or Cherie's, or whether they're less dramatic, it's important that you focus on how others perceive you. Armed with an understanding of what you've said and done, you can begin to identify whether what you do instinctively is working for you or not. If not, maybe it's time to think about what you can do differently.

FAQ: *Why should I defer to other people? Why shouldn't they defer to me?*

A: Practically speaking, you should defer to them because doing so increases the likelihood that your priorities will be met. I recommend that you take a pragmatic approach when interacting with others. If it works, keep doing it. If it doesn't work, don't do it again.

Easy-to-Make Changes

Change is hard, even frightening. When you're about to do something in a new way, often you feel vulnerable. What, you ask yourself, if the change is wrong? Maybe I'll look foolish, you think. Maybe you fear that what you do differently might lead to something worse than before. Maybe you think you don't know how to change. Or what to change.

Good news! Most of the changes we're looking for are small and manageable in scope. No major personality shifts or anything of that nature. You don't have to change who you are. You don't have to change your values. You can keep your job, your family, and your friends. Probably, however, you do have to change some of your behaviors. The good news is that every change, no matter how small, will help you in expected and unexpected ways.

The first step is analyzing *which* behaviors you need to consider changing. By honing your ability to read other people's signals, you're likely to discover that you react in predictable ways to certain kinds of people. Once you know:

- which personality attributes in other people bring out the best in you,
- which behaviors in other people give you trouble,
- how to reliably recognize which people possess those qualities,

you can experiment with different approaches that compensate until you find the one that's best for you.

Simple Changes Result in Major Benefits

Marcia, an elder-care social worker, put it this way. "I'm completely, a hundred percent, intimidated by *Producers*. I used to dread meeting this one doctor, Dr. Rogers. He's a terrific doctor, a geriatrician, and a lot of my older clients see him. But he's *so* impatient, I'd freeze anytime I got around him. I took it personally. I thought this man had it in for me. It was only after I learned to recognize personality types by what seems pretty superficial stuff—appearance and environment—that I realized, *aha!* Dr. Rogers is a *Producer*. Once I did, though, I was home free! I made a point of jotting down a few notes—the key points I wanted to make to him. What a simple solution. It works beautifully because I know that if I get intimidated and freeze, I have my notes to keep me focused and on track. You want to know something funny? I've *never* had to use them. It's the simple fact of *having* them that makes the difference. And I wouldn't have been able to come up with this idea if I hadn't been able to recognize him as a *Producer*.

"This positive experience set a new pattern for me. Having recognized Dr. Rogers as a *Producer*, from that moment on I routinely treated him as a *Producer*. Within a few weeks, my direct supervisor asked me what magic I'd worked with him. Apparently Dr. Rogers had just stopped him in the corridor and told him that I was a treasure. Can you imagine? From treating me with impatience to calling me a treasure in a matter in weeks.

"Talk about big benefits! My boss submitted my name to participate on a prestigious research committee, and he made specific reference to my having won over Dr. Rogers on my next performance appraisal. My career got a boost because I correctly recognized Dr. Rogers's personality type, and because I used the information to change how I interacted with him."

As Marcia noted, many of the clues discussed in this chapter *are* superficial—how people dress and what their environment is likely to look like, for example. There's no magic, and no guarantees. But by recognizing these easily visible clues, you give yourself a leg up in the process. And the rewards can be profound. Witness Marcia's success.

Easy-to-Recognize Clues Abound

George, CEO of an international education company, explained it this way. "I travel a lot on business. I always wear a suit. I believe I get better service, and am upgraded to first class more frequently. I believe that I'm treated with more respect simply based on my professional appearance. One of my senior marketing managers travels in jeans. His attitude is that he wants to be comfortable when he travels. So there we are, traveling together, me in a suit and tie, him in old faded jeans.

"Even at work he always dresses casually. I know this is the new trend, and I can see that it's appropriate for us—our target audience is teens, after all. I used to insist that he dress in a suit and tie. Finally I realized how it inhibited him. Now I take a different tack. I keep my opinion to myself. I admire and respect his abilities. He's terrific at building the relationships that make our business go. And I recognize that casual dress is *his* style. And here's the bottom line—as long as he does his job, makes his numbers, connects with the people he needs to reach, I don't care if he wears a paper bag."

Did you recognize George's personality? Take a moment and think about him. In Chapter 1 we reviewed how people are likely *to act*. Based on that, I'll bet you were able to correctly recognize that George is primarily a *Producer*. You can identify George as a *Producer* by his:

- clothing (*formal*)
- language (*"bottom-line"*)
- orientation (His focus is on *getting things done*. Note that he said, ". . . as long as he does his job, makes his numbers, connects with the people he needs to reach, I don't care if he wears a paper bag.").

How about the other fellow? He's:

- terrific at *building relationships*
- *casual in his style of dress*
- more interested in *comfort* than style.

Clearly, he's an *Accommodator*.

As you read the descriptions that follow, you'll recognize people with whom you work and socialize. Given that there are strengths and weaknesses associated with each personality type and combination of types, it's important to note that the issue isn't that you or others begin to adopt the style of what you deem the "best" personality to be, or that you shy away from those people who have personality types you don't like. The point is simple: once you know whom you're dealing with, you can change what you *do* (not who you are) to get the results you want.

Some people are good at this intuitively. They're "good with people," even chameleon-like in their instinctive ability to adapt and conform to changing circumstances. But wherever you fall on the bell curve of being able or not able to instinctively adapt, this ability can be learned. People signal their needs. You will be able to easily, quickly, and reliably recognize others' personality styles, and you'll be right most of the time.

As with the personality assessment found in Chapter 1, the clues that provide insights into how people want to be treated won't work all the time. If you are unable to determine a person's personality signals, defer to the *Producer*. It will never hurt you to do so, and doing anything else may harm you. If you treat someone as a *Producer*, and you're wrong, you'll receive immediate feedback that will allow you to adjust your presentation to fit the new information.

For example, if you say to someone whose personality you can't read, "Here's the update you requested. I summed up the three options," and they're not a *Producer*, they may say something like, "Looks like you did a lot of work. Come on in and tell me about it." His warm affirmation reveals that he's not a *Producer—but it didn't hurt you*. On the other hand, if you go in and say, "I need some help," and the person isn't an *Accommodator*—it hurts you.

The clues explained in this chapter will help you to quickly and accurately read people's signals. Deferring to people you can't read as a *Producer* serves as a safety net.

Knowledge You Can Use

During the holiday season, most of us have noticed a woman at the mall or walking through the city wearing red and green sparkly earrings that glow on and off. Her skirt is a little shorter than most women are wearing that season; she's wearing bright colors and jazzy patterns, like a leopard print scarf. She's walking quickly with a peppy bounce to her step. As soon as you see her, you recognize an *Optimist*. If you need to ask a stranger for help, perhaps for directions, she'd be a good choice. *Optimists* like to talk, assimilate information quickly (so she'd understand your request), and will cheerfully help. In other words, even in casual, everyday situations, using the personality information saves time (an *Optimist* will answer your question quickly) and reduces stress (interactions with *Optimists* are pleasant).

You won't simply understand how people tend to dress, how their office or homes are likely to be decorated and maintained, how they'll most likely sound on the phone, and how they prefer to communicate. You'll also be able to *apply the knowledge*. By sharpening your skills at recognizing others' styles—even in a fifteen-second phone call—and matching your responses to it, you significantly increase your chances of success.

Why People Dress the Way They Do

People adopt a style of dress based on many factors, including inclination, habit, culture, and environment. Personality is one of many variables that unite to create a "look." Do you wear clothing to help you create a certain image? To be alluring? To signal success?

Have you ever tried on an outfit that didn't feel right? If so, you understand the impact of these variables. It doesn't matter whether that outfit makes you look terrific, is flattering to your body type, creates exactly the image you need or want to create. What matters is how it *feels* on some intuitive level. A person's appearance matters. How you appear to others affects how they perceive you and how they treat you.

Preference, culture, image, choice, personality . . . all of these factors influence the decisions people make. How well-groomed a person is, how stylish and well tailored their clothing, and the variety of outfits they own and wear signal how they want to be treated—if you can recognize the clues.

Friendly and Conservative *Accommodators*

Accommodators tend to dress traditionally and modestly. They're not trendsetters; they are most comfortable presenting a conservative appearance. Note that this is not a comment on whether they are stylish or unstylish. Rather, it is an observation about the way they present themselves to the world; their grooming, cleanliness, clothing, every aspect of their outward appearance, is understated and quiet.

Accommodators choose clothes for coverage and inconspicuous conventionality. They don't want to stand out in any way. They want to be perceived as one of the group. Note that the style of dress reflects an *Accommodator's* attitude toward life: they prefer not to stand out.

Think of conventional business clothing. For a man it might be a navy blue blazer, gray slacks, and a burgundy tie. The blazer may be an old favorite of such traditional styling that it looks professional and appropriate year in and year out, season after season. Or it may be this year's style. Whether single-breasted or double-breasted, whether it features two or three buttons, it is, to an *Accommodator*, a uniform. But it is a uniform that can be customized. Perhaps he's added nautical buttons, or replaced the nautical buttons with ones supplied by his alma mater. Or maybe he wears the blazer with a school tie. In other words, while an *Accommodator* gentleman wears traditional styles, his individuality may also be displayed, especially to show the groups with which he's affiliated. When you meet a woman *Accommodator*, you notice her neatness and modesty. She may well be dressed in a stylish manner, but her skirt reaches to the long end of the range of this season's hem lines. Her V-neck sweater doesn't plunge, or if it does, she's wearing a blouse or turtleneck jersey underneath.

An *Accommodator* woman working in a formal environment would wear a traditionally tailored suit or a dress with a conservative blazer. Perhaps she's added a lace collar. She may be wearing pearls. Certainly her jewelry is conventional and unobtrusive.

If your company is one of the many that has embraced casual dress as its dress code, you will notice that *Accommodator* men wear conservative khakis and polo shirts; *Accommodator* women wear tailored slacks and blouses.

Both men and women *Accommodators* prefer traditional colors, including maroon, hunter green, navy blue, tan, and white. Whatever they wear, whether for work or play, their clothes are crisply pressed, meticulously clean, and very comfortable.

Rose-Marie, a second-grade teacher, explained that she had been looking forward to participating in her school's "Everyone Wears Shorts" day. The annual event allowed teachers, who were expected to maintain a professional style of dress, to come casually dressed. "I'd pressed my shorts—very pretty flowered Bermuda shorts—the night before. And then at breakfast I dropped some egg yolk in my lap, so I couldn't wear them. My kids—my students—were disappointed that I didn't wear shorts, but I explained to them that I just couldn't, not when they were soiled and I hadn't pressed another pair. I had some bike shorts I'd considered wearing, but I decided they were a little too much for school. They were tightly fitted and just not appropriate for a work environment."

Notice that Rose-Marie is displaying typical *Accommodator* behavior—organized, prepared, neat, and modest.

Jimmy, a lawyer with the Legal Aid Society and a strong *Accommodator*, believes that his casual yet professional appearance helps him do his work. "If my clients saw me wearing an expensive pinstripe suit, they'd lose confidence that I understand their lives."

Jimmy's suit is clean and neat, but neither expensive-looking nor symbolic of power. It's tan, lightweight wool, simple in design and construction, and emblematic of an *Accommodator*. "If I wore a power suit, people might be intimidated. Wearing this," he concludes, "reassures my clients that I'm a good guy, that I'm one of them."

He might be right; certainly his success in his career supports his statement. Perhaps, however, it's a case of what *feels* right *is* right. In other words, his success derives from his abilities, and his abilities spring from his personality (among other things). That he dresses as he does is an natural outcome of his personality, a function of who he is. It's not a pose.

With the modesty typical of an *Accommodator*, Jimmy stated he wears casual suits on purpose to appeal to his clientele. Perhaps, though, his appearance genuinely reflects who he is, and that he is not aware of it doesn't mean he's faking it. His *Accommodator* nature led him to pursue the law in a helping environment; it is a logical outcome for a hardworking and caring *Accommodator* to be successful in his career. Maybe Jimmy is putting the cart before the horse. By highlighting his appearance, he's implying that his success is due in part to how he looks. It is more likely, however, that his appearance is simply the outward manifestation of who he is—a strong *Accommodator*—and that his success comes from the proper fit of personality and job duties.

Regardless of why he's wearing what he does, you take one look at him, and you conclude that he's an *Accommodator*.

Playful and Lively *Optimists*

An *Optimist*'s appearance is marked by bright colors and a sense of drama. They, more than any other personality type, are very aware of fashion. Style is their middle name. They tend to be flashy dressers. They window-shop a lot, buy often, and enjoy wearing the latest styles.

"I'm a single mom," says Karla, a sales clerk, "which means I can't afford all the clothes I want. But I sure love looking! And I'm a clever shopper. For instance, I love animal prints, and I've been looking for months, but I can't afford a new outfit. But wow! Just yesterday I bought some really cheesy leopard print earrings. They were only a couple of dollars, but they are so jazzy-looking—it'll give a simple black outfit a whole new look. I put them on, I feel like strutting! I know I'm looking good."

Ignore Karla's budget; pay attention to her outfit. Leopard print earrings at work? Dead giveaway: you're looking at an *Optimist*.

Optimists don't just prefer bold clothing; it *hurts them* to wear clothes that aren't highly individualistic. *Optimists* are sensitive to atmosphere and environment. To wear a conventional outfit upsets and inhibits them—both psychically (they feel bad), and literally (it reduces their productivity by inhibiting their ability to think and work).

"When I first started as a broker, I had a real shock. I walked into the brokerage house, my first day on the job," Brian explained. "It seemed like it was 1959, not 1999. Everyone was wearing the same thing. No joke! It was a sea of gray suits and white shirts; everyone of those guys wore a maroon or yellow tie. Boring!

"Well, here's the shocker. I walked in that first day, it was about a week before Christmas, wearing a jingle bell tie, bright red and green—and guess what? My boss told me to use my lunch hour to buy a new tie. I didn't last even a month at that place. It was not a good fit for an *Optimist* like me.

"Don't get me wrong. I'm a hundred percent professional in all my client interactions. But this is *my* style and it works for me. Luckily I found a job that's perfect for me—it's a really laid-back place where all us brokers are welcome to be ourselves—ourselves as individuals.

"Here's why I think it matters so much—my work as a broker depends on building good, solid relationships with my clients. It's hard for a lot of people to talk about their finances, especially to a stranger. They meet with me and I'm wearing a jingle bell tie at Christmas time—well, guess what, the ice is broken. It's a great conversation starter."

Brian is very persuasive (an *Optimist* characteristic). Note, however, that though he may have good, sound logical reasons for dressing as he does, his reasons are irrelevant. *Why* he does what he does doesn't matter. What matters, for our purpose, is that his style of dress reveals him to a savvy observer as an *Optimist*.

Raquel, vice president of a music company, wears brightly colored suits with short skirts and high heels. Her long hair falls in lush waves beyond her shoulders. Her makeup is heavy. Her smile is broad, she talks a mile a minute, and she laughs easily. "My style is *my* style," she says. "Sure, I'm in an industry that allows individuality. But that's not why I dress as I do. I wear the clothes I wear because when I do, I feel like a million bucks. And when I don't, I don't."

Raquel would dress this way regardless of her industry's mores. It's how she wants to present herself to the world. When you notice the colors (bright), the hemline (high), the hair (unconventional in business), and the makeup (bold), that she is an *Optimist* becomes clear. Treat her that way, and she will respond in a positive way.

In casual-dress environments, *Optimists* generally feel the challenge of maintaining a professional image. Christi, a supervisor for a small rural utility company, couldn't believe her eyes. "I'm going back years, when dress-down Fridays first started at our company. Now we're a hundred percent casual. But then this young woman blew me away. We created an entire dress code because of her.

"She was a customer service rep," Christi explained. "I mean, she greeted customers who walked into the facility to pay bills, set up a payment plan, ask for an environmental review. She *was* the company in our customers' eyes.

"My thinking was that in the summer women wouldn't have to wear hose. And guys could skip the tie. Man, was I out of touch! First dress-down Friday we had, she's wearing a T-shirt and jeans. The T-shirt says, 'Same shit, different day.'

"Can you imagine? Of course I challenged her. She thought it was funny. Really. She did. When I pointed out to her how a customer might perceive a customer service rep wearing a T-shirt like this, she blushed; she turned white; she gasped. She asked for permission to dash home and change. Of course, I granted permission. Do you know, it never occurred to her that not everyone would share her sense of humor?

"She still works for us. She's been promoted to senior citizen advocate. She's a doll, very upbeat and warm. Our older customers love her; she genuinely empathizes—I mean, she cries at their hardships, and is very creative at helping them find solutions.

"But we, as a company, have a policy that you can't wear *anything* that has a saying on it, unless the company provides it, because of her!"

In casual environments, *Optimist* men wear the latest style of jeans or casual slacks, muscle man T-shirts, and bold-print shirts (in whatever bold print is trendy—an aloha shirt, a retro fifties floral pattern, etc.). *Optimist* women wear midriff-baring tube tops, skimpy sundresses, thong bikinis (probably in an animal print), along with long scarves and big earrings. *Optimists* are attracted to impish details like kitten buttons on a sweater or dalmatian puppy cuff links.

Often they appear to be hedonistic or decadent because of the emphasis they put on their appearance. *Optimists* may try on fifty outfits before finding just the right one. (And all the discarded pieces will be scattered throughout the room.)

Well-Dressed Producers

Unlike quiet and conventional *Accommodators* or bold and festive *Optimists*, *Producers* dress for show. When you see a *Producer*, you think, "Wow!" *Producers* look well tended. Their clothing is expensive, their accessories perfectly matched, their grooming impeccable.

It's not that they overspend on clothing. Rather, these are the folks who perceive the value of one good suit rather than two or three of lesser value. *Producers* judge others by appearance and expect others to judge them the same way. Therefore they take decisions about appearance more seriously than any of the other personality types, and spend a great deal of money, time, and/or energy selecting their clothes.

Rhonda, president of a rehabilitation company affiliated with several hospitals and skilled nursing facilities in the Midwest, said, "I drive a Cadillac. I wear designer brands only. I shop at Tiffany's in New York. I'm not just a corporate CEO, I'm also a role model. My employees—mostly women—look up to me as one of them, an occupational therapist who's done good, who's made it big. I hear all the time how they love to see what I wear. They ooh and ahh over my outfits. Another reason I dress this way is that I meet with hospital administrators and government officials day in and day out. It's important that I look terrific all the time because when I'm out in the world, *I am* the company."

Notice that Rhonda has a clear understanding of *why* she dresses as she does: to signal success to both employees and outsiders. It's interesting, but understanding her motives isn't necessary. In fact, even knowing her motives isn't necessary. All you need to know is *how* she dresses and what that implies, not why. Rhonda is dressing as we would expect a *Producer* to dress.

So is Dwane, a middle manager at a major pharmaceutical company. "I directly supervise eight folks in the marketing department: copywriters and graphic designers. In other words, there's a lot of creativity knocking around. But I don't care about their moods and emotions and all that. Being creative— *that's their job*. Let me put it another way. My focus is on getting results. We produce marketing material—our goal, our entire purpose is to produce marketing material that generates results. Creative—yeah, right. Irrelevant. I don't care what they wear. I don't care what hours they work. All I care about is that they write and design promotional material on time and under budget that works. But me, I've always been a sharp dresser. It's important when I go into a presentation or a meeting. 'Clothes make the man,' right?"

Thoreau might agree. In "Economy," from *Walden*, he wrote, "It is an interesting question how far men would retain their relative rank if they were divested of their clothes."

If someone is a sharp dresser, that someone is almost assuredly a *Producer*. There are plenty of other clues, of course. Notice Dwane's words: all he cares about is results. He expected his staff to be "on time and under budget."

Joanne Sieck, an accomplished stay-at-home-mom and former dental hygienist, put it this way. "All my life, I've spent the time to dress well. I never leave the house until I'm properly dressed. I want to look my best, so I do it. I put on the makeup. I wear the beautiful clothes. Although I think first impressions matter, it really has nothing to do with that. It's not like I think I'm going to meet Joe Blow's sister-in-law at the grocery store or anything. It's just who I am—it's me. It's how I want to be perceived by the world. And I think it translates into self-esteem. When I look good in the mirror, I feel good about myself. And the better I feel, the more I do."

Producers are doers. They tend to be quite formal in presentation. These are the folks who wear the pinstripe suits with starched shirts and the cashmere (not simply wool) coats; for them, casual means tailored outfits. Whatever they wear, it will be of the finest quality.

Julie Chan, who owns a custom jewelry store, wears beautifully tailored suits every day. "My clerks dress well because they have to. I require dressing properly as a condition of the job. I mention it as part of the interview process. We're a high-end shop located in an expensive shopping district. But you can always tell who dresses right because they want to and who dresses right because they have to. And when I see how some of them dress—some of my staff arrive in blue jeans and change in the bathroom. Fine with me, as long as they look professional and polished when on duty."

A *Producer*'s appearance sends clear signals. *Producers'* shoes will be polished; their hair won't simply be cut, it will be styled; their nails will be manicured (or at least well kept); every aspect of their physical appearance will be put together attractively and well.

"I buy my shirts in Hong Kong," says Don Riddleson, an engineer with a telecommunications firm. "Most of the people I work with are techie types—me too, I guess, but I want to be seen as more than that. I want to be seen as a leader. Notice the monogram on my cuffs? I love that monogram."

Thoughtful *Data-Collectors*

"I never think about clothes!" exclaims Jerry, an analyst with a major insurance firm. "And I'm always astonished when I realize other people do. Who cares? I just want to be comfortable."

Practical *Data-Collectors* choose clothing for practical reasons: warmth, utility, durability, tradition, or versatility. Often their outfits are perfectly coordinated; they dislike shopping so much, they find helpful salespeople and allow them to match the pieces. There's a clothing product line for kids comprised of symbols so that kids can easily identify which bottoms go with which tops. A *Data-Collector* would love a grown-up version. They want to avoid shopping, and if they do shop, to have the process be systematic, efficient, and organized.

For instance, when Mack, an engineer, discovered a hole in the elbow of a sweater, he was shocked. "I went right to my bureau, and looked at every sweater and guess what? There was a trend. Hole after hole. I couldn't believe it! But then I realized, I hadn't bought any sweaters in over twenty years." It took Mack more than a month to research sweaters. "My first decision was whether to repair or replace the sweaters. I like the professorial look of elbow patches, and I liked my sweaters, so I thought I'd quickly found an efficient solution. But the tailor at the dry cleaner—you know, the guy who does minor repairs on things—he pointed out to me that the sweaters were all pretty far gone.

So I bit the bullet and began the research. There are so many de-cisions! Wool versus cotton, department store versus off-price store versus direct mail versus the Web. It was an awful process! When I finally made my decision, I bought eight sweaters—one in every color—so I wouldn't have to do this again for another twenty years."

FAQ: *I wear a wide variety of styles of clothing. How could anyone recognize my personality type when I'm all over the board?*

A: I wonder if you wear different styles of clothes at cer-tain times or in various environments. In other words, maybe you're bringing forth different parts of your persona in dif-ferent circumstances, which is pretty typical. And it would make sense that you'd dress to suit these different personas. Regardless, if someone can't recognize you based on your clothes, they should defer to the *Producer*, and then adjust as they gather additional information from your words and mode of communication. Also, remember that adapting to personalities is an inexact science. Your goal is to use person-ality clues as a management tool, not to predict the future.

Very typical *Data-Collector* behavior. Until they decide which is best, they simply don't have a preference. Preference is based on intellectual judgment, not visceral reaction.

Data-Collectors are eminently practical. As a general rule, they have little style or color sense. Their favorite outfits are the most suitable ones for the circumstances. Chad, for example, chooses to wear one flannel shirt (of the six he owns) over and over again. When asked why, when the others are equally attractive and newer, his response is very telling. "I work outside and it gets pretty dusty. This one doesn't show the dirt." He added, "I'm going back to the store where I got it to buy two more of the same. It's a good shirt, perfect for me. I wear the others. Like if we go out to dinner, or if we're going to the movies. But for work, this one's the best."

Plaids, stripes, dots, floral patterns—*Data-Collectors* don't understand the complexity of matching different colors and patterns. Their outfits therefore tend to be quite simple and straightforward.

Their hairstyles are also likely to reflect this simplicity and in-difference. Women tend not to feature complex do's. No mousse, styling spritzers, gels, or fancy blow-drying techniques for a *Data-Collector*; no hour-long consultations with the premier hairstylist. These folks are more comfortable getting the quick and inexpensive cut at the cut-rate salon in the mall, or walking into a no-appointment-necessary barber shop. *Data-Collectors* are definitely low-maintenance.

Andrea, a law professor, says, "I've had enormous trouble over the years choosing clothes. I just don't care—but I wanted to look professional and polished! I used to think it was a failing in me that I hated to shop and couldn't care less about clothes. I re-member being a teenager—the other girls would spend hours poring over the latest fashion magazines. I never got it. I thought it was all completely boring. Now I finally understand—there's no right or wrong, it's just a personality thing. I'm a *Data-Collector* through and through. I'm as womanly as the next woman, but the only reason I wear nice clothes is for my career.

"Thank goodness I found this wonderful store with knowl-edgeable sales clerks who select outfits for me and make sure everything matches. They know what I like and what I need, and they make the whole awful process as painless as possible. The last time I was in there, this one clerk, she told me to take my shoes to the cobbler because they needed new heels. New heels? Who notices heels? If she hadn't told me, I would never have noticed. Heels on shoes? Who cares?"

Notice that Andrea has found a practical solution to the prob-lem: she delegated the responsibility. What a good idea. She al-ways looks professional and put together. But no one would mistake her for a clothes horse. While conservatively and attrac-tively dressed, you see no mark of individuality. No trademark scarves or hats. No special jewelry. There is no flair.

Because of *Data-Collectors'* indifference, they often have missing or broken buttons, threads hanging, hems pinned up (not sewn), or small rips and tears. They may present a rumpled appearance. But they will always be prepared for the weather.

Their forethought means they'll know if it's due to rain (and therefore they'll carry an umbrella); they'll wear layers in fall (because the weather is variable); and they sport galoshes in winter to protect their shoes (because they don't care if they look nerdy).

Anne, a computer programmer, said, "People laugh at me about my boots. I know they're rubberized and look like they belong on a seven-year-old. But they're fleece lined, so they're very warm; they're double insulated so my feet never get wet, and look, they reach to my knees—I can walk through snow and stay warm and dry. So what if I look like a doofus?"

Decor Reveals Personality

The appearance of a person's office, cubicle, or home also provides personality clues. Some people thrive in chaos. Some people need meticulous order. There's no right or wrong way to be, although, just as with clothes and grooming, the way your office looks creates an important first—and lingering—impression.

"The way I like to work is that I sort through everything, creating piles of work by category," explains Brittany, a TV producer. "I'm very organized, and this way everything is visible. So it blew me away when my boss told me that every time he passed my door and saw the disarray, it set his teeth on edge, and that if I didn't want everyone at the station thinking I was an out-of-control loser, I'd straighten up my office. I couldn't believe it! I thought he was joking. He made it clear, though—he wasn't joking. So I straightened up. I never liked it, but I did it."

Clutter versus neatness; personal touches versus utilitarian; coordinated versus ad hoc—each of these qualities reveals clues about personality. Some people are sensitive to environment, and others don't even notice. Become alert to the clues, recognize others' styles, and you'll be in a good position to manage *your* priorities well.

FAQ: *My boss makes all employees keep their desks clear, and we're not allowed to have anything personal anywhere in sight. How could anyone visiting me recognize anything from my environment?*

A: Even people in the most structured environments leave clues. First of all, *Producers* and *Optimists* rarely last in dictatorial environments such as you describe. As soon as I walked into an environment and saw that everyone had a uniformly clear desk, I would expect long-term employees—and by long-term, I mean anyone who made it out of their probationary period—to be either *Accommodators* or *Data-Collectors*. How would I distinguish between the two? I'd look for family photos. *Accommodators* are likely to have found a way to position at least one somewhere visible (say a wallet-sized snapshot tucked into a corner of their computer monitor). If there are none, I'd conclude the person was a *Data-Collector*. Note my logical approach. While nothing says I'm right, as I gather additional information in the course of our meeting, I can adjust my response.

Home and Hearth for *Accommodators*

Accommodators thrive in friendly environments, and so they usually create one for themselves.

"I'll never forget Shawna," Chuck said. "I own a machine shop, and she was the bookkeeper for years. There's oil and grease everywhere. My office furniture is old junk. I mean, I invest in machine tools, but a nice desk set, forget about it. Within a couple of days after she started, her corner of the office—not just her desk, but the whole darn corner—looked like it came out of *House Beautiful* or something. We all used to joke about it. 'Shawna,' I'd say, 'this is a machine shop!' She just laughed."

Here's what Shawna's corner of the shop looked like: she brought in a lamp from home for her desk and put a small braided rug in the area in front of the desk. She always had a bowl of candy beside her stepped vertical filing holder, and framed pictures of her children in a neat arrangement on top of her computer monitor. She used a rolling file cabinet to keep track of her payables (blue folders), her receivables (red), tax material (manila), and other items of interest (yellow), all placed in a thirty-one-day tickler file. She had plants lined up on the windowsill, all of which were thriving. One glance, and you knew that she was an *Accommodator*!

Here are some of the qualities you can expect to find in an *Accommodator*'s office:

- signs of *family*, such as photographs or children's drawings posted to a bulletin board
- *neatness,* indicated by ample storage or visible filing systems. There will be no clutter
- *friendliness,* indicated by bowls of candy or an uncovered guest chair
- *comfort,* relaxing elements, such as a lamp or plants, or favorite items brought in from home, such as a needlepoint sampler

When trial attorney Beth McCoy, a *Producer*, walked into Judge Martin's chamber for the first time, she stopped short. "It took my breath away. Here's this famous and important judge known for his crisp, no-nonsense manner. His office looked like a colonial home, and it was filled with Depression glass. There were countless vases and bowls displayed everywhere. I'd been assuming he was a *Producer*—after all, he *was* no-nonsense—but then I realized he was an *Accommodator* who had *learned* to control his courtroom.

"I shifted immediately. Instead of striding in and saying, 'Your Honor, I insist on something or other,' I said, 'Your Honor, your office is beautiful. Is collecting a hobby you share with your family?'"

"We chatted for a few minutes about his collection. When I made my request, he was all ears and smiling at me. No, I don't think my request was granted because I chatted with him first, but I guarantee you, it didn't hurt."

Beth's assessment was right on the mark, and her adaptation

served to create a feeling of friendliness and mutual cooperation. There's no magic in what Beth did; however, she was able to give herself a leg up in her dealings with a judge with whom she can expect to interact several times a year for her entire career.

Fun-Loving *Optimists*

You can recognize an *Optimist*'s office by the fun spirit. There may be photographs of family, for example, but they definitely won't be formal portraits. The photos will be of last summer's white-water rafting trip or the kids in their Halloween costumes.

"I have so much fun with it," exclaims Amelia, administrative assistant for an editor. You walk into her cubical, and the first thing you notice is that one entire wall is covered with montages of photographs arranged asymmetrically. "I love arranging all the photos—and my husband and I take enough of them. We must have thousands of my kids. You can see I do one montage a year. I'm so good at procrastinating, it takes me the whole year to do it! It's a lot of fun!"

Amelia's cubical is messy, papers scattered seemingly at random across her desk. Pens and paper clips and rubber bands mix with papers; there are stacks of file folders, a half-eaten sandwich, and two magazines strewn across the desk. Trolls sit on her computer, and she has cartoons taped to her monitor and pinned to a wall. There's a general sense of fun and disarray.

Most *Optimists*' environments will incorporate several of the following qualities:

- symbols of *fun*, such as Happy Birthday balloons pinned to the wall, cartoons, or games
- *offbeat* items such as a Zen rock garden or a Slinky
- *mess* or disorganization
- *bright colors* of the latest hue. They may bring in a length of fabric to personalize their office, for example, and tack it to a wall; they're likely to change the fabric every season, exchanging eggplant for sea foam, or whatever the latest color is that season

- *stylish* items; they prefer the most modern of materials and design

---

FAQ: *A coworker has trolls hanging off her computer, so you'd think she's an* Optimist, *but she also has photos of family on her desk, and she's really organized, so I think maybe she's an* Accommodator. *How can I tell?*

A: Sounds like she's a combination of the two. Try approaching her using techniques likely to appeal to each part of her persona, and evaluate which one generates the most positive response. For example, does she display more enthusiasm if you request an answer then and there as opposed to sending her an e-mail with your question in advance? If so, she's acting more like an *Optimist* than an *Accommodator*. Also, remember that *Optimists* and *Accommodators* share the qualities of enjoying social activities and interactivity, so any focus on those shared qualities is likely to appeal to both parts of her personality.

Kitty Allen, an *Optimist*, knows that her lack of innate organizational ability has the potential to hurt her career. "Luckily, I'm in a creative job—I'm a graphic designer, so people expect a little flakiness. The truth is, I'm not the least bit flaky, but I do tend to be messy—call me 'clutter girl.' Given that I work in the finance industry, I interact with a lot of *Data-Collectors* and a lot of *Producers*. It's clear to me that my messy nature creates a perception of disorganization. What's that old saying? 'A messy desk is a sign of a messy mind.' I don't mean to be sassy, but do you know what I've always wanted to ask the neatniks around? 'Well, then, what is an *empty* desk a sign of?' But I never have.

"My solution? Fun stays. Chaos goes. The way I did that was to buy these really cool fluorescent-colored boxes. I keep them on a shelf in back of my desk. Inside each box is a hornet's nest of mixed-up junk, but from a visitor's point of view, my office looks neat and orderly. I keep my huge silver jacks and my Disney posters in plain sight. It cheers me up. It boosts my happiness quotient just to look at my fun things."

Kitty's smart. It isn't *only* that she knows herself well enough to understand in what of environment she's most comfortable working, but also that she's aware of how others are likely to perceive that environment.

It doesn't matter that Kitty's office is neat. You would still be able to recognize her as an *Optimist* by the signs of fun on her desk and walls, and by the bright, colorful storage boxes.

Accomplished *Producers*

There will be no mistaking a *Producer*'s office. It will proclaim accomplishment—whatever the level of the employee.

Nathan, in his first job out of college, is on the fast track, a management trainee in a year-long program offered by a major consumer-products company. A *Producer*, he has a small cubical, and big plans. "I want anyone walking by to see that I'm a winner," he explained. "I keep a softball trophy on my desk. I won it in college. It's not that big of a deal, but it's sure a conversation piece, and it's a symbol that says I'm focused, that I like to win."

Here are some attributes you can expect to see in a *Producer's* environment:

- symbols of *success*, as represented by degrees, certificates, or plaques
- *signs of affluence,* in whatever manifestation the individual chooses, be it Oriental rugs or leather-bound books
- an appearance of *richness*, whether jewel toned accessories or lush, sink-to-your-ankles carpeting
- *serious,* purposeful decor. The computer will be the latest and best model available, and the plant will bloom all year round (or it will be promptly replaced).

Bob, an analyst (and a *Data-Collector*), explained that his boss told him to attend a meeting in the executive vice president's office starting in thirty minutes, and that he would be expected to report on European sales.

"I wasn't ready. I knew the numbers, of course, but I would have vastly preferred the opportunity to think it through before I had to do a presentation for the top brass. No such luck. My boss told me that if I did a good job, there might be a promotion in it for me. I didn't know what was so urgent; I didn't know what the problem was. All I knew was I had to show up and do a good job. Right away.

"The minute I walked into his office, I felt intimidated. I mean, this was the most incredible place I'd ever seen. It's on the sixty-seventh floor of the Empire State Building; there's an unobstructed view all the way downtown to the World Trade Center. Unbelievable. When I finally forced myself to stop looking outside, the view inside didn't help with the intimidation factor. This guy is the executive vice president, and I'm an assistant to an assistant director—this is a *major* player. I felt completely inadequate. They called on me first, and I made my report—poorly, I might add—and then they told me to leave. No, I didn't get the promotion."

We don't know—just as Bob didn't know—why he hadn't been given time to prepare. Many people might think that the situation was unfair, but that isn't relevant. It happened.

Having to deal with the unexpected (and undesired) is not unusual; it has happened to most of us, whether it's an unexpected guest knocking on the door or a customer showing up without an appointment. Had Bob been able to recognize the executive vice president as a *Producer*, he would have had a less stressful experience, and perhaps he would have been more successful.

Bob was intimidated by a *Producer*. It's easy to understand why. The *bottom-line* and *urgent* nature of the report, and the office that shrieked *accomplishment*, all signaled that the executive vice president was a *Producer*. If Bob had been able to recognize the office as such, and had known what that meant, he could have conducted himself differently. Before arriving for the meeting, he might have known to be prepared for an impressive office. He still would have been impressed, but not intimidated. Bob would have understood to focus on the bottom line, keep his report concise, and avoid overexplaining, a *Data-Collector*'s natural inclination.

Analytical *Data-Collectors*

Data-Collectors aren't affected by environment as are home-loving *Accommodators* and sensitive *Optimists*, nor do they use their environment to signal success, as does a *Producer*. It isn't that *Data-Collectors* don't care per se; they never think of environment at all. If you ask them what a new friend's home looked like, for example, they're unlikely to be able to tell you. Frequently, they just don't notice.

As a result, their environment is often messy, dirty, or chaotic. Or it may be completely empty, even austere. *Data-Collectors'* offices usually include lots of tools that provide information. There may be reams of paper, shelves of books, an extra computer, data printouts piled high, and stacks of manila files. Because of the Data-Collector's relative indifference to appearance, however, the files may be strewn across the desk; the books left on the floor, open and spine up; and the walls covered with computer schematics, tacked up with bits of masking tape.

The following attributes are commonly found in a *Data-Collectors'* office:

- *information* sources, such as magazines and books, especially on technical subjects (i.e., not *Desktop Publishing for Clothing Designers*, but rather *Software Implications in Desktop Publishing Applications: Fashion Details*)
- *reports,* such as computer printouts and ledgers, stacked high and well thumbed through
- sophisticated *research* tools, including encyclopedias (probably with a volume or two lying open on the desk or floor)
- *technologically sophisticated* materials, products, and equipment, such as the newest model of whatever they're personally interested in (stereo equipment perhaps), or those items their work requires (samples of plastic treated with the latest resin)

Clarise, the national sales manager for a midsize chemical company, and her assistant are both *Data-Collectors*. "My boss is all

Producer. Within a week of my starting the job, he came into my office and said, 'This place looks like a pigpen. Clean it up.'

"Needless to say, I was shocked. I looked around, and all *I* saw was an office being used—you know, sales reports on one side of the desk, stacks of competitive updates on the other. I called my assistant in and asked if she knew what he meant. She laughed and told me that it was pretty chaotic-looking. So I straightened it up, you know, stacked files, put books back on shelves.

"When my boss stopped by that afternoon, he said, 'I thought I told you to clean this dump up. I meant *now*.' Before I could ask him to be specific, he was gone. I had my assistant send for a rolling two-drawer file cabinet, and from then on, I kept everything except for whatever I was specifically working on in the cabinet. I had my assistant do the same thing with her work—not with a file cabinet, because she didn't have room for one, but with stacking shoe box–sized plastic containers. They fit on her cubicle's built-in shelf."

Clarise's strategy worked. "My boss hasn't said a word about my office—which I take to be good news because I know that if he had something to say, he would."

Data-Collectors and *Optimists* both work well in clutter, so simply seeing a messy environment won't reveal the personality. With *Data-Collectors*, you're much less likely to see anything personal. The photographs, cartoons, games, and artwork that are so important to *Optimists* are not important to *Data-Collectors*.

Color choice doesn't matter much to a *Data-Collector*, and fretting about decor or furniture styles simply doesn't happen. Tallia, a media research executive, explained, "I know myself. I just don't care. I go to work to work. But clients come to my office. Many senior meetings are held there, so I *had* to care. I hired an interior decorator. She gave me four or five options, I made the decisions in two minutes flat, and ba-boom, I have a decorated office.

"I love it, actually. Makes me feel very adult to have a decorated office, and I get a lot of compliments. But to tell you the truth, I never notice it unless someone calls it to my attention."

Even How You Sound on the Telephone
Provides Clues

Even talking to someone for the first time, you can make an educated guess about their personality. Within just a few seconds a person's rate of speaking and tone of voice, their inclination to interrupt, and the expressiveness of their voice allow you to make inferences about how best to treat them.

Customer-service professionals, technical representatives, sales-people, information specialists, and others who spend time on the telephone will find themselves more successful by adapting their conversations to suit the people to whom they're speaking.

Charlie Winslow, educational coordinator in a children's museum, explains, "Most of the calls I field are standard. Teachers want to know our exhibit schedule, how to arrange a field trip, and the like. Even dealing with calls so similar as to be routine, using this approach works.

"I've come to realize that some people I talk to are no-nonsense, some are more chatty. By recognizing the difference, I can provide better service."

Karen Proctor, senior vice president of the American Association of Advertising Agencies, puts it this way. "Some people want you to be brief; others prefer a little conversation with the information."

Becoming sensitive to their styles allows you to adapt. Here's how various people are likely to sound on the phone.

1. *Accommodators* are the best listeners, and their excellence at encouraging others to speak freely translates to the tele-phone. They're the best at *active listening* techniques, whether one-on-one or on the phone. You're talking, for instance, and they're going, "ahah," "hmm," "interesting," "really?" or "mmm." These little noises punctuate their lis-tening and convey the message that someone is interested in you and what you're saying. They're likely to speak in a soft voice and slowly—though not in a monotone. They'll remember your family members' names and ask after them. They'll ask, "How are you?" and wait for you to answer. If

you remember their family members' names, they will feel valued.

2. The cheerfulness that marks *Optimists* is noticeable on the phone as well as in person. They speak with almost a bubble of laughter in their voice. They chitchat, they interrupt (in a friendly way), and they tell jokes. They don't mind if you interrupt them either. The only thing that inhibits an *Optimist* is if you force them to get down to business before they're ready. If they have a half hour to do business, they may well spend twenty-five minutes of it socializing, and then focus in on business for the remaining five minutes. It's important to note that they're *not* wasting time. Rather, this is how they create a reservoir of goodwill so that business can be accomplished quickly and efficiently.

3. *Producers* want to know about the bottom line—and that's all. This mentality affects their behavior whether they're writing or on the phone. In fact, they often skip the polite pleasantries considered by most people to be part of a phone conversation; they may not even say hello or goodbye. It's important to realize that while a *Producer's* behavior is often perceived as tactless, it almost never is intended that way; it isn't personal. They're all business, and so tend to focus strictly on acquiring information. But *Producers* don't consciously ignore the common civilities—it simply never occurs to them. They're likely to interrupt you if they feel you're overexplaining, or if you provide information they don't find relevant. There is no humor in their voice.

4. On the phone and in person, *Data-Collectors* tend to speak slowly, even in a monotone. They're polite and pleasant, so they don't interrupt you, and they don't like being interrupted themselves. In fact, if interrupted, they may—after a pause to get their thoughts back in order—start over. They expect a lot of specifics, and tend to provide an abundance of details themselves. They are matter-of-fact and methodical in their delivery, often prefacing their statements with background or context. It is unlikely that they'll ask any personal questions; they're private themselves, and unlikely to indulge in small talk or irrelevant chatter.

Identify the Person, Adapt the Message

Consider that you are applying for a job with a textile manufacturer. You have experience in your field, let's say as an event planner, but none in this industry. Your first interview is with the human resource manager.

What would you expect his personality to be? You have no hands-on knowledge; your appointment was made by his assistant, so you haven't even spoken to him on the phone. Think about it—what sort of person is likely to be in that job?

Did you answer, *Accommodator*? It's a logical conclusion. When you think of a human resource manager's duties, certainly working with people comes to mind. So too does smoothing ruffled feathers, improving morale, helping people flourish in their jobs by providing training, and inspiring personal and professional development. Every one of these tasks commonly associated with human resource management would appeal to an *Accommodator*.

You introduce yourself to the receptionist. The manager's assistant comes to greet you and leads you to her boss's office. As soon as you step over the threshold, you notice the dingy darkness. Shades are drawn, the light is dim. Computer printouts are piled on one corner of the desk alongside bound directories, manila files, and open magazines.

The manager stands up, smiles, and shakes hands. You notice that his slacks are wrinkled and there's a thread dangling from his shirtsleeve.

Have you changed your mind about his personality?

FAQ: *I can't tell! What do I do if I can't assess a person?*

A: If you still can't tell after listening to the words they use and their mode of speech, and considering what job they're in, how their office looks, and what they're wearing, defer to the *Producer*. Doing so won't hurt you, whereas doing anything else might. As you receive additional information, immediately adjust your response to suit.

Did you conclude he's a *Data-Collector*? Think of all the human resource responsibilities that fall in the arena of data and analysis: benefits calculations, tax and reporting requirements, procedure and policy manual development, and monitoring of various compliance issues.

Don't panic! By understanding how to recognize different people's signals, you give yourself the opportunity to quickly modify your communication style to fit and thus to create the best first impression *with this specific person* that you can.

Instead of announcing that you want this job as an event planner to *help people* (which would speak to an *Accommodator*), for example, you might elect to say that you want to *systemize the process*. These two phrases are saying the same thing. By choosing your words carefully, you'll convey the message you want to convey, and your message will be understood by the other person. Consider how to impress a *Data-Collector*:

- Instead of providing only a standard one-page résumé, how about offering to send additional data sheets covering specific aspects of your background and experience? For example, you could say, "Here's my résumé. If you're interested in more information, I'd be happy to send you detailed data sheets that I've prepared about my accomplishments, education, and volunteer work." (Notice that you shouldn't replace the standard résumé. Doing so would be risky for two reasons; first, you could be wrong— maybe the person you're interviewing with is *not* a *Data-Collector*; and second, perhaps he has a *Producer* boss who would be turned off when shown a multipage résumé.)
- Instead of answering questions quickly, it would be better for you to pause and think about your answer before responding.
- Instead of speaking rapidly, you should speak slowly.
- Instead of making light-hearted jokes, you should speak seriously about everything. (*Data-Collectors* don't lack a sense of humor; they're just unlikely to bring it to a job interview.)
- Instead of emotionalism, you should moderate your

language. For example, instead of saying, "I loved my summer job as a lifeguard," you should say, "Every summer in
college I was fortunate enough to serve as a lifeguard."

There's no question that you will do a better job in managing
your priorities by modifying your presentations to suit other
people. Discovering others' personality styles by noting their
clothing and their environment, by observing how they process
information, and by paying attention to the words they use will
enable you to frame *your* messages so they'll be heard loud and
clear.

The grid on the next page summarizes the clues so that you'll
be able to quickly read people's signals. Take a look at it, then get
ready to consider communication styles, discussed in Chapter 3.

Tips

- Once you become adept at reading personality clues, you'll
  be able to make smart adjustments. By discovering how
  people dress, decorate their office or cubicle, talk, process
  information, and act, you'll quickly recognize how they
  want to be treated.

- Just because you like a lot of detail doesn't mean your boss
  does. Or vice versa. Just because you're a quick decision-
  maker doesn't mean your colleague is. Or vice versa. Detail
  or big picture, quick or methodical—nobody's right, just
  as no one is wrong. Knowing your differences allows you
  to modify your message—to speak their language.

EASY-TO-USE SUMMARY CHART

	Accommodator	Optimist	Producer	Data-Collector
Style of dress	Conservative	Playful	High-quality	Indifferent
Style of decor	Homey	Modern	Traditional	Indifferent, technical
Style on the telephone	Friendly and interested	Cheerful and fast-paced	Impatient, even brusque	Methodical and well prepared
Examples of words and phrases you're likely to hear	Help, need, support, feedback, share, work together, smooth out the rough edges, collaborate, build consensus, improve morale, teamwork, family, let's talk about it	Fun, wacky, offbeat, kinda on the wild side, just take a sec, chill out, brainstorm, innovate, create, pick your brain, it'll be painless	Get it done, hurry up, stop complaining, solve the problem, bottom line, reach the goal, work, do it now, profit	Data, analysis, facts, detail, think about, consider, evaluate, review, outline, curious, a surprise, interesting, research

CHAPTER THREE

✦

Communicate More Effectively to Meet Your Goals

Let People Know What You Need

Once you are able to recognize people's personality types or personality mixes, you will be able to present your ideas, make your requests, frame your offers, and convey your messages in ways that are specially tailored to each person or each group of people, dramatically increasing the likelihood that you'll get your needs met. The secret lies in *applying* the personality information by presenting your ideas appropriately.

Mary M. MacDonald, managing director and CEO of D'Arcy Directory Marketing, explains, "I present most information targeting each person's personality. If there's a new policy, for example, I'm aware that some people hear the new policy, and that's that. They understand it and have no questions. Other people need a lot of hand holding, a lot of reassurance. I'll go into their offices—I'm always careful not to call them into my office, I go on their ground—and ask if they're comfortable with it. I'm willing to do what's necessary to get them comfortable, because if they're not, their work suffers."

Bernadette Grey, editor-in-chief of *Working Woman* magazine, told me, "I've concluded over the years that most conflicts between people come from bad communication. By adapting to other people's communication styles, I've seen difficult situations completely turned around. It doesn't just turn around the performance—it also helps improve the relationship.".

She added, "I see it with my children too. My daughter, Lili, is like me. I can say to her, 'Get ready for school,' and she gets it. She's only five, but she knows what that means. Luke, my son, is seven, and he doesn't respond to a verbal instruction. I got him a Filo-fax and we created a list defining what exactly I mean by 'Get ready for school,' and it's working."

Applying these techniques assures *you* of success. In this chapter you'll learn *how to present* your ideas and what *words and phrases* to use. The examples highlight how various personality types and personality combinations respond to different presentation approaches and vocabulary, so you'll be able to select the approach that's most likely to work for you.

Methods of Communication

Should you write it down? Should you attach the documentation that supports your point of view? Should you use big words or everyday language? Should you speak especially slowly, or should you rush through your points? Should you pick up the phone or send a quick e-mail?

By making sensible and timely decisions, you equip yourself for success. In contrast, providing information or trying to persuade someone *without* considering their personality style risks irritating or offending the person—which almost certainly ensures failure. In the descriptions that follow, you'll learn the various personality types' preferred communication styles. It's another clue to help you recognize people, and it translates into successful interactions—whereby *your* needs get met.

Accommodators Prefer Time to Consider

Accommodators aren't comfortable under pressure. They like a little time to get their thoughts in order. Think about this: if you rush in, state a problem, and demand a solution, you're challenging an *Accommodator* to do something for which he's just not equipped.

In a recent interview Richard Archer, retired president of Dun & Bradstreet Europe, Middle East, and Africa, gave as an example a country manager he eventually had to dismiss. In this very responsible position, the manager took the time and care to develop an enormously loyal and devoted staff. He was a truly nice, warm, and giving man, Archer said. "He knew every employee's birthday—over a hundred of them—and he personally placed a birthday card on their desk on the proper day. That's showing extraordinary care for a man in his position. But his personality style finally proved to be his undoing.

"A subordinate would come into his office with a question or problem, and he felt it was incumbent on him to solve it then and there. Frequently with disastrous results. He felt he *must* help." When told to slow down and think things through, the manager was unable to do so. He was so focused on the people's needs, he lost sight of the issues at hand. His concentration was on the person, not the business.

Accommodators will give you a more thoughtful and higher-quality response if not asked to do so under the gun. In other words, put it in writing. The document can be quite informal, a handwritten memo, an e-mail, or a sticky note annotating a letter. Solicit their help, but give them time to think it through and frame a response.

Sammy, an *Accommodator*, remembers his favorite coworker. "Her name was Angelina. I was a new supervisor, untrained and scared I was going to mess up. She was older, and she could tell I was insecure. The first time she needed me to give her some direction—specific instructions on a big project—she handled it so perfectly, so completely perfectly, that for the last ten years I tell this story to every new employee. It's important, I think, that they know how to get the best from me.

"What Angelina did was so simple. She popped her head into my office and said, 'Got a minute? I need a little help. I jotted down a few notes, and if it's all right with you, I'll grab us a cup of coffee while you take a look at it, then maybe we can talk.'

"Do you see the beauty of what she did?"

Notice how Angelina put together her request, deftly targeting an *Accommodator*. Capitalizing on attributes common to an *Accommodator*, she:

- put it in *writing* (an informal handwritten note)
- positioned their meeting as a *friendly* interaction (the cup of coffee)
- gave him a little *time to think* (while she went for the coffee)
- solicited *help* (a powerful motivator to an *Accommodator*)

FAQ: *My boss says that a customer letter has to be answered in writing. I think it's a waste of time to write a letter in response to a customer's complaint when it's quicker and easier to just pick up the phone. What do you think?*

A: I think it's likely that you're very comfortable on the phone. I recommend, however, that you decide based on what is most likely to appeal to your customer, not simply what suits your own inclination. In communication there's an important principle called *parallel construction*. If she called you, it makes sense to call her back. But she didn't. She wrote you. Therefore, probably the best response is to write her back.

Optimists Aren't Readers

"If I need Raquel to answer a question, or if I have a problem that needs solving, I never write it out," explains Sue-Anne, an assistant in the music company where *Optimist* Raquel is vice president. "Not even an e-mail. Raquel hates reading reports. So what I do is to make a point of putting a smile on my face and talking to her in person. I try hard to avoid putting things in writing. I also make a point of adding some goofy words. It works," she insists. "Otherwise, you end up having a conversation about what's wrong, or how you're feeling, or if everything is okay.

"For example, just the other day I went into Raquel's office and said, 'Are you ready for a question from funky city? You're not going to believe what's happened now! I lost July's data—did it come running in here?'

"It was great! She laughed and told me how to easily re-create the data. The situation went from one of looming disaster to no big deal. I could have said, 'We have a problem.' But why would I do that? By keeping it upbeat and fun, even when there's a problem, I get what I need more quickly and with less effort than if I did anything else."

When interacting with *Optimists*, try to eliminate paper. *Optimists* tend not to be readers. Perhaps they're less visual; maybe they're more audio-oriented. Regardless of why they don't read very much, the point is that they don't. Don't expect them to read long memos, reports, or analyses. They won't review the training manual in advance of the workshop, no matter how firmly the memo instructing them to do so is worded. Try adding graphs and charts or cartoons to reports to lighten up the material and make it more accessible to an *Optimist*.

Lauren recalls the days when she was design manager for a major fashion house. "I'll never forget the look on this one guy's face. He was new; I'd just hired him as an inventory control analyst. After he'd been with us about a month, he walked into my office with a stack of computer printouts and a dreary look on his face. I chased him away," she adds, laughing.

" 'Go away, you *fiend*!,' is what I said. He blanched. I told him to take whatever he planned to tell me and distill it down into two to three sentences. 'Think of it like headlines,' I said, 'then be prepared to answer all of my questions about it.'

"I could tell that he thought I was a fool, but I'd been manager for a lot of years, and I hated bad news. Still do, in fact. So my attitude is, give it to me short and sweet, and let me get going on the fix.

"He didn't like it, but you know what, he did a great job. And he learned to respect that that approach works well for me. The proof is in the pudding! I'm now president of the company, and he's now my CFO. We're a heck of a good team!" Lauren was smart in knowing her information needs and in communicating her needs well.

Notice that Lauren capitalized on her *Optimist*'s abilities to:

- *assimilate information quickly* (she knew she'd understand the basics with an explanation of just a few paragraphs)
- *optimistically move forward* (she wanted the bad news out of the way, so she could get to work on fixing it)
- *rely on other people* (she trusted a new employee to distill the situation down to its salient points)
- *work well with a variety of people* (she's able to bring out the best from someone profoundly different from herself)

Producers Want News Quickly

Karen Proctor, the senior vice president of the American Association of Advertising Agencies whom we met in the last chapter, understands the power of adapting the delivery of information. She says, "I consciously make judgments about people's personalities, and adjust what I say to fit. I don't merely change the words I use, I also adjust the style—how I present information. For example, when talking to a *Producer*, I think it through carefully, say it quickly, and get it in writing."

For *Producer* Dwane, the middle manager overseeing creative work in a major pharmaceutical company, quick does *not* equal sloppy. "When I ask for an update, I want it quick *and* I want it right. I tell my staff, give it to me in writing. I don't care if you send it by e-mail or put it on paper. I tell them that for two reasons. First, I think it makes people more careful to write it down. They're not so likely to throw facts and figures around if it's going to be in black-and-white. Second, I'll have proof in front of me if I ever discover there was a problem."

Notice that Dwane knew himself well enough to take advantage of the following *Producer* qualities:

- *Speed* matters. (*Producers* think quickly and don't want details.)
- *Accuracy* matters. (Because they *do* things, *Producers* need to be able to rely on the integrity of others' work.)
- *Trust* is not automatically given. (Many *Producers* truly think other people are lazy, that they're naturally inclined to slack off; therefore, it's logical that *Producers* are most comfortable with written documentation.)

Most *Producers* won't read the report. But until they develop a lot of confidence in the people generating the report, they won't trust that they have done their homework unless it's long and comprehensive. They may find the bulk of the document reassuring, however.

One sure-fire way to win respect from *Producers* is to start sentences (whether spoken or written) with verbs. Sounds simple, and it is. Sentences spoken or written using this technique—the imperative—sound brusque to non-*Producers*, but *Producers* don't hear it as harsh or tactless. Instead of "Would you mind calling Mr. Smith?" say, "Call Mr. Smith," or if that's too strident to *your* ear, add the word please. "Please call Mr. Smith." It's focused, directive, and effective in getting the best from *Producers*.

FAQ: *How can I speed up conversations with someone who drones on and on?*

A: Overexplaining is a *Data-Collector* quality. Given your question, I would guess that you're an *Accommodator*. *Accommodators* are polite and considerate listeners, and they hate to interrupt. By learning to interrupt politely, which is considered perfectly acceptable in our society, you exert control over your information needs, and thus take charge of your time. Use the four-step process discussed in this chapter to interrupt the conversation without alienating the person.

Data-Collectors Think It Through

Elinor Basso, senior vice president, business development, for Dun and Bradstreet Business Education Services, explains, "Over the years I've learned to tailor my style to the person I'm working with; I have a certain antenna that goes up. In order for my employees to succeed, I must tailor what I do and say. For example, one person who works for me is quite literal. I can't give vague or general directions. They like it when I'm very specific, detailed, and directive—they don't think I'm being pushy or bossy. I see their comfort level increase the more specific I become."

Notice how Elinor capitalizes on her *Data-Collector* employee's methodical qualities:

- She provides *detailed* instructions (and avoids general ones).
- She is not *vague*. (Instead she's highly specific.)
- She appreciates their *literal* nature (and doesn't dismiss it as a lack of imagination, instead providing adequate direction).

Elinor adds, "On the other hand, there's another person who works for me who feels insulted if I provide step-by-step instructions, as if I think they're stupid, that they require hand holding and can't be relied on." Do you recognize this doer, this "I get it, I get it, let me get going already" sort of person? Clearly Elinor was speaking of a *Producer*.

"I'm a scientist," explains Terry, a professor at a small Midwest college and a *Data-Collector*. "I don't have a big staff, and my lab work depends on my generating funding. My inclination as a scientist is always to provide full and complete details. I've had to struggle over the years to develop a writing style that suits *their* [the grant providers'] information needs, not my own.

"For example, I hate it when a paper starts with a summary. My attitude is whoa, slow down. But I've come to realize that busy people need the synthesis quickly, and that I'm in no way shirking my duties as long as the summary is followed by adequate backup and full documentation."

There is no such thing as too much detail for a *Data-Collector*. They're curious about everything and value nuance and specifics. As a result, they often provide overwhelming amounts of details; they overexplain. Here's a polite and socially acceptable way to interrupt a *Data-Collector* and regain control of the conversation. If anyone (*Data-Collector* or not) is going on and on and on—this technique works.

For example, if an employee is overexplaining a computer bug, providing far more detail than you need to make a decision about repairing or replacing the unit, you can interrupt by:

1. Saying, "Excuse me."
2. Announcing what you're doing and why.
3. Asking a specific "closed-ended" question, if necessary.
4. Thanking them or otherwise ending the conversation.

In this example, you might say, "Excuse me, let me jump in here because I have enough information at this point to make a decision. Let's get three quotes on a new machine. Can you do that by a week from today?" If they answer, "Yes, I can," you can finish the conversation with, "Thanks for the update. Let's meet at two-thirty one week from today and decide which machine to purchase."

Focus on *Them*, Not Yourself

Applying this material requires practice. No matter how comfortable you are with the *theory*, you need to methodically analyze what is likely to work in getting what *you* want or need from others. Take the time to work through the logic, then use those approaches that are likely to work, and the entire process becomes more ingrained and habitual.

Let's say that you (an *Accommodator*) want to propose outsourcing certain functions that are currently done in-house to your *Optimist/Producer* combination boss. You determine that finding vendors for some payroll and graphic design tasks will save your department $10,000 a month. Your first decision needs to be *how* to present your initiative.

As an *Accommodator*, you prefer informality, and therefore you might feel that a quick e-mail is best. After all, you say to yourself, you and your boss are on the same team, right? What's the big deal? you ask yourself. Why does it need to be formal? You believe that your proposal will save the company money, reduce missed deadlines, and improve morale. You honestly can't imagine why the company *wouldn't* do it.

However, you realize that you need to consider your *Optimist/Producer* boss's personality—is he a reader? Will he trust your recommendation, or will he demand evidence that you've done your homework? You decide to select the best approach using a methodical process of logic. As you focus on your boss (not yourself), and review how he typically reacts to presentations and proposals, you identify five qualities that sum up his preferences:

- He wants the big picture, and he wants it quickly, succinctly, and with vivid clarity.
- He resists reading and likes visuals.
- He wants to get to the bottom line painlessly—he doesn't want to struggle.
- He's articulate and direct, even combative; whatever you say or do, he's likely to zoom in looking for flaws and weaknesses in your content, organization, presentation, and conclusions.
- He thinks you're lazy—not you personally, all employees, all people. You need to convince him with everything that you do that you're not lazy.

Take them one at a time.

1. How would you get him the big picture?
   How about something called a "Snapshot," or a "Summary"?
2. He doesn't want to read—he prefers to look at pictures.
   How about adding visuals to the proposal?

3. He doesn't want to struggle to get the information.
   How about a sidebar highlighting the key benefits?
4. He wants to be able to challenge you here and now.
   How about a live presentation?
5. He thinks you're lazy.
   How about providing all of the documentation?

Now, put it together. You need to sell your ideas during a short, live presentation with a thick document for backup that features exciting visuals. A comprehensive proposal featuring colorful graphics and a concise summary page—that you hand-deliver during a short presentation—has a much better chance of winning *you* respect and getting *your* ideas implemented. In other words, in order to manage *your* priorities, you must present the data *his* way.

As you further analyze his preferences, you realize that there are two good options for the proposal format:

1. Start with a strong graphic and a short, pithy caption. Subsequent pages of your proposal would include sufficient detail to satisfy his *Producer*'s need for evidence of your work (although he probably won't read it), and have enough white space (empty space) and visuals to make it not intimidating for his *Optimist* side.
2. Design a layout for the proposal with one narrow column (like a sidebar) and one wide column. On every page of the proposal, label the narrow column "Executive Summary," "Examples," or "Key Benefits." That way he can quickly scan the entire proposal and garner the salient points, or he can delve into the detail positioned in the corresponding wider column if he's so inclined.

With either alternative, you'll be making a live presentation with the written document as backup. By identifying your boss's combined personality, and methodically working through the logic of what that assessment means to *you*, you avoid communicating in the mode *you* prefer, and instead develop and deliver a presentation in the mode *he* prefers. How could you not do a better job?

Karen Quinn, a vice president at American Express, successfully applied this principle in a similar situation. "I once worked for a senior vice president who only responded if you had two or three words on a page, while you would elaborate verbally. He also responded when there were pictures on the page. So, when I was selling my ideas, my presentations contained few words and loads of pictures. Any other way I would try to present an idea, his eyes would glaze over." She was able to sell *her* ideas by presenting them *his* way.

Colleen, a product designer in the petroleum industry, and a strong *Optimist*, understands the importance of this approach. "Years ago I worked for a guy named Ralph. He was a great guy. He was part *Data-Collector*, part *Optimist*. When I started at the company, I assumed he was just like me—after all, we hit it off so well. We spent a lot of time chatting, getting to know each other.

"I learned the hard way to have all my ducks in order *before* I went into a meeting. After I'd been there about a month and had completed an initial design based on some recommendations from the field, I was invited to present it at the monthly product-review meeting.

"I knew the meeting was a big deal because I'd been hearing people talk about it for the month I'd been there. It was supposed to be a very high-pressure 'watch your ideas die' sort of thing, but I felt no anxiety. I knew that I'm good on my feet, and I knew that my boss, who chaired the meeting, loved me.

"When it was my turn to present my drawings, I breezed in with a cheery 'Howdy!' and I was off and running. I was done with my entire presentation in about three minutes; I told them the purpose, described my thinking, showed the initial drawings of the product I was recommending, and—between you and me—I thought I'd done a great job. *Not.* Boy, was I out of touch.

"I'd finished with my presentation, and Ralph said he was going to open it up to questions, after he asked two. *I couldn't answer either one.* And it was downhill from there. There was no rhyme or reason to the questions; there was apparently no logical sequence, no order—these guys just fired question after question at me. It was awful. I looked like a fool.

"It became clear that I had made a terrible mistake. I wasn't supposed to have gone in there with an *initial* drawing; I was supposed to have gone in there with a fully developed product plan that I could defend. Their attitude was, why assign a product manager to a product—the next step in bringing a product to market—no matter how good the marketing prospects look, if the person who developed the product can't even defend it.

"It was a nightmare. Nightmare! I couldn't answer ninety percent of their questions. I was embarrassed and ashamed. The only good news here is that I handled it really well. I stopped the meeting after about ten agonizingly long minutes. I apologized for taking their time when I obviously wasn't properly prepared and asked for an extension, at which point I promised to be completely ready.

"They said okay and—just to finish the story—I did a much better job at the next meeting. As it happened, the product never was approved, but that's neither here nor there. The point is that I did a good job. Had I known the personality approach—and therefore been aware of Ralph's personality mix—I wouldn't have been surprised that he switched gears. My mistake was in preparing for a meeting of *Optimists* instead of a meeting *chaired* by a *Data-Collector/Optimist* mix and including a lot of technical experts, mostly *Data-Collectors*.

"I should have known," adds Colleen. "If I'd thought about it at all, I would have realized what I should do." Here's how Colleen summed up her boss's (and his colleagues') information needs:

- He expected her to deliver a fairly short presentation featuring a quick abstract of the project (for the *Optimist* part of his persona), followed by an organized and methodical summary of her thinking (for the *Data-Collectors*).
- He expected the report to provide support documentation (for the *Data-Collectors*).
- He anticipated seeing many charts and graphs detailing her analysis and showing a logical sequence leading to her conclusion (for the *Data-Collectors*).
- He expected her to field questions deftly (the immediacy

appeals to the *Optimist*, and the detail associated with each question appeals to the *Data-Collector*).

- He expected that her peppy and charming personality would showcase his department well to his colleagues (appealing to the *Optimist* part of his personality).

"Once I considered his *total* personality, not just the part I personally found so appealing, as well as the other people attending the meeting, it was obvious," Colleen explained.

Improve Your Presentations

The bulleted lists that follow summarize how the various personality types most effectively communicate in groups and when making presentations. Use it as a guide as you develop strategies for yourself.

Accommodator

- Informal in tone, media, and style. The tone can sound chatty and relaxed; the media can be as informal as a hand-written margin note, a sticky note, or e-mail; the style can be bullet points or phrases instead of formally constructed sentences.
- Written, so that they have something to refer to and consult.
- Comprehensive. Don't belabor the details, but include enough information so the scope of the project is clear.
- Social or interactive, allowing time for questions and examples.
- Low or no pressure. Be sure there's sufficient time for actual discussions and review, as well as time for them to think about it. Try to avoid deadline pressures.

Optimist

- Informal is preferred, but formal (and the pressure associated with it) presentations are acceptable.

- No written material, although if written documents are needed, e-mails work well.
- Graphics or visuals, especially if they're fun, like cartoons or crossword puzzles.
- Interactive. Meetings in a social environment (such as a breakfast meeting, for instance) are best, although phone and e-mail communications can work well.
- High pressure, such as a deadline or the presence of high-level people, adds spice.

Producer

- No-nonsense. Use the imperative; that is, begin sentences with verbs to maintain a focused and directive tone.
- Short and concise. Use an Executive Summary or other short and snappy synthesis device.
- Significant documentation to prove your points. Isolate the extra data, however, so readers can skip it if they choose.
- Distilled to its essence. Avoid adjectives and unnecessary details, background, rationalizations, or justifications.
- Confrontational. State your desired outcomes with the bottom-line consequences likely to result from each. Make clear recommendations as you play devil's advocate to alternative approaches.

Data-Collector

- Advance notice preferred. They're not comfortable responding unless they're fully prepared.
- Complete documentation. Add appendices, annotations, attachments, and supporting data.
- Low-pressure. Avoid deadlines, last-minute or urgent requests, and challenging them to defend a position unless they've had time to prepare.
- Fact-based, not opinion. Provide references and supporting data.
- Demands time to get thoughts in order. By allowing adequate time, they will read up on the project, review

previous systems, and study alternatives, thus bringing insights to the interaction that might otherwise be missed.

FAQ: *I have to make a presentation to a group. Presumably there will be all sorts of people there, people with all sorts of personality mixtures. Whom do I target?*

A: In a presentation to a mixed group, defer to the *Producer*, and then weave in references that appeal to the other personality types. By targeting the *Producers* first, you will keep their interest. By appealing to the other three types shortly thereafter, you don't risk losing anyone else's attention.

For combination personalities, combine the appropriate lists and reconcile differences. For example, Andrea, a *Data-Collector* law professor, determined that her boss (the dean of the law school) was an *Optimist/Accommodator/Producer* combination. She had always submitted course or curriculum recommendations by writing a detailed proposal.

"I realized that I had been writing it for *me*. I *like* that sort of detail. My boss doesn't. Never did. I'd hand him a recommendation, and you could almost see him sigh. I realized I had to change my approach: create a summary sheet in addition to the primary document that would feature bottom-line statistics and facts, and present my ideas in a short, snappy presentation over a cup of coffee. Guess what? It worked. My new course idea was approved in half the time it had ever taken before, and my boss congratulated me on doing such a good job."

Vocabulary Creates the Emphasis You Want

In addition to decisions about how best to present your information, you need to select the *best words and phrases*. There are generally several ways to say something. For *Accommodators*, for instance, you might ask for:

- "Help in sorting through the options."

For *Optimists*, you might phrase the same request as:

- "Help! I have too many good choices . . . let's brainstorm which option is best."

For *Producers*, you could say:

- "Here are three options with the bottom-line consequences of each—pick one and I'll get going on it."

For *Data-Collectors*, you may decide to request that they:

- "Think about the options."

Once you understand the different words and phrases that speak to each personality type, you can formulate your sentences—whether in writing, in person, or on the telephone—to suit the situation. You don't, however, have to memorize pages of words and phrases.

How about making notes on four index cards, one for each personality type? Use the list below as a guide and jot down words that speak most powerfully to each of the personality styles. Add notes about prefered communication methods, and summarize presentation styles. You're now equipped to convert theory into practice, to employ the knowledge for your own success.

For instance, let's say your *Data-Collector* boss tends to intimidate you (an *Accommodator*). If you have a one-on-one meeting scheduled, you may be dreading it. You're afraid you'll forget data that you know well, focus on morale, not financial factors, and generally create a bad impression.

How about pulling out the index card that corresponds to your boss's personality type and spending ten minutes before your meeting reviewing the clues, reminding yourself of the specific language to use? Rather than allowing the newfound knowledge to simply simmer on the back burner of your mind, you're bringing it to the forefront, where it will empower you to communicate effectively, adapting what *feels* right to *you* to what will *actually work* with your *boss*. You'll do a better job of meeting your boss's expectations and needs. The meeting will run more smoothly, you'll conduct yourself with more confidence, and the outcome will be more positive.

> **FAQ:** *I told a colleague that I couldn't meet with her right then because I was too busy. She got mad. What did I do wrong?*
>
> **A:** Think of the implication of the phrase "I'm too busy." You told your colleague that her needs were a lower priority than whatever else you were doing. Next time, turn the statement around and make it positive. For example, you could say, "This is so important, I want to give it the time it deserves."

Here are some words and phrases that speak to *Accommodators*:

- Help, support, guidance, feedback, and direction
- I need you. I need your help. I need your support.
- We're all in this together. Collaborate. Unify.
- We're on the same team. We're like family.
- Avoid confrontation, irritation, anger, a breakdown in communication, or ill will. Smooth out the rough edges.
- Build consensus. Work together.

For an *Optimist*, your guide might include these words and phrases:

- New, innovative, creative, unexpected.
- It's fresh, the latest, high-style, agile, high-spirited.

- Brainstorming, or any creative or idea-generating exercises or processes
- Fun, whacky, wild, funky
- Inspiration, vision, illumination

The following words and phrases will be most likely to speak to a *Producer*:

- Bottom line, profit (surplus), revenue, percentage change, market share, money, dollars
- Goals, objectives, purpose, achievement
- Mission, aim, target, ambition
- Solution, resolution, answer
- Get it done. Be productive. Finish it.
- Hurry up. Here's the "Quick and Dirty . . ."
- No excuses. No explanations. No blame. No comment.

For *Data-Collectors*, use the following words and phrases:

- Facts, data, analysis, evidence, statistics
- Tested, known, proven, studied, researched
- Documented, demonstrated, reported
- I think you'll be interested in this. This was a surprise. This is curious. This deserves further scrutiny, examination, study, research, review, or analysis.
- Think about it. Consider it. Determine whether it is true.
- Detail, minutia, enumerate, catalogue, itemize

Adapt and Get Your Priorities Met

Sometimes it's easy to adapt, and solutions are simple. Consider Cathie's situation. Cathie, a *Data-Collector* office manager for a large sports medicine company, explained, "My boss used to read the first page of anything—and that was it. I used to get so frustrated, because on page one I was just warming up. Then a lightbulb went off over my head. I learned about this personality approach—and I recognized my boss as a *Producer*.

"Now I start every report—even a short little e-mail—with a bullet-point summary. He reads what he wants—the bottom-line stuff. From his point of view, he thinks I finally 'get it.' "

The change Cathie needed to make was easy to understand and easy to implement. Other times, the secret is in the messages we tell *ourselves*. Mary Magruder, owner of a flower shop, discovered the importance of perception only after hours spent worrying. She explains it this way: "One of my really good customers called the other day. I answered the phone the way I always do: 'Hello, Magruder's Blooms. This is Mary. How may I help you?'

"He said, 'Where's my plant? It was supposed to be here an hour ago.' No hello, no how are you. Luckily, I recognized his voice. With no apology, I explained where his plant was—my delivery van had had a flat—and then I told him that I'd already called his office and explained what had happened to his receptionist half an hour ago. He grunted and hung up.

"It sounds a little odd, but the truth is, once I learned not to take his brusqueness personally, I realized that I'm really glad to do business with him. He never wastes my time with idle chit-chat, and he always lets me know when there's a problem—which means I have the opportunity to fix it. We get along very well. That he grunted and hung up didn't mean he was dissatisfied. It meant that he'd gotten the information he wanted and was done talking to me. He has no social graces. So what? I couldn't care less about social graces in business. I feel gratified that my flower shop is good enough to enjoy his repeat business.

"I used to fret. I used to think that I ought to be more conciliatory, that I ought to do things differently, that I was going to lose his business. Then I realized that *he* liked doing business with me just as much as *I* liked doing business with him."

The utter lack of defensiveness shown by Mary Magruder is a hallmark of people who manage priorities well. Karen Quinn, the vice president of American Express who succeeded with an *Optimist* boss by using visuals, told of another success in which she adapted the presentation of her ideas to suit a boss's preferences. "I recently had a conversation with my current boss where he told me he didn't need as much detail about my projects as I was telling him. I appreciated the feedback, and now I'm streamlining my communications with him to suit the level of detail he needs." Notice that she *appreciated* the feedback. It is her ability to adapt that made the difference.

FAQ: *Given that we're all working for the same company to get the job done, why does communicating well matter?*

A: There's evidence that in certain industries and in specific occupations you don't need to be a good communicator to everyone. You merely need to be a good communicator to a few people. For example, the entrepreneurs behind some highly successful Internet start-ups are notoriously terrible at communicating in general. However, they excel at communicating their vision to the technical people whom they need to execute it. Most business activities require that you're able to get your ideas across in a persuasive manner to a wide variety of people, whether they work within your company or not. If people don't understand you, or if they aren't convinced you're right, your priorities won't be met. Ensuring you're understood and that people will support your efforts demands excellent communication skills.

Knowing your abilities is a key to success. For example, Sally, an *Optimist*, who is the marketing director for a family-owned food company, knew her limitations. "I was scared to death to ask, but I knew I had to," she explained. "As an *Optimist*, I *hate* details. One of the reasons I left my last job is that my boss was always asking for these stupid reports. It all felt like make-work to me. I *hated* it!

"I made a commitment to myself when I was interviewing for jobs that this time I'd check it out in advance by asking straight out—how many reports does the job require? I'll tell you why I was scared. I really liked this company. I really liked the man I was interviewing with. But I knew how much it mattered to me. So there I am, in an interview for a fantastic job, and it's going really well . . . and I swallow twice, smile and I ask, 'So, as far as updates and reports, how many are required?'

"I had my fingers crossed. He gave just the right answer. He said, 'I'll expect you to give me a one- or two-sentence verbal report. You'd just better be able to answer any follow-up questions that come up.' That was perfect for me! I was offered the job and I took it. I've been here three years, and we're still working well together."

The ability to assess what *other* people need or want enables you to achieve *your* priorities. Doing so is easier for people who are balanced in their personality mix, but everyone can do it when they perceive the benefits, and when they approach the process in a methodical manner. When someone's personality integrates all four personas, they're better able to see others' points of view, adapt as needed, and patiently and persistently achieve their goals. Given that everyone, to a greater or lesser extent, is a mixture of all four personality types, we can all learn to bring forth each persona as needed, even if we're not intuitively used to doing so. Once the advantages are clear, the desired behavior becomes easier to implement.

You may recall Kya from Chapter 1. She was the woman who broke her finger, saw an occupational therapist, and grew very respectful when the therapist's *Producer* qualities helped her get better quicker. Kya is clearly an *Accommodator*. She was intimidated by the therapist's brusque manner, but did what she was told, looked for the best in the therapist, and had something nice to say about her.

Imagine how much more comfortable and motivated Kya would have been had her therapist treated her as an *Accommodator*. Think about the occupational therapist's job. In addition to offering therapy, she needs to motivate her clients. Put yourself in her place. What would work to motivate a client of each personality type?

If she had perceived Kya to be an *Accommodator*, she might

have said, "Oh, I'm sorry it hurts. But I'm watching carefully, and you're not doing any damage. Could you try squeezing a little harder? I'm right here and I'm watching. I won't let you hurt yourself."

If Kya were an *Optimist*, perhaps the therapist might have said, "Ooh! Does it hurt? You squeeze and I'll tell you about this great movie I saw over the weekend. Come on now—if you don't squeeze, I won't tell you! And it was *gooood*!"

To appeal to a *Producer*'s competitive spirit, the therapist might say, "Interesting that it hurts. I treat a half dozen people a month with injuries like this, and most are further along than you."

For a *Data-Collector*, the therapist might enlist their interest in the process by saying, "Pain is expected, and the amount you're feeling is within the normal range. It indicates stretching. There are several articles I can refer you to, if you'd like, which provide additional details."

By changing her words, shifting the emphasis, and focusing on her *clients'* needs, the therapist would be more likely to achieve her own objective—helping her clients' conditions improve.

Freelance musician Joseph Stanko, a member of the touring company of the Broadway hit *Les Miserables*, finds that his ability to be, as he described it, "chameleon-like" serves him in good stead. "When I begin a job, it is important that the ensemble sound unified as quickly as possible, and that I make adjustments to the other musicians in order to achieve that unity.

"For example, upon joining the *Les Miserables* orchestra, a problem had to be worked out. The two trumpet players and the one trombone player—me—sat next to one another. Three days into my first week, the first trumpet expressed concern about the volume—not the quality—of my sound. Since the three music stands were positioned so that they're practically touching, my sound was reflecting off the stands and coming across at him, like the sun reflecting off a mirror. I was able to solve it by turning to the right and changing the angle of my bell. It took me a little time, moving my seat, changing the direction my mike was pointing, and so on, but the problem was solved to everyone's satisfaction.

"As a result, I was able to play at the volume I wanted, the conductor was very happy, and so were the trumpet players. Given that I was quick to respond, and took the time to ask how the changes were working out, I was appreciated and respected professionally, and personally, by both the conductor and the trumpet players. All because I took the time to adjust, and then followed up by expressing my concern that the other players be comfortable."

That Joseph Stanko is mostly a *Data-Collector* isn't relevant; what matters is that he was able to bring forth enough *Accommodator* to express his concern to his colleagues, enough *Optimist* to happily and quickly adjust, enough *Data-Collector* to carefully assess the problem, and enough *Producer* to persevere until reaching his goal.

In recounting the incident, he explained that he hadn't noticed a problem, but once the issue was raised, he immediately worked toward fixing it. How could this cooperative attitude not help him succeed? His priority was fitting in quickly as a respected member of a prestigious orchestra. By being sensitive and responsive to others' needs, *his* priorities were met.

The grid on page 106 summarizes communication styles. In Chapter 4 you'll learn a methodical approach to applying this information, and you'll meet several people who've used the tools successfully to manage their priorities.

Tips

- Should you be no-nonsense? Or will an indirect approach help you win people's support? For group presentations, where you anticipate multiple personality styles, use more than one approach. For example, in writing reports or proposals targeting a mixed group, you could combine a sidebar of short bullet points with longer, more detailed, narrative text.

- Watch your words. Vocabulary is powerful. If you tend to focus on facts, for example, and the person you're trying to persuade focuses on people getting along, you may be perceived as cold. If you talk about how the facts affect the people, you're more likely to succeed in your persuasive efforts.

EASY-TO-USE SUMMARY CHART

	Accommodator	*Optimist*	*Producer*	*Data-Collector*
Overall tone	Informal	Informal best, but handles formal well	To the point, tends to prefer formal	Matter-of-fact
Ideal Method	Written	Oral, or if written, visually exciting	Written: summarize with documentation as backup	Written: data and supporting documentation should lead to conclusions
Preference regarding pressure	Low or no pressure	High pressure	High pressure	Low or no pressure
Level of detail desired	Medium	None	Extensive, but won't be read	Extensive, and will be read

CHAPTER FOUR

✦

It Works!
Celebrate Success

Succeed with a Step-by-Step Approach

Applying the techniques discussed thus far will become easier with practice. In the case studies that follow, take an analytical approach. When questions are posed, consider several options before answering. As alternatives are reviewed, speculate on possible outcomes. Don't fall into the trap of thinking there's only one way to achieve an objective. There's no way of knowing how different approaches would work, of course, but it's a safe assumption that various approaches *would* work, and probably would work well.

When Helene, for instance, talks about providing her boss with a spare to-do list, pause and ask yourself what you think his reaction will be. Will he be grateful? Will he use it? Will he even notice it? When Lois is considering ways of getting what she wants—being a central figure in her grandchildren's lives, while avoiding what she *doesn't* want: feeling like a doormat and taken advantage of—ask yourself what you would do. As each case study unfolds, answer the questions, list what you perceive as viable options, and speculate on how each alternative would likely work.

By using a methodical approach, you increase your chances of success. Don't focus on what you *feel*. Focus instead on reaching your goals in a systematic way. You'll notice that each case study presents a situation that is successfully resolved using a three-step process:

- ✔ State your desired outcome.
- ✔ Analyze the personality styles of the people (including yourself) involved.
- ✔ Determine how to best communicate what you need others to do in order to reach your stated goal.

Case Study 1: Helene Capitalizes on Her Boss's Strengths

"My boss is driving me crazy!" explained Helene. "He's completely disorganized. I have to figure out how to get him to be more organized because *I'm* beginning to look bad."

Have you ever been in that position? Someone else's missed deadlines make *you* look bad. Helene knew from experience that she couldn't get her boss to be more organized. She'd been trying for years to do so, and everything she'd tried, failed. "What I've learned," she said, "is that no matter how badly you want them to do something, and no matter how convinced you are that it's in their best interest to do it, unless *they* want to, they won't. Period. End of discussion."

As a paralegal in a midsize city's district attorney's office, Helene was assigned to support the prosecutorial efforts of one of the assistant district attorneys. In addition to her research duties, she was also responsible for maintaining the integrity of the office. It was her responsibility, for example, to see that their budget was submitted on time, that phone calls were returned, and that her boss attended various departmental meetings.

"I love working for him," she said. "He's absolutely the best guy in the world to work for, but he makes me nuts!" She explained that he had a great sense of humor, a kind heart, and that he was a terrific prosecutor. "He makes *me* look good, because *his* track record is good. He's very effective in court, and he's good at bringing out the best in others. For example," she went on, "when I'm researching a case for him, sometimes he'll just stand at my desk and brainstorm. He'll free-associate ways he might proceed with the prosecution, one idea bouncing off another. He'll think of a case he prosecuted five years ago. He'll remember a citation from law school, for goodness' sake, and all the time he's doing it, I'm there taking down notes. He makes my life easier by doing this—it gives me a head start on the research I need to do—and it's good for him too. It helps him clarify his thinking.

FAQ: *My boss pushes all of his work down to me. He's mostly an* Optimist, *but he has enough* Producer *in him to make him really demanding. I don't have enough time to do my own work, let alone his. How do I handle it?*

A: First of all, be sure your assessment is accurate. You may not be privy to all of what your boss does. It's also possible that you're mistaken about the scope of your own job. Second, recognize the tribute your boss is paying you in showing such confidence in your abilities to juggle priorities. Finally, if there's not enough time to do all of your assigned work, you need to document it. For instance, time yourself doing things to demonstrate where your time is going.

"There's no doubt we're a terrific team. But here's the problem. He's not very good at keeping track of details, and he's pretty disorganized. Let me restate that: he's terrible with details and utterly, completely disorganized. I send him off in the morning with a to-do list with twenty items on it. Guess what? He loses the paper.

"I've taken to sneaking a second copy into his briefcase. Can't you just see him when he finds the second copy, saying, 'Oh, my God! It's back!' I don't know what to do with him. But here's what I do know. When he doesn't answer my budget questions, *my* budgets are late. Who looks bad—him or me? Me. When phone calls aren't returned, who looks bad—him or me? Me. There has to be a way to get him to be more organized."

The first step in resolving this dilemma is to identify *what the problem is*.

✔ State your desired outcome.

How would you sum up Helene's situation? In one sentence, state her desired outcome.

Here are several statements Helene considered and rejected:

1. Help him to become more organized.
2. Help him to understand his problem.
3. Teach him organizational tips.
4. Get him to stop missing deadlines.
5. Stop looking bad to my coworkers.

She wisely rejected these because they focused on getting someone else to change, which can't be done, or they stated her desire as a negative as opposed to a positive goal.

After consideration, Helene stated her desired outcome as:

Make my deadlines and build my reputation as a reliable administrator.

As long as the statement is positive and states behavioral (not emotional) changes within *your* control, *it will work*.

✔ Analyze the personality styles of the people (including your-self) involved.

Can you identify their personalities or personality mixes? Did you recognize the clues? Let's start with Helene's boss. What sort of person is driven to win? Which of the personality types would perch on the corner of a desk and free-associate, brainstorming aloud? Which type is likely to be disorganized?

It's safe to assume, isn't it, that you're dealing with a *Producer/Optimist* mix? Think about that—isn't that exactly the sort of lawyer you want representing you if you're ever on trial? Someone who's able to adapt and adjust to the jury's mood, quick on his feet, articulate—and a winner?

Now think about Helene. What sort of person is organized, research-oriented, methodical, and systematic?

Did you decide that she's a *Data-Collector*? Can you see the dilemma she faces? She's very good at coming up with alternate methods of organization, new systems or procedures, and step-by-step approaches for tracking details. None of which her boss has ever used. As Helene's frustration grew, so did his. And she knew it. "He told me last week that it was my job to see that the details were taken care of. I was speechless! All I do is try to take care of the details, but he thwarts me at every step along the way."

"So I took a deep breath and reminded myself of the proper approach. Stop looking at the situation from *my* point of view—look at it from *his*."

✔ Determine how to best communicate what you need others to do in order to reach your stated goal.

"Finally, it dawned on me to go with his strengths," Helene explained. "I really thought about it, and I realized that as a combination of *Producer* and *Optimist*, he's hardworking and motivated to do even more. I knew he'd be responsive if I offered him a way of becoming more productive. And he has a great sense of humor!"

She developed a form (perfect for a *Data-Collector*!). She called it her "Nag" form. Inch-high letters read, "Nag, Nag, Nag" across the top. She ran it off on hot pink paper. No longer was her boss given a to-do list with twenty items on it. Instead, she'd leave him twenty little pieces of hot pink paper with specific actions she needed him to take. On one was a handwritten note to return a phone call; on another was a reminder about a time change for a deposition; on a third was a two-line summary of a memo from the district attorney concerning a change in policy regarding expense submissions.

"First, I told him the truth. When I heard Jane's seminar, she made a real point about the benefits of telling the truth, and I love that. What a relief to be able to tell the truth! You just have to watch your words—to be sure and position your message in a way that the person you're talking to is likely to be receptive to.

"What I said was, 'You're wonderful to work for and a marvelous prosecutor, but we both know you're disorganized. You've told me that it's my responsibility to keep us organized, so I've come up with a new idea that I think will help you be more productive. I'm hoping you'll agree to try it for a month.' Wasn't it brave of me to say it straight out like that? You know what? He *loved* that I said it so directly. He asked why he should try *anything* for a month. I said, 'Because that's how long it takes for a new thing to become a habit. Let's see if it works . . . let's give it a fair shot.'"

Helene was wise to speak directly because *Producers* and *Optimists* prefer a frank delivery. Also, notice the *words* Helene used. She said that she had a "*new* idea," which speaks to the *Optimist* persona. She added that she thought her idea would "*help you be more productive.*" That's a direct appeal to the *Producer* part of his personality.

"Here's why I think it worked," Helene explained. "First, the pink paper stood out on his desk—a very practical advantage to a disorganized person. Second, the deal we made was that he wouldn't leave the office until all his pink pieces of paper were gone. The implied deadline pressure appealed to him. He thought it was fun! I mean, really, I couldn't enforce a deadline—I worked for him! Third, he thought it was funny that I was nagging him. And fourth, he found great satisfaction in the accomplishment, in that he was in fact getting a lot done. Also, he felt good because he perceived that he was doing a lot.

"It worked so well, he was accomplishing so much more than he ever had before, and he was feeling so proud of himself, you know what he did? Within a week he bought himself one of those executive basketball hoops that go over trash cans. His reward for finishing a task was to crumple up the paper and throw it through his hoop!"

In other words, Helene's idea worked. She got *her* priorities met, not by converting him to *her* way of thinking, not by teaching him to use *her* systems, but by capitalizing on *his* strengths. She embraced the three principles: she stated her desired outcome; she analyzed her boss's and her own personality styles; and she determined how to best communicate what she needed her boss to do in order to reach her goal.

She combined those three central principles with two others.

1. She told the truth.
2. She broke what her boss perceived as an overwhelming project into smaller units.

Telling the truth. So simple. Choose your words so the person listening to you is receptive to your message. Often, an effective technique is to employ the RAF principle: the Rule of Affirmation First.

Note that when Helene told her boss the truth, the first thing she said was, "You're wonderful to work for and a marvelous prosecutor, but we both know you're disorganized." She said something positive first. It's often easier for people to hear a negative when it follows something nice.

Also, she was not critical, she was constructive. She wasn't complaining, arguing, or trying to avoid responsibility, nor was she defensive. She offered a specific, practical, and well-thought-out suggestion for fixing the problem.

In other words, it's not simply that she told the truth. She told the truth in a positive and constructive manner, positioning herself as someone wanting to solve a problem.

She combined telling the truth with another important principle—*baby steps*. When you can't think what else to do, try breaking things into smaller units. Breaking responsibilities into baby steps helps any task become more manageable and less intimidating. Instead of a to-do list with twenty items on it, she provided twenty little pieces of paper.

Case Study 2: Lois Creates a Plan

Lois was doing well at work. "I'm an office manager for a technology company. And I like it. I've been there for years, through two owners and three reorganizations. I've survived it all, and I still like my job. But in the last few months I've found myself having trouble concentrating. And it's all because I'm about to become a grandmother. I'm a widow and my own sole support. Which means I better not screw up my job. And when you're an office manager responsible for ordering equipment, services, and supplies which add up into the thousands, screwing up can have major consequences quickly. So, I decided I had to act sooner rather than later."

Successfully managing priorities at work requires success in managing priorities at home. If you're not able to juggle your responsibilities successfully in all arenas, something has got to give. Therefore, it behooves you to make sure your personal priorities are managed as effectively as your professional priorities.

Lois explained that she had, as she put it, "doormat proclivities." She was determined to find a way to be a baby-sitting resource for her grandchildren—her priority—without feeling taken advantage of. "Not that my daughters would ever consciously take advantage of me. That's not it. It's just that I have a terrible time saying no. My daughters would be behaving normally, and I'd end up feeling like a doormat. I'm not exaggerating—here's what would happen: one would call and ask if I could baby-sit, and I'd say yes.

"I'd say yes because I wanted to baby-sit, and I'd say yes because I just automatically say yes. I hate the thought of disappointing people, especially my girls. I'm a classic *Accommodator*. It's a real problem for me. I get myself into trouble a lot—I'm always spread too thin, and it doesn't matter that I know it's my own fault, I keep doing it. And then what happens is that I start resenting the people who've got me into the situation. I know, I know, no one but me has got me into the situation. It doesn't seem to matter. I still resent them. I didn't want to end up resenting my daughters, and I didn't want to screw up my job, so it was very important to me that we get started on the right foot."

Lois didn't want to risk alienating her daughters with what felt to her—an *Accommodator*—like a confrontation. *Accommodators,* more than other personality types, avoid confrontations, or anything they perceive as a confrontation. And *Accommodators* typically perceive confrontation in interactions that other people simply don't. Which means they may well delay confrontation long beyond when it might be in their best interest.

"That was in my mind. That no matter what I did, I'd lose some of my daughters' affection. I was very troubled, very conflicted. I knew I had to take control of the situation, or it would be an ongoing problem. Also, I think it's terribly important to teach children respect for other people's time. As an *Accommodator*, I know how easy it is to let other people control your time. And if they get your time, they get your energy. My only hope was to cut them off at the pass—*before* there was a problem.

"The first thing I did was refer to Jane's three-step process, which is so helpful in working through difficult situations:

- ✔ State your desired outcome.
- ✔ Analyze the personality styles of the people (including yourself) involved.
- ✔ Determine how to best communicate what you need others to do in order to reach your stated goal.

"I thought that stating my goal would be easy, because I had a picture of it in my head. I could envision my grandkids in my house. It was great! At first I couldn't do it at all. It surprised me to find how hard it was to do. I found it a real struggle to state what I wanted in a positive way. When I first started formulating my goal, everything I came up with was negative. I had a lot of fears and concerns which I didn't even know I had until I started this process. But *finally* I did it—I wrote a goal that was accurate *and* positive."

How would you frame Lois's objective? Write one sentence that defines her goal.

"Here's how I thought about it," Lois explained. "First, I just stated it flat out: *I want to be a frequent baby-sitter for my grandchildren, but I never want to feel taken advantage of.* As soon as I put it that way, I realized that I needed to get more specific. What, I asked myself, would make me feel taken advantage of? I'm embarrassed to admit it, but it was quite a list! Here's what was on it.

"I will feel taken advantage of if:

- They ask me to baby-sit at the last minute.
- They ask me to baby-sit every day.
- They never say thank you.
- I hear them telling people, 'Sure, we can go . . . no problem, Mom will baby-sit.'
- They expect me to commute long distances in order to baby-sit.
- They expect me to cancel other things so I can baby-sit.
- They assume baby-sitting is all that I want to do in life."

Do you notice a pattern? Lois did.

"As soon as I read over the list, I realized there was a pattern. I would end up feeling taken advantage of if they didn't respect my busy schedule and accommodate *me*.

"So now my goal became: *I want to be a frequent baby-sitter for my grandchildren, but only at my own convenience.* Well, that was the blunt truth, but I knew myself well enough to know that there was zero chance—no way—I could ever tell them that, at least I didn't think I could. But I felt good! I'd completed step one."

Step two invites you to analyze the personality styles of the people involved. "I stared at that check mark a lot," Lois said. "My daughters are wonderful women. Marianne is quite artistic and quiet, a very introspective person. Charlene is flamboyant and dramatic; she's a real go-getter."

What do you think their personality styles are? Take a moment and consider how you'd address the second step, which reads:

✔ Analyze the personality styles of the people (including yourself) involved.

Were you able to decide on their personality types? Here's what Lois said in explaining her assessments. "Marianne is part

Optimist—that's the artistic part of her persona—but mostly she's a *Data-Collector*. Charlene is primarily a *Producer*—very focused and goal-oriented—but she presents herself as an *Optimist*—her sense of drama and her flamboyance are evident in everything she does. Because that's how she presents herself, that's how I decided to treat her in this interaction—as an *Optimist*. Me, I'm easy—I'm all *Accommodator*."

The third step in the model reads:

✔ Determine how to best communicate what you need others to do in order to reach your stated goal.

"This one got me," confessed Lois. "I didn't even know where to start."

When you're stymied, take a methodical approach. Don't expect answers to come to you fully developed. For instance, try listing as many implications of the personality type or types you're trying to work with as you can. Take each personality or personality mix one at a time and then look for overlap or harmony. For instance, Lois listed that Marianne, her *Optimist/Data-Collector* daughter was:

- highly organized
- rational and reasonable

and Charlene, her *Optimist/Producer* daughter was:

- goal-oriented
- passionate

The question no longer is the broad "how can I best communicate what I need my daughters to do in order to reach my stated goal." Instead, Lois began thinking of a rational, organized way to express her goal clearly. Once she discovered the approach, Lois understood that she would need to express it reasonably, in a matter-of-fact manner to Marianne, and with great passion to Charlene. The process becomes easier, the more you understand what's involved.

"My first thought was to stop complicating my life. I have a wonderful and open relationship with my girls, so I decided just to tell them the truth. I knew they'd both understand. Keep it simple, I figured.

"But then I realized that telling the truth wasn't enough. That was just setting up a situation in which I'd constantly be saying no. How open our relationship was wasn't the issue. How much I loved them wasn't the issue. I forced myself to focus on my priorities.

"I wanted to set up a situation in which I'd constantly be saying yes, not no. And then it occurred to me. I didn't have a simple issue to deal with—I had three separate issues to deal with.

"First, I had to figure out how I could baby-sit but *not commute*. Second, I had to create a situation where I'd *avoid saying no*. And third, I had to create a situation in which I'd get the pleasure of *saying yes*.

"The commute part was easy. I decided to define how far I'd be willing to travel day in and day out as an always available baby-sitting resource. Both of my daughters live nearby, but in today's world moving doesn't seem to be as major an issue as it used to be. I didn't want to be in the position where my daughters had relied on me as a baby-sitter for a few years, and then they move two hours away, and expect me to keep up the same baby-sitting schedule.

"Isn't it funny the worries that come into your mind? I was fretting about something—whether they'd move far away—that I had no reason to anticipate. It didn't matter whether it was rational or not—it was worrying me, and I wanted to deal with the possibility, even if it was only a slight possibility.

"The other two issues were hard. I spent a lot of time thinking about them, and I realized that maybe I could achieve them simultaneously because they're related. It wasn't *only* that I didn't want to say no, also *I wanted to say yes*. So if I could find a way to say yes a lot, maybe I could build in ways of not saying no. That was my thinking. I considered it all step by step.

"Here's what I did. I got a huge white board calendar and mounted it on my kitchen wall. I mean, it's so big it takes up almost one whole wall. I did this with some trepidation because all of the time-management books I've ever read warn you against trying to maintain more than one calendar, and I understand that. But this idea worked for me.

"I put *everything* that was on my personal diary on the white board, so that at any time my daughters or the kids could come into the kitchen and slot themselves in. I put everything on the calendar, even an informal lunch with a friend. If my granddaughter wanted me to go to her ballet recital on Saturday, for example, she'd see that my bridge club met at seven, and that that was the only thing on the schedule for that day. That meant she could write in that the ballet recital begins at noon. Then when I came home, I'd transfer the recital to my diary. It was a lot of work, but it has been so worth it, I cannot tell you! And it was so cute to see the little ones. They were so eager to be able to write things on the calendar themselves. My granddaughter was five when she had her first ballet recital. She wasn't able to write 'ballet recital, noon.' So she drew little ballet slippers on the board. So cute! Then my daughter added the time."

She phrased the offer to each daughter differently. She invited each daughter—one at a time—to her house, and over a cup of coffee in the living room, she delivered her prepared speech. Midway through, she took them into the kitchen to see the white board.

Here's what she said to Marianne: "I've been thinking about baby-sitting now that you girls are both married and Charlene is pregnant. I want to be a baby-sitting resource for you both.

"But I have so much going on in my life, what with work and my other activities, that it occurred to me I need a system so that I can spend as much time as possible baby-sitting—being a part of my grandkids' lives. Here's what I came up with. I don't want to spend my valuable baby-sitting time doing anything else than being with my grandkids. So as long as you live within this school district, I have an offer to make you. I'll baby-sit anytime you want if I have the time available. And here's how you'll always be able to tell."

Showing her the white board calendar, Lois explained, "I'll keep the calendar up to date. All you have to do is find an available slot, pick up the marker, and write yourself in. That's it! If the time is open, you'll know it, and my time is yours."

Notice how Lois satisfied all three components of her goal, which was: *I want to be a frequent baby-sitter for my grand-children, but only at my own convenience.* Specifically, she wanted to:

- Not commute. She satisfied this by defining her limit as *"live within my school district."*
- Not say no. There was never a question of saying no, be-cause she cleverly *avoided having her daughters ask*.
- Say yes a lot. By allowing her daughters to write them-selves into her calendar, she was providing plenty of *"yes, I'll baby-sit"* opportunities.

The language she used in talking to Marianne, whom she de-cided to treat like a *Data-Collector*, was crafted to appeal to her. Lois spoke of creating a *system*, and she described it in a *methodical* manner. She showed her a calendar which was *tangible*, the visual element of a *plan*. The calendar as well as Lois's *rules* served as a *blueprint* for more than the use of time—it was a *blueprint* that defined Lois's future relationship with her daughters, *setting limits* and *offering options*.

Compare this presentation with what Lois said to her *Optimist/ Producer* daughter. You'll recall that Lois decided to treat Char-lene as an *Optimist*.

Lois said, "I've been thinking about baby-sitting now that you girls are both married and you're pregnant. I want to be a baby-sitting resource for you both. I'm so excited, I can hardly stand it!

"But I have so much going on in my life what with work and my other activities—you know how I'm running all over all the time—that it occurred to me that we need to find a way to keep track so that I can spend as much time as possible baby-sitting—being the grandma of my dreams! Here's what I came up with. Tell me how this idea strikes you. I want to spend all the time I can with the babies, so as long as you live within this school dis-trict, I have a promise. I'll baby-sit anytime you want if I have the time available. And here's how you'll always be able to tell. Come with me to the kitchen—you'll love this!"

Showing her the white board calendar, Lois explained, "Look at this. I'm color-coding work versus pleasure—don't you love the purple marker? So here's how easy it is—check out my schedule, find an available slot, pick up the marker of your choice, and *poof!*—you've got yourself a baby-sitter. That's all it takes! If the time is open, it's yours—guaranteed."

Lois selected words and phrases to appeal to the light-hearted, passionate Charlene. She spoke not of creating a system, but of her *excitement*, not of a blueprint, but of being the *grandma of her dreams*. She spoke of *colorful markers*, and appealed to Charlene's dislike of organization and details with the phrase *"we need find a way to keep track."* Lois used playful language like *poof*, and asked Charlene for her feedback on a new idea.

Note that when talking to Marianne, Lois used the pronoun *I*, reflecting a *Data-Collector's* self-reliance, but to Charlene she used the pronoun *we* because *Optimists* crave interactivity. This simple vocabulary shift increased the empathy between each daughter and her mother.

Lois reports that her offer was happily accepted by both daughters, that the calendar worked exactly as she'd hoped from the first day she tried it, and that it is still working, six years after she first proposed the approach.

"My eldest grandson is now in junior high, and one of the first things he does when he comes over to my house is run into the kitchen to see the calendar. He'll call out to me, 'Grandma, you're coming to my game on Saturday!'

"You know what I'm most proud about? As part of my offer, I required that everyone physically be in the kitchen writing themselves up on the white board. They couldn't just call and have me do it. There were two reasons for this, and both reasons translated into important and long-lasting benefits for us all. First, I wanted the kids to see that Grandma had a busy and full life. The second benefit—and this is where I confess to feeling very clever—is that because I required that they physically be there, well, *they were!* Which means that they are in my kitchen a lot!"

FAQ: *Where do I begin in trying to get my staff to work more as a team?*

A: First, state your desired outcome. Why do you want them to work as a team? Is it because you want to increase sales? Improve inventory control? Or reduce absenteeism? In the three-step process discussed in this chapter, the point is made that you can't solve a problem unless you're clear about what the problem is. Once you know that, you're in a good position to achieve your objective.

Case Study 3: West Cancels Training and Boosts Sales

West (his nickname, and how he prefers to be addressed) supervises thirty-five sales representatives in three regions for his midsize Internet start-up. "It's an impossible job," he explains. "I remember learning in B-school, in some management course, that the span of influence is eight. The most any one person can effectively supervise is eight people. I have thirty-five."

It was the example of the flat tire that started West thinking. "That woman, Kim, the *Optimist*, whose cell phone was always dead? That's my entire sales staff. In that one example, I recognized my staff. They're always dramatic, they're terrible at paperwork. I'm always dealing with their angst. Motivating and supporting *Optimists*—that's my life.

"When I learned the personality information, it was a revelation. What was most compelling to me was understanding that I should stop trying to change them. It was a relief, I've got to tell you, because the truth is that I'd been trying to get them to change for months, and it wasn't working. Nothing I did seemed to have any lasting effect.

"So I sat back and considered what *I* could do differently. Guess what? It worked. And it worked in a very straightforward and predictable manner. I realized that I needed to change—I needed to stop yelling at them to recharge their batteries. It wasn't simply that my doing so wasn't working; it's that the constant anger was lowering their spirits.

"I changed the policy. Salespeople are no longer responsible for recharging their own batteries. Now it's our job at headquarters to do it. We'll send them two fresh batteries a week by overnight delivery with a prepaid form to get the old ones back. How simple and efficient. It was easy to justify the expense. All I had to do was spend a week tracking the number of times I couldn't reach them, and calculate the opportunity cost. Suddenly the cost of overnight delivery seemed cheap.

"It didn't take me long to realize something else. It was no accident that their paperwork was always late, and that a lot of the time it was filled out wrong. My sales staff is terrible with all details. Forget their expense reports! They have trouble with all kinds of follow-up. I had ninety thousand dollars budgeted to bring the thirty-five of them in one more time for training— to beat them up about the paperwork—and then it occurred to me that it wouldn't be likely to work this time any better than it had in the past. I considered the situation, using the three-step process:

✔ State your desired outcome.

How would you sum up West's goal?

Here's what he said. "At first I thought my goal was to get them to fill out their paperwork properly, but then I realized that it wasn't." I realized that *I want the paperwork filled out correctly*. That's the bottom line. I don't care who does it."

✔ Analyze the personality styles of the people (including yourself) involved.

"My impatience with the salespeople is no surprise when you recognize I'm a *Producer*. I just want it done. Done right, done quickly, done without fanfare. But none of that matters. My job is motivating and supporting *them*, so I have to work to reach them. Not myself. Here's how I summed up their personality style as it relates to this issue. I determined that they needed help with:

- details of client contacts
- follow-up of client contacts
- proposal submissions
- tracking sales trends and patterns
- expense report submission
- activity report completion
- everything, in other words, that wasn't direct client and prospect contact

✔ Determine how to best communicate what you need others to do in order to reach your stated goal.

"I realized that I could take an entirely different strategy. Why not take that ninety thousand and hire a couple of administrative staffers? People who were good with details.

"Think about it: not only will my paperwork be done better, but I'm freeing up my salespeople to do what they do best—sell. How can I lose? And the best part is that it doesn't require additional funding. My annual sales training budget will more than cover all of the expenses associated with the increase in head count, even overhead." West's success serves as a good example of using the three-step process well.

FAQ: *As a* Data-Collector, *I'm pretty efficient. My problem is my boss. How can I get her—a* Producer—*to be more organized?*

A: Think of her, not yourself. *Producers* aren't interested in being organized. Being organized is what motivates you. Try phrasing your requests as enabling her to become more productive—that's what motivates a *Producer*.

Case Study 4: Jessica Gets the Room with the View

Jessica had to force herself to use the three-step process. "I hate this sort of thing," she said, laughing. "It's a nightmare for me to approach anything in a methodical manner, but I did it because what I'd been doing wasn't working. If I, a strong *Optimist*, can do it, trust me, you can too! I may never like doing it, but the truth is, it was easy and it worked."

Jessica had been thinking she was going to break up with her boyfriend. She explained, "We were going on vacation—combining it with a business trip. I'm in cosmetics and my company was holding its winter meeting at a resort in Barbados. What a perk! They'd booked us rooms for Monday, Tuesday, Wednesday, and Thursday. My idea, which Pete, my *Data-Collector* boyfriend, thought sounded fine, was that we arrive early and leave late. But here's the thing. The rooms they booked were the cheapest available, on a low floor and looking out over the parking lot.

"I wanted to upgrade. The resort was kind of pricey, but given that my airfare was paid for, and our hotel room was covered for four nights, we could afford it. But I wanted a better room. A hotel room that looks out over a parking lot, well, to me that just kind of spoils the whole thing. It never even occurred to me that Pete would object. I said, 'I've got a great idea! I'll get us a room with an ocean view.' You know what he said? 'Why waste the money? It's just a place to sleep.'

"I felt like he'd doused me with a bucket of cold water. 'Just a place to sleep?' I couldn't believe he said that to me. But then I learned Jane's system, and I realized that he was saying *oil* and I was hearing *water*. When he said 'It's just a place to sleep,' I heard that sentence as *he didn't love me*. Now I understand that when he said 'It's just a place to sleep,' he meant that *'It's just a place to sleep.'* He had no hidden agenda. He's a *Data-Collector*—duh. I've come to understand that they're very literal folks. But knowing that doesn't solve the problem. Sigh! I went back to the three-step process looking for help."

✔ State your desired outcome.

How would you frame Jessica's objective?

Here's what she said about her goal. "That was easy—*I want the room with a view, and I don't want Pete to have an attitude about it.*"

✔ Analyze the personality styles of the people (including your-self) involved.

Like most *Optimists*, Jessica was sensitive to the personalities around her. Once she learned the material, she was intuitively aware of its implications. Here's what she determined was rele-vant in solving this problem.

For herself, an *Optimist*, she realized she needed:

● a hotel room with the good view
● a loving interlude with Pete with no ill-will

For Pete, she perceived that he needed:

● not to feel bulldozed into a hotel room he didn't want or value
● not to feel as if he were wasting money

The third step was to consider how to reach her goal and sat-isfy all four of the needs she identified above. Here's what Jessica said about the process.

"Taking the exchange out of the arena of hurt feelings and power plays enabled me to negotiate a settlement that worked for us both. Here's how I worked the logic.

1. I want a ocean view.
2. I made a mistake in presenting it as a done deal, as a great idea. Given that it's a shared vacation, it would have been better had I consulted Pete rather than dictated to him. I didn't mean anything by it, but I still should have realized he might feel differently about it.

3. It's reasonable that Pete wouldn't want to pay for something he didn't value. Who'd want to pay for something they didn't want? No one.

"I told Pete the truth, in just that way, and I offered to pay the differential in the room charge, because it was *my* issue, not Pete's.

"He told me that he had felt resentful every time he thought of it. He agreed that it seemed fair that I pay the difference. Now we're both happy. He's not spending money on something that seems wasteful to him, and I'm getting the view I want."

FAQ: *My boss is a great guy, a lot of fun, and very upbeat all the time. When I try to tell him some bad news, such as we may not hit our projections, for example, he simply won't listen. It's a serious situation. Once he understands an issue, he's terrific at rallying the troops and coming up with ideas. But how can I get him to listen to me sooner and without such a struggle?*

A: It sounds as though your upbeat and fun-loving boss is an *Optimist*. Typically, *Optimists* shy away from bad news, so it's not a surprise that he avoids talking to you about the budget projection being in jeopardy. It's also not a surprise that he rises to the occasion beautifully. *Optimists* generally excel under pressure and are terrific at coming up with new ideas. To get him to listen with less of a struggle, start by saying something like, "Good news! You're about to have another opportunity to save the day! I need two minutes to review some budget info with you. It'll be painless, I promise!" Hand him a one-page summary of the specific issues, using charts or illustrations if possible.

Remember Jessica's objective: *"I want the room with a view, and I don't want Pete to have an attitude about it."* By identifying her personality strengths and his, she knew *why* the problem occurred and *what to do*. She defused a situation that could have mushroomed until it ruined their vacation.

She added, "Now that I know this important difference between us, and that there's no right or wrong point of view, it's just that we're different—I can anticipate problems, and we'll be able to avoid disagreements in the future."

Case Study 5: Veronica Stops Nagging

Veronica was surprised to discover how using this process got her exactly the result she'd long sought but had never achieved. Her husband of ten years, Gus, thought she was a nag. They'd had many arguments about it, and she just didn't understand what he objected to. Her position was that if she didn't remind him of things, he forgot them. In their busy lives, she needed him to do his part. She felt trapped. On the one hand, she understood how irritating it was to be constantly reminded of things, but she felt she worked hard not to "nag," but simply to "remind." On the other hand, she resented his criticism of her. If he'd do his share, she thought, I wouldn't be in this position in the first place.

Here's what she would have said to him before learning to use my approach: "Honey, you know how we're meeting the Smiths for dinner? Well, I know you're busy, and I don't want to be a nag, but I have to remind you of something . . . and I know you probably would have remembered on your own, but I felt as if I ought to say something just in case it had slipped your mind, which is understandable of course because you're so busy . . ."

Do you notice she still hasn't actually reminded Gus of anything? All she's done so far is apologize and talk about feelings—typical *Accommodator* behavior. Which, she confessed, for the ten years of their marriage had driven her *Producer* husband insane.

Finally, after apologizing for disturbing Gus at work and focusing on their emotions, she concluded by saying, ". . . but I hope you don't forget to bathe the dog and clip his nails."

"I knew that what I was doing wasn't working perfectly," Veronica said, "but I was worried about changing in any way. The status quo might not have been ideal, but I knew what to expect, and we seemed to get along all right. My decision to go ahead and try a new approach was because of what happened at work.

"I got yelled at by my boss for the same reason Gus yells at me. And I said to myself, whoa, girl. This is not just a minor issue between me and Gus. This is a problem in other areas of my life.

"What happened is that we were planning a conference. And the negotiation between us and a hotel wasn't going well. I knew I needed to tell my boss, and I knew he'd be angry. He's a *Producer* too. He's a great guy, just like Gus, but wow, when he gets angry, you know it! So I avoided talking to him as long as I could, hoping that somehow something would happen to make it okay. But, of course, no miracle occurred. So when negotiations broke off, I went and told him. Here's what I said. 'I know you're working on all sorts of projects, so I don't want to bother you, but I think you probably—well, maybe—need to be aware of a potential glitch, but with any luck, it won't be such a big deal . . . but just in case, I thought I ought to alert you to the possibilities.' Oh, God, isn't it awful! I was just going on and on and on and not saying anything. Finally, he did the hand gesture—you know the one I mean—where he's saying, 'What, what, what? *What's the bottom line?*' So I told him, and he exploded. I mean, he exploded! I had just had the frustrating conversation with Gus, and I realized it was about *me*, not them. Yeah, maybe they could both be more patient, maybe they could be more sensitive and understanding, but what I realized was that I was exacerbating the situation. And given that I couldn't get them to change, my only hope was to change myself. So I went back to the three-step process, which seemed to work so well with others."

The first step is:

✔ State your desired outcome.

How would you state Veronica's goal?

Veronica said that her goal was simple. *"I want Gus to bathe the dog and clip his nails."*

✔ Analyze the personality styles of the people (including your-self) involved.

"Are you kidding? I know, as an *Accommodator*, what matters to me:

- that my husband doesn't feel pressured
- that I don't offend him

"And, I've learned that, as a *Producer*, my husband:

- doesn't want to waste time chitchatting
- doesn't want to feel stupid

✔ Determine how to best communicate what you need others to do in order to reach your stated goal.

"After taking Jane's seminar, I knew what to do. I just didn't want to do it. But I've learned my lesson. When interacting with *Producers*, here's what I'll do. I'll be direct. I won't delay delivering an obligation. I won't delay giving bad news. It's hard. So hard. But it works. Clearly. Immediately. It's astounding.

"Let me give you an example. Three months later, the dog needed his bath again. This time I called Gus and I said, 'Honey, we're meeting the Smiths for dinner at seven. Before then, please bathe the dog and clip his nails.' And you know what he said? 'Oh, thanks for reminding me! I'll do it!'

"Can you believe it? I was direct and to the point, and I got a compliment.

"This approach worked well at work too. The very next day, a prospective client called to cancel an appointment. I knew my boss would be upset, so my natural inclination was to put off telling him. Instead, I walked into his office, and said, 'Mr. Browning just canceled and doesn't want to reschedule until at least next week. I told him we'd call him on Monday. Is there anything else you want me to do?'

"Guess what? I didn't get yelled at. My boss nodded, thought for a minute, and said, 'Good. Make a note for me to call him first thing Monday.'

"Adapting my message to suit my boss's style worked. I actually was able to do it, and do it well. Once you understand what to do, it's easy to apply the principles."

FAQ: *My boss is obviously a* Producer, *very impatient and aggressive. I freeze when he yells at me. What can I do to get him to talk to me with respect?*

A: Remember that while a *Producer's* approach feels intimidating and off-putting, it's not personal. Because *Producers'* personalities are focused so intently on the bottom line, they tend to ignore social niceties, chitchat, even common politeness. The best way to get your boss to talk to you with respect is remain calm, no matter how explosive and aggressive he becomes, answering all questions with as few words as possible, and phrasing statements in a direct manner yourself.

Three Steps to Success

Whether the problem is simple or complex, whether it's occurring at home or at work, these case studies prove that the three-step process used throughout this chapter works. It's a tool to help you manage *your* priorities, by finding ways to get from others what *you* need.

Remember the three steps:

- ✔ State your desired outcome.
- ✔ Analyze the personality styles of the people (including yourself) involved.
- ✔ Determine how to best communicate what you need others to do in order to reach your stated goal.

Take the time to assess the situation and apply the logical approach, and you'll enjoy the same positive results as did Helene, West, Jessica, Lois, and Veronica, and countless others. And as you'll discover in Chapter 5, there are practical tools to help you do so.

Tips

- Whether your priority is increasing your department's training budget or booking a room with a view, analyzing other people's personality types, and positioning your requests in a way that fits their communication needs, increases the likelihood that your request will be granted.
- Learn from other people's successes. Observing other people who have succeeded in ways you want to succeed enables you to analyze their actions with an eye to adopting their best practices. What did they do? How can you adapt their behavior to your circumstances?

PART TWO

✦

Convert Dreams into Action

✦

CHAPTER FIVE

How to Set Goals with CAN DO! and *"In Order to . . ."*

Think Big! Dream Big!

There you are, walking through the office with two pieces of paper in your hand, both related to crucial projects, both with looming deadlines. How do you decide which one to work on first? When everything feels like it has to be done right away, how can you—how should you—make judgments about priorities?

Think long-term. The first thing to do in determining priorities is to envision your desired outcome. Go ahead and dream. What do you or your organization want to accomplish? What is the ultimate goal? Once your end result is clear, work your way backward. Think long-term, and let that lead you to the short-term. You must start with the macro—what you and your organization consider of most value—before you can consider the micro—what should I do this minute?

It's easy to get caught up in the minutia of day-to-day living. Running from task to task to task, fielding whatever balls are tossed at you, who has time to consider the big picture? If you're competent, you might conclude that you're productive. However, productivity means more than getting through a pile of papers or responding to the phone calls as they come in. In evaluating your level of productivity, be sure you don't lose sight of the big

picture. Consider your day-to-day business life. Don't you sometimes feel as if all you do is put out one fire after another? As if
you're barely keeping up? Many people never think of their priorities at all. They're too busy simply getting through the day.

In your business, what's meant by long-term? What does the
phrase mean to you? Is it an hour? A year? Three years? Your lifetime? In many businesses it's normal to have three- to five-year
objectives. Let's say your company sets three-year goals. Doesn't
that tell you where you should be after one year? A third of the
way there? And if you know where you should be in a year, doesn't
that imply where you should be this quarter? And this quarter
leads to this month and this month leads to this week. Only now
can you create a to-do list for today. How can you possibly create
a to-do list for today if you don't know where you want to end up
in three years? The only effective way to manage priorities is to
set priorities. Setting priorities requires that you set goals. Set
goals in the longest of long terms and work backward.

Once you know your long-term goals—over whatever time
frame you select—not only can you rationally set today's to-do
list, you can also defend your decisions. Because the actions you
take today relate to the big picture, they're rational and thus
they're defensible.

Think long-term in your personal world as well. Why not write
a list of things you want to do before you die? Perhaps you want
to climb Mt. Everest. Doesn't it make sense that before you tackle
Mt. Everest, you should first climb Mount McKinley? And before
climbing Mt. McKinley, doesn't it make sense that you should
climb Mt. Washington in New Hampshire? When you see that
your local YMCA is sponsoring a mountain and rock-climbing
workshop, signing up becomes logical. In other words, knowing
what to do in the short-term becomes clear and easy to justify as
soon as you know your long-term goals—in this case, that you
want to climb Mt. Everest before you die.

You can apply the same logic at work. Let's say you have a goal
to create and implement a marketing plan that results in an increase in revenue of three percent in three years. You expect the
majority of the revenue increase to occur in years two and three,
after the redesigned sales literature and advertising campaign

has a chance to kick in. In year one you expect that revenue will increase only .05 percent.

Remembering the time early in your career when you okayed an innovative brochure design only to discover that off-the-shelf envelopes didn't exist—and especially remembering the cost of designing and producing custom envelopes—you know that you need to consult with your design team to ensure they're working with the printers *now*—this quarter.

If you need to consult your design team—some of whom are based in another city—this quarter, you'd better start arranging meetings this month. If you want to start arranging meetings this month, you need to contact your team leader, get an update on the project, and start him organizing the coordination process.

Now today's to-do list begins to come into focus—all with an eye to meeting your three-year goal. You have a busy day—four client meetings in your office are on the schedule, and an angry client called and left a voice-mail message saying he was waiting by the phone for your call back. You make the call, attend the meetings, do all your other work, and realize you haven't called your team leader. You think you'll put off making the call until tomorrow. But because you know your long-term goal, and because you know your short-term goal, you are able to recognize that this one call, while not associated with a specific deadline, is nonetheless critical to your success. You make the call today.

Have you read Lewis Carroll's *Alice's Adventures in Wonderland*? At one point Alice comes to a fork in the road. That's where she runs into the Cheshire Cat. She asks him which way she should go. "That depends a good deal on where you want to get to," said the Cat. "I don't much care where—" said Alice. "Then it doesn't matter which way you go," said the Cat.

On some level, isn't that life? We face forks in the road every day. Big forks with major consequences, minor forks with irrelevant consequences, fork after fork after fork. If you don't know where you want to end up, how can you make decisions about which fork to choose? If you don't know—clearly—which fork is the one likely to take you where you want to go, how can you possibly make decisions about what to do day in and day out?

Goals are statements of direction. When you have goals,

you're declaring which fork or forks you intend to take. The more clearly you keep your goals in mind, the easier day-to-day decisions become. The entire-priority setting and priority-managing process must evolve from long-term goals.

A Goal Is Not a Vow

Writing your goals down will help you remember them. Unless you're strongly an *Optimist*, it makes sense for you to write them down. (*Optimists*, of course, are unlikely to write goals down, but it's more important to have them than it is to write them down. For everyone else, write them down.) Seeing them in print makes them real. It also helps to defeat Murphy's Law—haven't you ever noticed that it's the *good* ideas that evaporate? Writing them down helps you keep track of them.

But write them in pencil, not ink. See goals for what they are—a statement of intent, not a lifelong commitment. *A goal is not a vow.* As you'll learn from the examples in this chapter, there's value to the goal-setting process, even if you start working toward a goal and decide early on that it's not for you. Likewise, there's value to the process even if once you get there, you say this is for the birds. There's value in the *process*.

FAQ: *I've set goals in the past and never looked at them again. If I set goals now, how can I be sure I'll refer to them?*

A: If you don't refer to your goals frequently, it's easy to let them slip away. To ensure that you integrate goals into your daily life, annotate your calendar with a reminder to take a look at them periodically. Some people like to do so monthly or quarterly. At a minimum, review them twice a year. Putting a note on your calendar to do so when you change your clocks or on your birthday and half birthday will help the activity become a habit.

Easy Ways to Keep Goals Current

Take a look at your goals frequently, at least a couple of times a year. Doing so will help you keep them in the forefront of your brain. Notice what you've accomplished. Consider which goals need to be modified, adjusted, deleted—see what you've done and consider what you haven't even started.

As a general statement, the busier you are, the more frequently you will want to review your goals. Busy people, people who run from one task to another, barely pausing to take a breath, are most likely to lose sight of the big picture. Consulting your goals frequently will help ensure that they're fully integrated in your day-to-day decisions.

Consider looking at your goals on your birthday. That's the beginning of your new year. When you do so, go forward in your calendar six months, and make a note to take another look on your half birthday. Or you might connect your biannual goal review to the equinox. When you change your clocks, take a look at your goals. There's something pleasing about the relationship to the time change and taking a fresh look at your goals.

Nadene R. Cole, human resource director of Barclay White, said she and her husband review their goals when they make their estimated tax payments—four times a year. "It's a good time to sit back and sift through our goals—individually and as a couple," she explained.

Whenever you do so, and however frequently you do so, it's important that your goals stay fresh, not static. Don't write a list of your goals and simply tuck it away in a back corner of your desk to gather dust. Look at your list frequently and evaluate what you've done, what you haven't done, even what you haven't thought about at all. Ask yourself what needs to be changed, added, or deleted. Decide what's still relevant for you, and what you no longer want to work toward. Use the opportunity to see what you've accomplished, and determine what still needs to be done.

How Productive Are You? A Self-Assessment

Be careful of generic terminology. When you state that you want to become more *efficient, organized, professional,* or *productive,* you're setting yourself up for failure. These terms don't describe behaviors—rather, they describe a category of behaviors. For example, many organizations prohibit the use of the word *attitude* in performance appraisals (as in "you have a bad attitude"); the thinking is that with the best will in the world, many employees won't know what you're talking about. Instead of saying, "You have a bad attitude," you might say, "You need to answer the phone on the second or third ring." You're describing a behavior that can be changed. Consider how challenging yourself to become more productive, efficient, or organized is likely to leave you frustrated, not motivated. Certainly you want to manage priorities better—you're reading this book, after all—but what does that mean?

As we discuss the specific tools for goal setting, priority setting, and priority management covered in this chapter and in the other chapters of Part Two, you'll be encouraged to describe *behaviors* and to make goals tangible in every way that you can.

FAQ: *I've set a goal to become organized for years, and I've never reached it. What am I doing wrong?*

A: In order to become organized, you have to define the behaviors that contribute to your being organized. In other words, do you mean that you need to put files away in a place where you can find them again? Do you mean that you need to balance your checkbook every month? Until you define exactly what you mean by the term *organized*, you're not likely to achieve it.

The exercise that follows will help you identify what you're doing now that leads to productive behavior, and what you're doing that inhibits it. As you respond to the ten statements that follow, consider how you conduct yourself at both home and work. Use a scale of one to ten. With one being never true and ten being always true, choose the number that best reflects what you believe to be accurate about yourself.

- If you score a statement as a ten, you're saying, "Yes, it's always true."
- A score of seven, eight, or nine reflects a range of uncertainty. You might conclude, for instance, "It's often true, but not always, or it's not completely true."
- If you believe that the statement is correctly answered with "Sometimes it's true and sometimes it's not true," or "Maybe it's true, but I'm not sure," then you would score it as a four, five, or six.
- A score of two or three indicates an answer of "It's rarely true."
- If you score a statement as a one, you're saying, "It's never true."

In reading the statements, don't be literal. You'll need to customize each statement to suit you and your circumstances. Once you've substituted examples that are relevant to you, evaluate whether or not the statement is true for you.

Statement 1, for instance, says that if your boss asks you for a report, you can put your hands on it right away. If you're a self-employed graphic designer, you don't have a boss. Substitute *client* for *boss*, and ask yourself whether you could put your hands on a design if a client asked for it.

In statement 10, for example, you're asked to consider whether you're likely to subscribe to a music series if you like classical music. If you're not a classical music fan, don't get distracted. Instead, substitute what's relevant to you. If you love bowling, ask yourself if you participate in a league. If you're a murder mystery reader, consider whether you spend adequate time reading your mysteries.

After evaluating the ten statements, tally your score. The most you can score is a hundred (ten questions multiplied by ten points equals a hundred).

1. I'm really well organized. For instance, I can put my hands on my last three years' tax returns, I know where insurance documents are stored, and my boss can ask me for any report, and I know I can put my hands on it right away. There's time on my schedule to put things away, and everything has a place where it belongs. Even if I like to work in chaos, I know that many people perceive a cluttered desk as the sign of a cluttered mind, so I make a point of keeping my work area neat and orderly. The same applies at home; my possessions and papers are where they should be. My dining room table is not covered with paper, for example, and my books, videos, or CDs aren't scattered across the room.

2. My priorities are clear to me. I know what qualities I most value in my personal relationships. I understand the relative significance of my various tasks and projects at work. I know how to evaluate anything because I know what matters to me.

3. I have written goals that I refer to regularly and strive to achieve in a methodical manner.

4. I can say no tactfully. My experience has been that I am able to say no and people don't hold it against me.

5. Delegation is a strong suit of mine—whether I like or respect the person or not, I am able to engender cooperation. For instance, when I need feedback, direction, or guidance from my boss, I get it. In fact, I'm able to assign specific tasks to my boss. My colleagues and peers frequently assist me, and those people (if any) who directly report to me understand their responsibilities and do their work well. At home, the same is true. If I need to arrange an appointment with a plumber or a TV repairman, for example, and I'm unable to be there, I'm able to negotiate with my spouse, roommate, friend, or partner to cover for me in such a way that they feel no resentment.

6. I'm able to control my time and energy. For instance, I

know how long my various tasks take, so I can schedule effectively. I know when my energy level is highest, so I schedule around my down times. I close my door for quiet periods of concentration, or if I'm in a noisy and distracting environment without a door to close, I'm able to either get away (I go to the library, for instance, or to the cafeteria, or I borrow someone else's office), or if I must stay put, I've developed the ability to concentrate in chaos.

7. I'm sensitive to issues of time. I keep my appointments. I'm never late. I make my deadlines. When a request for information is made, I respond promptly. I'm up-to-date on my reading, telephone callbacks, and e-mail.

8. I focus on the "next step." When I read a letter, for example, I make notes in the margin (or highlight key passages or annotate it with sticky notes), so when I come back to it again, I don't have to reread it. I apply the same principle to voice mail—I strive to move the conversation on to the "next step." My messages aren't long, but they're detailed—in fact, I number all content so the person I'm leaving the message for can easily take notes. By helping them get organized, I know I increase the likelihood that they'll respond to me. For instance, here's a message I might leave: "Hi, Joe. It's so and so from the such and such a company. My phone number is area code and number. I'm calling about invoice 123. I have three questions. . . ."

9. I plan. I know what I'm doing and when I'm doing it (with as much empty time for unanticipated work and unplanned relaxation as I want or need).

10. My skills in my field and about what interests me are up-to-date. I know what I need to know to do my job well. If I lack knowledge, I get myself educated by consulting a librarian, taking a course, reading up on the subject, or speaking with experts. I never let ignorance stand as an excuse for not doing something. Whatever my hobbies or personal interests are, I stay up-to-date with them as well. For instance, if I enjoy classical music, I make a point

of subscribing to a chamber music performance series each year.

Add up your score. If you scored ninety or more, that's excellent. That suggests that you are highly efficient, organized, and productive. Now review your scores for each statement. Consider which questions earned your lowest scores. Changing behaviors associated with these low-scoring questions is the most efficient approach to becoming more productive. Instead of trying to be more productive, concentrate on the specific *behaviors* associated with the generic term more productive.

Consider Oskar's success. An architect in a busy office, he explains, "Of the ten questions, my lowest score was for question eight—I gave it a two. My office is chaotic, really busy. We're all running all the time. It never occurred to me that there was value in slowing down, in taking things to the 'next step.' I assumed I'd be most productive if I spent as little time as possible with each task.

"After taking this assessment, and learning what my low score implied, I decided that, starting right away, I would commit to annotating my mail. Within just a few days I evolved a system that works really well for me. When I open my mail, I write notes to myself on blue sticky notes. I use blue ones so they'll stand out. I write the notes as I read each document. For instance, two weeks ago I reviewed an RFP (request for proposal). As I read it, I made notes about how we might approach the bidding process. I positioned the sticky notes so my comments were clearly associated with the sentence or paragraph to which they applied.

"Before I started using the sticky notes, I would have had to reread the entire RFP. Even though it's been two weeks since I read it, all I had to do was review my sticky notes and I was up to speed, ready to write.

"The net result? Hours and hours saved. I'm producing proposals faster. Time that had been allocated to working on proposals is now freed up and available for other work."

By considering your low scores, you can do what Oskar did: identify behavior that you want to modify. In other words, the assessment helps you understand an ideal and see how to achieve it. Once you know how an efficient, organized, productive, and focused person is likely to act, both personally and professionally, you can begin to translate those standards into the action steps that will make those ideals happen for you.

Take advantage of this assessment as a tool to identify what you're good at (the high scores) and where you're weak (the low scores). Focusing on your lowest scores gives you a leg up in the goal-setting process.

Even when you know that the changes you're considering are in your best interest, often it's hard to get started. Once you start, sometimes it's hard to sustain the change. Habits are entrenched, the unknown is frightening, and anticipated benefits can seem too abstract to motivate you. Good news! The tools that follow will help you change your behavior more effectively and quickly.

FAQ: *We're making our deadlines, but only at the last minute. The stress is nearly unbearable. What am I doing wrong?*

A: As explained in the "*In Order to . . .*" model, start at the end and track *who*, *what*, and *when*. If you frequently almost miss your deadlines, you're scheduling improperly. Don't neglect to add twenty percent to all resource allocations at each step. This isn't padding. Rather, by doing so, you're anticipating things that might happen but which you can't predict, such as people getting the flu.

Chart Your Course with CAN DO

Ship captains set sail with carefully drawn charts. These charts show coastlines, water depth, and other information of use to navigators. As you set sail on your adventure of change, think of yourself as the captain of your own future. The CAN DO model will help you create your chart. It will alert you to unforeseen dangers, highlight opportunities, indicate the shortest route to your objectives, and protect you from false readings.

In the examples that follow, you'll see how people set goals using the five steps of the CAN DO acronym—Concrete, Attainable/Realistic, Narrow, Deadline, and Objective form of measurement—to achieve success. When you use the CAN DO navigational tool, you'll set goals that are framed correctly, in such a way that you're set up for success, not failure. Consider each of the five factors one at a time. Once your goal is properly set, your future is charted, and you will be able to proceed with confidence.

The acronym CAN DO stands for:

- *Concrete*
  Do you know what your goal means *and* how to accomplish it?
- *Attainable and Realistic*
  Are you capable of doing it, and have you overcome avoidable obstacles?
- *Narrow*
  The more specific the goal, the more likely you are to achieve it.
- *Deadline*
  If you don't have one, how will you know when to do anything?
- *Objective* form of measurement
  Set unique standards so you will know when you've succeeded.

Step 1. Have You Defined the Goal?

The C stands for Concrete.

Do you know what your goal means *and* how to accomplish it?

There are two standards associated with the term Concrete, both of which must be met. First, you must know *what* the goal is about, and second, you must know *how* to achieve it. Consider, for example, the declaration: *I want to go on a long walk.* Is that Concrete? No, it's not. How one person defines long is defined by another person as medium. It's not clear what's intended. What if I say that *I want to walk to San Francisco?* Do you see the difference? Specifying the end result—San Francisco—makes it Concrete.

Let's say that your boss calls you into her office and says, "Good news! The board has just approved a new computer system, and I've selected you to do a comprehensive needs assessment. You'll do a formal presentation at the November 15 meeting. Congratulations! It's a great opportunity for you to shine." You thank her and run back to your own office, realizing that you have no idea how to do a needs assessment, and you don't know much about computers.

In other words, the goal as currently framed is not Concrete. Doesn't it make sense that the first thing you should do is go into the files and review last year's needs assessment on telecommunications? The content may be different, but think of what you'll learn. You'll see how many vendors were consulted, how many proposals were solicited, how the various company departments were surveyed. You may even find a copy of the actual needs-assessment form, which you can use as a starting place to develop your own form. You also may learn what's meant by the generic term *a formal presentation.*

After that, wouldn't it be logical to ferret out a computer consultant—either internally or externally?

FAQ: *How do I get information I need when I know nothing about the subject, can't tell a soul I don't know whatever it is I don't know, and have no clue how to proceed?*

A: Ask your local librarian. For those of you who are able to access the Internet, consult the Web sites of major newspapers. Most maintain an easy-to-use archive and offer reasonably priced librarian services.

Ignorance has a bad reputation in our society. Many people are ashamed to admit that they don't know something. While there may be good reasons not to confess to your boss, your friend, your spouse, even to your mother that you don't know something, tell *yourself* the truth. It makes no sense that you wouldn't. How can you proceed when you don't know *how* to proceed?

Perhaps part of the issue for some people is a lack of understanding of the meaning of the word. Ignorant does not mean stupid. Ignorant means *uneducated*, *unaware*, or *uninformed*. Stupid means *lacking intelligence*, *slow to learn*, or *worthless*. These are very different words. There's no shame in ignorance—get yourself the knowledge that you need. Here are several ideas about how to approach the process of educating yourself:

- Go to the library and ask the reference librarian for help (for free).

Sometimes people feel intimidated by libraries. When you don't know how to use their resources, the array of books and periodicals, microfiche machines, and computers can seem overwhelming. Sometimes librarians' training is spotty, and often you don't even know the questions to ask.

It's possible, however, that you'll meet a knowledgeable librarian who can direct you to exactly the information you seek. If the librarian can't do that, perhaps the staff will know where you can begin your search. Conducting research using computerized card catalogues is generally straightforward. Most systems are user-friendly.

- Use newspapers' Web sites' archives to search for relevant articles (and then print them out for a dollar or two each).

All major newspapers maintain a Web site. Usually they're easy to find; simply type *www.thenewspaper'snamehere.com*. Look for a link called *archive*. Easy-to-complete search forms allow you to locate headlines that correspond to your research needs.

For instance, if you're trying to find out suitcase sales in China last year, you'll select appropriate key words (i.e., "luggage and China") and set the search time line to a year. If you find articles of interest, you have the option of printing them out for a small fee. Many libraries offer this service for free.

- Take a course.

Local community colleges, YMCAs, churches, and temples offer credit and noncredit courses on a wide variety of subjects. Get training through seminars, industry conferences, workshops, and suppliers.

- Hire an expert.

Identify experts by asking vendors for suggestions. Scan bookshelves or bookstore Web sites for authors who have written on topics that are relevant to your research. Ask department chairs at colleges and universities. Many authors and professors consult in their fields. However you locate expert help, often the consultation fee buys you information or an approach to solving a problem that saves you countless hours of toil.

Let's return to the original discussion of how to make goals Concrete. Consider this sentence: *I want to change my appearance to be more professional.* How would you make the goal more Concrete?

Were you able to visualize a professional appearance? If so, you might have rewritten the sentence to say: *I want to buy a new suit and have it fitted by a professional tailor* or *I want to buy a leather briefcase.*

Consider this sentence: *I need to increase the productivity of the technical staff.*

How would you rewrite it?

Ask yourself what you mean by productivity. Perhaps you realize that you want your staff to make more calls per day. Doing so requires that they spend less time on each call. Thus, the Concrete goal becomes:

✔ Reduce the average call from one hour to fifty minutes.

By avoiding vague statements, and by ensuring you know how to proceed, you can be certain that your goal is Concrete.

Step 2. Can You Reach the Goal?

Attainable and Realistic

Are you *capable* of doing it, and have you *avoided* being stymied by obstacles that you may be able to overcome? Once you have confidence that you know *what* you want to do and *how* to do it, you can consider whether the goal is both Attainable and Realistic.

Attainable relates to capability. Can you do it? Are you able? Is it possible? Consider my long walk—now defined as a walk to San Francisco. Can I—a non-athlete of normal health—walk to San Francisco? Certainly. Given that I live in New York City, can I get there by next Sunday? Of course not. That's the difference between Attainable and Realistic. Be careful not to confuse the two. Evaluating whether a goal is Realistic often involves assessing the limitations associated with physical parameters. How easy it would be to give up on goals that seem impossible. Consider my walk to San Francisco—I've established that I cannot walk to San Francisco from New York in a few days. How tempting it would be to say, "Oh well, too bad, can't be done." This is an inaccurate statement. Just because I can't get there by Sunday doesn't mean I can't get there at all. Don't give up too easily.

Before giving up, it makes much more sense to see what you can shift or adjust and preserve the essence of your dream. You may not be able to achieve your goal *as you first stated it*, but perhaps you can keep more aspects of it than you thought. It's not black and white. For instance, if you say, "I can either walk to San Francisco by next Sunday or I'm not going," you're missing an opportunity to retain the core of your goal. How about restating your goal as, "I can walk to San Francisco by a year from Sunday." That's Realistic, and all you did was adjust the deadline. Just because you determine a goal isn't Realistic when you first evaluate it doesn't mean that it's hopeless. Anytime you're allocating limited or scarce resources, you're dealing with priority setting.

Given that there's never enough time, never enough money, never enough of whatever resource you need, you must choose how to distribute what is available. Only you can choose how to use your resources. Your choices require that you know what is a priority to you and your organization. Chapter 7 addresses this process.

It makes no sense to set goals that can't be met. Doing so leads only to frustration, and ultimately to quitting. Why bother striving to reach a goal that, no matter what, can't be met? If I clung tenaciously to my stated goal of wanting to walk to San Francisco by this Sunday, failure would be inevitable. My frustration would be inevitable as well.

The process of allocating resources requires wisdom and judgment. Knowing whether any resource or any combination of resources is adequate for the project under consideration demands experience and research. For example, how can you decide if a deadline can be met unless you know how long the tasks required to meet the deadline take?

If a teacher is responsible for educating only one student, he could do a superb job. If you were hoping to sell only one piece of luggage, you could manufacture a suitcase of the highest possible quality. But neither situation is realistic. Teachers must educate hundreds of students, and luggage manufacturers must sell hundreds of thousands of pieces of luggage. It is this balancing act—producing acceptable levels of output at acceptable levels of quality—that keeps businesses solvent and nonprofit organizations functioning.

How many times have you heard older people dismiss as impossible (i.e., not Realistic) a goal typically pursued by younger people? Don't give up so easily. The oldest sheriff in the Los Angeles County Sheriff's department was fifty-four when he joined the department near the top of his class as a rookie. The oldest first-time flight attendant to join Delta was in her mid-fifties as well. President Bush has sky-dived in his seventies.

Consider Ruth Chessman's experience. She was sixty-five when she decided to become a psychiatrist. She had no college degrees—although she had taken two courses back when she was eighteen. It didn't take much research for her to learn that going to medical school in the United States was probably impossible. She considered going offshore, but decided that would raise an overwhelming set of problems. At this point, many people would have said, "Oh well, it can't be done."

"I focused on the end result," she explained. "What did I want to do? I wanted to be a therapist. I wanted to treat a certain kind of client. I realized that I didn't need to become a psychiatrist. By focusing on the behavior—on what I wanted to do—my decisions became clear.

"What I needed was to achieve a certain level of education, to develop appropriate professional relationships, and to maintain the necessary affiliations. What I didn't need was a medical degree."

Ruth went back to school at age sixty-six, graduated with a master's degree at age seventy, and hung out her shingle. She maintained a private practice for fifteen years before retiring and moving to Florida.

We're all getting older. Don't let your age determine your future. Let your aspirations and ambition set your path. Given that none of us knows how much time we have, the best approach is for each of us to spend our time doing exactly what we want to be doing.

Consider this sentence: We want to break into the Asian market by signing a contract with a suitable distributor within a month.

Upon learning that it took your competitor two years to achieve this goal, and knowing that you have no resources that they didn't have, rewrite the goal to ensure that it's Realistic.

No matter how much you *wish* you could do it more quickly, it is accurate to state the goal as:

✔ We want to break into the Asian market by signing a contract with a suitable distributor within two years.

Step 3. Think Small to Achieve Big

Narrow

The more specific the goal, the more likely you are to achieve it.

Consider the walk to San Francisco from New York. It's a daunting endeavor. Think of the logistics. (Where will I sleep? How will I stay in touch with my family? What will I take with me?)

What about the logistics associated with walking a mile? Isn't that less daunting? There's an old saying that the longest journey begins with a single step. Think about it—if you take one step, and then another, before you know it, you'll be across the room.

It's much easier to motivate yourself to do something small than something large, in part because it's less intimidating. Also, it's easier to envision a more specific task than a big-picture goal.

No one says you have to do things all at once. This is another example of the power of baby steps. Take a big-picture goal and break it into smaller units.

Max, a supervisor in an environmental lobbying group's Information Technology (IT) department, received the assignment to investigate new technology options. "I didn't know where to begin. Don't get me wrong. I love keeping up with the latest technology, so this was a great opportunity. While I can always use more hands, I had adequate staff and it was a non-critical assignment, so there was no break-your-neck deadline. The problem was the scope of the assignment. It was just too broad.

"No matter how I approached it, I couldn't seem to get a handle on it. I had three people working on it. After about a month, when their preliminary reports began to come in, I realized there was a major problem. Overlap. Because my assignment to them was broad, they were focusing on areas of personal interest to them—and they shared some of those areas.

"I stopped them then and there and rethought the assignment. The first thing I did was list categories of technology. I thought about approaching it by internal department needs, but decided that might limit us. Just because a department manager told me that he needed new PCs for everyone in the department doesn't mean it's true. New technology changes everything. In this case, everyone in the department got new laptops—not new PCs.

"What I did was stop the staff from investigating new technology and put them on the task of investigating existing technology. Once we knew what we were doing now, I broke it into categories. Only then were we ready to investigate new technology. We ended up with small assignments, like investigating options in Internet service providers and pricing alternatives for cell phone service.

"We got it done quicker and with less overlap because I converted a big-picture assignment into Narrow components."

Experiment with applying the principle. Consider this big-picture objective: *I want to increase revenue by four percent.* How can you make this goal more Narrow?

Let's assume that this is a Concrete goal; that is, let's assume that you know enough about your industry and how it works to have confidence that you can reach this revenue projection. Let's also assume that you have assessed your available resources and have determined that you have adequate staff and budget to achieve the four percent increase. In other words, the four percent increase is both Attainable and Realistic. Given that you've satisfied the first two steps of the CAN DO model, you're ready to evaluate the third. How would you rewrite the goal to incorporate specifics, to make sure it's Narrow?

As you consider how you'd rephrase this goal, use your own industry, or make one up. Don't worry about whether your assumptions are grounded in reality. For the purpose of this exercise, simply focus on stating the same goal—increase revenue by four percent—in as Narrow a manner as possible.

What does it take to accomplish it? Think of journalism's five W's—who, what, when, where, and why (and maybe *how* too)—and analyze your options.

What did you decide? Did you focus on *how* to achieve the four percent increase? Did you determine *who* would help you achieve it? There are, of course, many good answers to the challenge. Here are some examples of statements that serve to make the big picture Narrow. Each of these statements would work:

✔ I need to attract a hundred new customers.
✔ I need to acquire a harmonious company, maybe a competitor, with sales of at least $500,000 a year.
✔ I need to increase our average sale to $500.

Think small. Small accomplishments accumulate and lead to big achievements.

Step 4. Keep the End in Sight

Deadline

If you don't have one, how will you know when to do anything?
There are three reasons why having a deadline is essential to goal setting (and thus to priority setting):

- desired results provide your starting point
- deadlines help you avoid procrastination
- deadlines force you to get yourself educated

First, it makes no sense to begin the process of breaking any goal—even a properly framed goal—into smaller units (which is the next step in achieving your objectives) until the end is in sight. How can you? In order to work backward, by definition, the starting place is the end. Without an end, therefore, there can be no start. You *must* have a deadline.

Second, it's easier to justify a delay in working toward your goal if it's open-ended. Without a deadline, there's less motivation to begin. You can keep telling yourself that you'll get to it when you get a chance. *Accommodators* are very good at tracking pending items and tend to be self-starters. The other personality types have more trouble avoiding procrastination. Here are some things to consider when evaluating whether you have a problem with procrastination. Keep in mind that just because you think you have a problem doesn't make it true.

Sometimes the issue is that your expectations for yourself are unrealistic—and are all in your own head. Kimiko, for instance, learned this lesson after many years of beating herself up for procrastinating.

She had become, as she put it, "The designated Christmas cookie baker in my close-knit and large family. I guess it started because I liked to cook. But then I got married. And had kids. And got a full-time career. You can imagine! Each year I hesitated to set a deadline because I'm so busy. Each year I put it off later and later. I ought to win a Procrastinator of the Year award for last year! It was two a.m. before I was done, and I told my husband 'That's it!'

"I lobbied all year to get him to tell my mother," she added, laughing. "I failed, and so this past October I braced myself and told her. I said, 'Ma, this year, instead of baking, I'm going to buy the cookies.' You know what she said? 'Sounds smart!' I couldn't believe it! I'd made up the entire problem in my head."

If you perceive yourself as someone who is a procrastinator, then identify what exactly the problem is, and consider that *maybe there's no problem at all*. Answer these two questions:

1. Are you missing deadlines at work and in your personal life?
2. Are you completing work and personal responsibilities at acceptable levels of quality?

If you're not missing deadlines, and the quality of your work is acceptable, it's possible that you're not procrastinating. If you *are* missing deadlines, make sure that there's not too much work. Maybe it's not your fault. How can you tell if you have a problem? By objectively analyzing your environment, your work load, and yourself. Likewise, if you think the quality of your work is inadequate, consider if it's the *Data-Collector* part of your persona coming forth. *Data-Collectors* have trouble assessing *acceptable* because of their attention to detail and inclination toward perfectionism. In other words, just because you think you procrastinate doesn't mean that you do.

As you assess your situation, consider the following:

- Think about how you spend your time. You'll be invited later in this chapter to time yourself doing things. Until you know where the time is going, you have no way of determining whether you're spending time wisely. Once you do know where the time goes, you'll be in a better position to compare your allocation of time for any specific task to your peers' and to the overall value of the task.

- Use common sense. Not all tasks are equally important. If you're procrastinating a task that has little value to you or your organization, maybe your problem isn't procrastination but faulty judgment. Did you ever see the bumper sticker that reads, "An immaculate house is the sign of a wasted life"? In other words, the fact that you're putting off cleaning your house isn't necessarily a sign of procrastination. Maybe it's an example of smart priority management, of wise judgment.

- Evaluate special circumstances—i.e., you missed three deadlines last month because you were covering for a colleague who's out on disability, your boss assigned you a special one-time project, or you were on vacation.

- Think about whether you spend more time on similar tasks than colleagues do. If you do, is there a logical reason (i.e., you're new on the job and still learning how to do things)?

- Ask yourself if your organization is one of the majority that have increased their expectations. Almost everyone agrees that they, and just about everyone they know, are working harder. One way to think about this is to consider whether most of your peers feel overwhelmed too, or whether it is only you who seems to consistently need to work longer hours than everyone else.

- Decide if you miss deadlines because you're defining "acceptable" by higher standards than anyone else. If this speaks to you, you're probably a *Data-Collector*. *Data-Collectors* have a lot of perfectionist in them. Once they identify the best way to proceed, they find it nearly impossible to back off. It's important to note that a *Data-Collector's* definition of "acceptable" is often approved by management (or agreed to by a spouse) because it sounds terrific. What most people would consider to be an unobtainable ideal, a *Data-Collector* identifies as the standard that must be achieved. However, their standards tend to be unrealistic. Do you consistently produce work to higher standards than anyone else? If so, you may be allocating too much time and effort to each project relative to its potential benefits to your company or family.

Maybe you're saying to yourself that you do make your deadlines, but hate always being up against them. Are you sure? Mary M. MacDonald, the managing director and CEO of D'Arcy, called herself a procrastinator, but was aware that she craved the excitement of deadline pressure, and accomplished her best work under that pressure. Therefore, there was no problem.

Working at the last minute to meet a deadline is commonly considered a symptom of procrastination. If only you'd planned better, many people are told, you wouldn't always be in a time crunch at the last minute. That's society's view. But think about your own particular approach to work. What for one person is procrastination is for another an efficient working style.

Data-Collectors and *Accommodators*, for example, are most comfortable when their work load is orderly and unhurried. Deadline pressure gives them considerable stress. *Producers* and *Optimists,* on the other hand, prefer a fast-paced, high-pressure environment.

If you decide that you do, in fact, have a problem with procrastination, use this checklist to alert yourself to potential pitfalls, and identify the best way to change your behavior.

- *Accommodators* tend to put off doing anything that's confrontational. Try trading off the task in question. Remember, it's acceptable to avoid problems. Teddy, for example, reports that she hates returning items at a store "more than anything." She says, "I know it's stupid, but it's how I feel. One day I realized that my friend Corey wasn't talking about fashions as much as usual. When I commented on it, she laughed, and explained that her second baby put a temporary end to window shopping. On an impulse, I offered to baby-sit for a couple of hours if she'd return a sweater for me. She was out of the house en route to the mall in about a minute and a half! It worked out great for us both."

- *Optimists* tend to put off doing anything they'd have to do alone. Try inviting people to join you. If you dread cleaning out your attic—and *Optimists* would dread that detailed, lonely work—have a pizza party under the rafters. Invite some friends to keep you company. Lorrie was surprised at how well this idea worked. "I tried it with my son, a strong *Optimist*. Afterward, he came to me and asked if I needed help cleaning out the garage!"

- *Producers* tend to put off doing tasks for which they perceive no benefit. They respond well to a risk/reward ratio. That is, ask the question, "What's the worst that will happen if I *never* do this?" They either terrorize themselves into action, or give themselves permission never to do it.

   Del reported she was procrastinating cleaning out the closet in the room she intended to use as a nursery. "It was liberating to pose the risk/reward question. I realized it's my house, my baby, my nursery—and if I chose to have a cluttered closet, who cares? When the baby is old enough to notice, then we'll talk!"

- *Data-Collectors* tend to put off tasks if the environment is chaotic, or if the assigned responsibility is ambiguous. They thrive in a culture that provides a lot of structure, and don't do well without it. Creating smaller units with baby steps (achieved by using the *"In Order to ..."* model explained later in this chapter) allows *Data-Collectors* to create a logical system of sequential tasks. A *Data-Collector* moves confidently from one step to the next until the end result is achieved.

   Yolanda, an engineer says, "I hate performance appraisals, but acknowledge that it's an important part of my job as a supervisor. My company requires that each employee receive an annual review using prescribed forms, but that's all they say. I created an eight-step list for myself, four steps that I need to complete before I sit down with my employee, three during the meeting, and one I do afterward. Baby steps. The whole process is easier for me now. I don't procrastinate. And I think I do a better job."

Third, if the goal is a stretch, many people hesitate to set deadlines because they fear that the deadline is unrealistic, and that if they set one, they may end up missing it and thus feel like a failure.

FAQ: *I feel frustrated every time I look at my goals—they seem impossible to reach. For example, one goal I have is to change careers, to become a broadcast journalist. What am I doing wrong?*

A: It sounds like your goals are too broad. Simply knowing that you want to be in broadcast journalism, for example, isn't enough. You need to translate your desire into action steps, or it will remain only a dream. Ask yourself a series of questions, each one of which begins, *"In Order to. . . ."* Doing so will ensure that your goals are narrow in focus and that you understand the specific steps you need to take to achieve them.

If you've never done a certain task, you might ask, how can you know how long it will take? Fair enough. Set a deadline anyway. *You can always change it.* Remember that we're writing our goals in pencil.

Nancy learned the importance of a deadline when starting her own business. "I wanted to start a business," she said. "I felt ready. But nothing happened. I felt like a huge procrastinator. I attended a lot of Expos and Business Opportunity conferences until finally I was ready to give up. I felt as if I was doing everything right, but still nothing happened. I just about convinced myself that I didn't have what it takes to go on my own. When I learned that I had to set a deadline in order for my goal to be a goal, as opposed to a dream, I recognized my problem. In my case, the first step was to file papers with the government, registering my company's name.

"As long as I didn't have a deadline, it was easy for me to avoid doing anything. Once I forced myself to set a deadline, my dream became a goal."

Consider this goal: *I want to produce a working document as soon as possible.*

How can you reframe it to add a Deadline?

Each of these satisfies the need for a Deadline:

- ✔ I want to produce a working document by Wednesday.
- ✔ I want to produce a working document by Tuesday's staff meeting.
- ✔ I want to produce a working document before I leave work today.

Be realistic about how long things take. It's often a good idea to time yourself doing them. It doesn't matter how long *you* think a phone call takes; what matters is the reality of how long it takes. Discovering that a "quick" phone call actually takes eleven minutes (the average business-to-business phone-call length, according to a major telecommunications company), you're better able to set deadlines you can meet.

Step 5. How Can You Tell When You Get There?

Objective

Set unique standards so you will know when you've succeeded.

You must be able to answer the question, "How can I tell when I've reached my goal?" And you must be able to answer it in a way that is unique to your situation. Just because you know what you intend to accomplish, and will know when you achieve it, doesn't mean anyone else does.

For example, how can I tell when I finish my walk and have arrived in San Francisco? Think about it.

Did you think, "When I see the Golden Gate Bridge?" Many people do, but *seeing* the Golden Gate Bridge won't work. Think about it—you can see it from afar, long before you arrive in San Francisco. Perhaps you said, "When I'm *on* the Golden Gate Bridge." But you can be *on* it on the Marin County side of the bridge.

Saying, "When I see the sign reading 'Welcome to San Francisco' " won't work either. You face the same problem with the sign as you did with the bridge: you can see it *before* you get there, you can *touch* it before you get there—do you see the complexity? Touching the *back* of the welcome sign would work. So would standing in or on or by a unique feature of the city such as Fisherman's Wharf.

When you are identifying the unique measure of success, there are two approaches to take. You can illustrate success with an example, or you can quantify it.

Regardless of which alternative you select, accurately stating the Objective form of measurement is essential for success. A manager for a major credit card company told me that he and his staff missed their Christmas bonus. They thought they were being judged by how many of their company decals they placed on merchant doors, but they weren't. They were being judged by how many of their company decals were placed on merchant doors that already had their competitors' decals on them.

There's another potential pitfall to consider as well. Just because you have established a quantifiable form of measurement doesn't mean it's understood by everyone in the same way. For instance, it's about three thousand miles from New York City to San Francisco. If you strap a pedometer around your ankle and head west, you might think that when it reaches three thousand, you're there. Do you see the problem? Maybe you drifted south and went to Santa Barbara by mistake. Or maybe you got really lost and walked to Key West and back to New York City. In other words, just because it's quantifiable doesn't mean it's measuring what you want measured.

Lester, a marketing analyst at an automotive parts manufacturing company, recalls when his boss assigned him a one-year goal. "I was to identify promotional or distribution weaknesses in our chief competitor's marketing plan. My boss made it clear that when I submitted my report, he expected me to have identified flaws in competitive systems that would result in our increasing revenue at least two percent.

"Unfortunately, he thought I knew that our division's thrust that year was international expansion, and that he meant the two percent should come from international opportunities. But I didn't. I had no idea. I missed my objective because I assumed he meant domestic, and I was wrong."

When your boss tells you to increase the number of grant proposals submitted, make sure he doesn't mean the number of grant proposals submitted to non-government sources. When your spouse tells you he or she wants to go out to dinner, make sure the vision of a candlelit dinner that's in your head isn't a vision of pizza and beer in your spouse's head.

Consider this statement of your goal: *I want to learn to draw.* How can you rephrase it so that it integrates an Objective form of measurement?

What did you decide? Each of these would work:

- ✔ I want to become familiar enough with anatomy and perspective so that when my friends say something about drawing, I understand what they're discussing, and so that if I'm asked a question, I can answer it.
- ✔ I want someone at the Art Institute to ask *my* opinion.
- ✔ I want to sign up for drawing lessons offered at the Art Institute.
- ✔ I want to be one of the ten students to qualify for the advanced drawing class.

There are countless ways of making the statement satisfy the final step of the CAN DO model, the Objective form of measurement. Any statement that either provides a *unique* example illustrating success (i.e., sign up for the course) or *uniquely* quantifies success (i.e., be one of the ten students to qualify) will work.

Confirm You've Set Goals That You CAN DO

Ask yourself the following questions to confirm that a goal satisfies the five steps of the CAN DO model. Once you say yes to every question below, you're putting yourself in a good position to achieve your objectives.

1. Does the goal specify an end result?
2. Does the goal avoid theoretical or generic terminology?
3. Does it describe a behavior?
4. Do I know how to do it?
5. Am I aware of the resources needed to do the job?
6. Do I have sufficient resources or, if not, can I acquire them?
7. Am I aware of what level of quality I expect—and can I define that level of quality in a unique way?
8. Does the goal refer to only one desired result?
9. Does it have precise parameters?
10. Is it explicit?
11. Do I have a time, date, or some other time frame illustrated or specified for when I need to be finished?
12. Do I know how I'm to be evaluated?
13. Can this measurement refer to nothing else except my specific goal?
14. Is the goal quantifiable or, in other words, is there an example of success that I understand, and that is unique?

Create Do-able Baby Steps Using "In Order to . . ."

"In Order to . . ."—three little words. Three of the most powerful in English. They allow you to take a properly framed goal and break it into the baby steps that provide the road map to achievement.

If your boss tells you on October 9 that she wants you to deliver a formal presentation to the board on November 15 summarizing computer needs assessment and making recommendations, the first step is to consider the CAN DO model.

Let's assume you know how to do a needs assessment and you know enough about computers to ask good questions. In other words, your goal is Concrete. You're about to learn whether it's Attainable and Realistic with the *"In Order to ..."* model. You'll know whether you have adequate resources to meet the deadline. It's appropriately Narrow in that it's not covering *all* technical issues, only computers. You have a Deadline of November 15. You decide to define your Objective form of measurement as the board saying yes. In other words, if the board endorses your recommendations, you'll know that you did a good job on the needs assessment and the presentation.

The *"In Order to ..."* model allows you to confirm that you have adequate resources to accomplish your goal. This simple project-management tool can be efficiently created using an 8½ x 11–inch piece of paper and sticky notes, although various cards-in-slots and computerized systems would work as well. Sticky notes are relatively inexpensive, come in various colors for easy color coding, are movable, and allow you to change your mind easily and throw them away.

Regardless of which system you use, follow these steps to complete the *"In Order To ..."* model and ensure that you know exactly what to do and when.

- After determining that the goal is framed properly using the CAN DO model, ask yourself a series of questions, each one of which begins, *"In Order to. ..."* The answers represent sequential tasks. Step by step, you'll learn where to start and what to do to reach your desired end result. You'll also identify glitches well in advance of the glitch becoming a problem.
- Assign responsibility for each task.
- Add twenty percent to every resource allocated at every step. By doing so, you anticipate problems. If you don't do so, you're almost assured of ending up in a crisis. What you've done is create a scenario where if everything goes right, you'll achieve your desired results. But things never go a hundred percent right. Think about it—printing presses break; people get the flu; and hurricanes and blizzards

strike without warning. Any of these might occur, or none may occur. It will be a crisis only if you haven't anticipated that they might happen. This is not padding. This is planning for the real world. Add twenty percent and you'll always come in under budget and before deadline.

Take a look at the graphic on page 167. Notice that the first sticky note—the last one on the page—reads, "Jane-Nov 15-Prez." I'm saying that I will do the presentation on November 15. That's my desired end result. When I pose the "*In Order to* . . ." question, I say to myself, "I want to rehearse. In order to do a good job at the presentation, I need to rehearse. I don't want to do this thing cold. However, by the time I'm ready to rehearse, I'll know the material inside out, so I won't need a lot of time. I'll just want to run through, check the A/V, and confirm that my timing is right."

I decide I need only a day. Adding twenty percent, I decide to call it two days. What if the A/V is wrong or my timing is off? The extra day gives me time to locate an alternative vendor or revamp my presentation. You'll note that the next sticky note reads, "Jane-Nov 13-Rehearse."

"*In Order to* . . ." rehearse, what do I have to do? I need the slides. Given that this is a formal presentation, I decide to have the Creative Department prepare slides, and Peter, the department head, has a rule that you have to give them two weeks in which to turn around any project. Call it seventeen days, and you'll see that the third sticky note reads, "Peter-Oct 26-Slides."

"*In Order to* . . ." get the slides from Peter's department, what do I have to do? Deliver a disk to Peter with the content that I want on the slides. It will take me only a couple days, I decide, to create the slides because by then I will have written the report. Call it three days. Note that the sticky note reads, "Jane-Oct 23-slide content."

"*In Order to* . . ." prepare the slide content, I have to write the report. I need a week, call it ten days. The sticky note reads, "Jane-Oct 13-report." "*In Order to* . . ." write the report, the information technology department has to finish their analysis. They need a week, so call it ten days. Oops.

Jane
Oct 13
Report

Jane
Oct 23
Slide
Content

Peter
Oct 26
Slides

Jane
Nov 13
Rehearse

Jane
Nov 15
Prez

Do you see the problem? I have to give the information tech-nology department the salespeople's presentations on October 3 in order for them to finish their analysis by October 13. And today is October 9. Which means *this isn't happening*. I just proved it.

The only good news here is that it's been only ten minutes. So I run—don't walk—immediately to my boss and ask if I can do the presentation at the February 15 meeting. Best-case scenario has my boss saying, "Sure. I'm glad you got to me before we pub-lished the agenda." Real-world scenario is your boss saying, "No. It's got to be on November 15."

This isn't bad news. This isn't a crisis. This is the real world. In every industry, at every level, throughout history, as managers move up in responsibility, they are increasingly responsible for al-locating scarce resources. There's never enough time. There's never enough money. Your staff is never large enough.

If you were a lawyer and were responsible for only one client, you could do a marvelous job. If you manufactured auto parts, and were responsible for producing only one unit, you could make an auto part of the highest quality. But you can't. Producing acceptable levels of output (be that consulting or professional services, manufacturing, tax collection, health care, or whatever) at acceptable levels of quality (however that is defined and mea-sured) is your challenge.

What this means to us as we strive to meet the November 15 deadline is that we need to identify any improper uses of re-sources. Plan A—our ideal scenario as we first envisioned and executed on the 8½ by 11 sheet of paper—isn't Attainable. We just proved it.

Two weeks seems like a long time for preparing slides given the convenience of commonly used and widely available soft-ware packages. Doesn't it make sense that before I approach Pe-ter and ask him to turn the slides around more quickly, I should first try to get a read of his personality? Think about my chal-lenge: I'm trying to delegate to someone over whom I have no authority. Peter is a peer. In determining his personality style, I'm trying to give myself a leg up. *My priority* is getting professionally prepared slides quickly.

If I decide that Peter is signaling that he wants to be treated as an *Accommodator*, I might say, "Peter, I'm really in a jam. I need some help." If I consider Peter to be an *Optimist*, I'd say, "Peter, brainstorm with me for a sec, will you?" For a *Producer* Peter, I'd phrase it as "Peter, can you speed it up? Bottom line—it's for the board." If I determine that Peter's a *Data-Collector*, I might say, "Peter, is there any way we can create a system that would speed this up?"

There's no magic. All I'm doing is trying to facilitate getting *my* priority met in the manner that I've determined is ideal. It's always possible, of course, that no matter what my approach, Peter might say, "Of course, no problem. With this much advance notice, we can turn them around much more quickly. Let's slot you in now." That's the best-case scenario.

Worst-case scenario is if Peter replies, "No. I was told no exceptions." If he refuses to cooperate, I have to face the fact that Plan B isn't going to work either.

Many people who have a good work ethic don't want to do less than the ideal. Many of you, for example, in reading this example, are now saying to yourselves, "Well, it's time to go to my boss and ask him to talk to Peter's boss." You probably shouldn't do this. It's probably time to crumple up Peter's sticky note and move on to Plan C. There are lots of good alternatives. Peter is not the one and only way of creating professional slides. Furthermore, this isn't life and death; this is business. Resist the urge to worry about it or to fret. It's probably time to move on. Remember, not all problems have to be faced. If Peter isn't cooperative, let it go.

Plan C might include taking a look at your budget. Time and money often trade off. For example, you can have slides made in an hour if you want to pay the rush fee. Peter's lack of cooperation is irrelevant unless you don't have the money.

Let's say you don't. Plan D is to ask the information technology folks to pump you out some pie charts while they're doing their analysis. They say no.

Plan E—do the slides yourself. But you don't have the proper software?

Plan F—you can do a marvelous presentation with no prepared graphics at all. An effective presentation depends on *you*, not your slides. You can make it interactive and engaging by jotting key points on a flip chart or acetate transparency as you're delivering your presentation. There's no doubt that dazzling graphics add sophistication and pizzazz. But the success of your goal—the board says yes—doesn't depend on any of them.

The beauty of the *"In Order to . . ."* model is that it alerted you to a problem well in advance. The issue isn't that you can't use a low-tech flip chart and do a good job at the presentation. The issue is that you don't want to be staying up all night the night before the presentation rehearsing because Peter didn't deliver the slides.

Patrick runs health care conferences. He explained that using this system provides him with a dozen or more summaries of what it takes to run a conference. "I have one sheet for the hotel negotiation, another for the printer, a third for the copywriter, and another eight or nine for all the other parts of making a conference go.

"It's very efficient. Each day I flip through all of the sheets of paper—I keep them in a three-ring binder—and at a glance I can tell *who* on my staff is due to do *what*. And I can see *when* they're due to do it. After the conference is done, I add a phone number or an e-mail address for each contact on the appropriate sticky notes. That means that six months from now, when it's time to begin planning next year's conference, I have a starting place—a skeleton—of what worked last time. Talk about *not* reinventing the wheel!"

The *"In Order to . . ."* model helps you manage priorities in three ways. You'll be able to:

1. properly sequence tasks
2. be alerted to potential problems in advance
3. replicate a process that led to achievement

Start by Dreaming

Managing priorities begins with dreams. It's a smart place to start. Let your mind go. What direction could your business take?

How might your organization evolve? Where might you direct your career if you had your choice? What kind of friendships would you develop? What would your romantic life be like?

Envision yourself in the future. Picture yourself as you'd like to be. Dream. Now take the dreams you really want to come true and use the CAN DO model to navigate your way from dreams to goals and the *"In Order to ..."* model to convert goals into action steps. To make optimum use of the goal-setting tools discussed in this chapter, you need to identify and integrate *Unspoken Expectations*, discussed in Chapter 6. You can do it! The tools provide the framework, but you provide the substance.

Tips

- When thinking about your priorities, envision your ideal future. Allow yourself to dream. Once you know where you want to end up, work backward to design a plan of action to achieve your goals. Long-term goals translate into short-term action steps. Simply taking action without a long-term context won't help your dreams become real.
- Make sure you know everything you need to know in order to succeed. Don't let ignorance hold you back. Treat getting yourself educated as a goal: first define your information needs, then go backward to identify the action steps appropriate to acquire the knowledge. Knowledge truly is power!

CHAPTER SIX

✦

Know Your *Unspoken Expectations*

Irrational but Influential—
Is It Perception or Reality?

When Leigh landed a desktop publishing job right out of school, she was thrilled. "I was so proud of getting a job in my field so quickly. I was hired as a design consultant at a major quick-print place in Chicago. My understanding was that I would be working with walk-in customers, the ones who came in needing a logo but didn't have a design in mind. I had visions of creative brainstorming sessions. Instead I discovered that what we were really talking about was generating business cards as quickly as possible.

"In the year and a half I've worked there, I've never met a customer. I get stacks of file folders dumped on my desk throughout the day. Each folder contains notes, instructions, and copy from the sales associate, and I'm expected to produce a business card—about fifteen an hour. Think about that. That's four minutes a card if I work nonstop.

"I just couldn't understand it. I knew that I'd been hired because they were impressed with my portfolio. Yet they didn't seem interested in my design ability. All they seemed to care about was speed. I asked my boss about it. He said I was wrong to think quality didn't mean anything. Quality meant everything, he said. He denied that there were production standards. No, he told me, I should take as much time as I needed to create each design.

"Maybe he *talked* about quality, but all I knew was that the folders kept coming. I had to design quickly, and I believe they expected it. For example, the deadlines written on the folders indicated that the business cards would be ready for customer pickup the next day. They couldn't possibly be printed in time for the customer to pick them up if I took longer than minutes to design them.

"Luckily, I realized what was going on and was able to adjust. In fact, it's been a great experience. I work on a huge variety of projects and have gotten very good at designing quickly and under pressure."

What did Leigh learn that transformed this potential nightmare situation into success? She learned to identify and then integrate an *Unspoken Expectation* into her daily life. She realized that her ability to generate quality designs was a given; she wouldn't have been hired without the talent and ability to do so. Her boss made it clear that she was expected to produce quality work. What remains unspoken to this day is the company's expectations regarding quantity.

The specifics of your situation are different from Leigh's, of course. What's the same is that you too have *Unspoken Expectations*, and that your success in all aspects of your life depends on your ability to recognize and integrate them into your day-to-day activities.

Unspoken Expectations can be defined as *that by which you are judged*. They're not necessarily what's on your job description, nor are they likely to be reported on last year's performance appraisal. They often seem petty or irrational. Whether they seem minor or not, whether they appear logical or not, their effect on your success—both personally and professionally—is major. That they exist is not in question. The only question is whether you're aware of them—and if you *are* aware of them, whether you've integrated them into your goals.

In order to effectively set goals that serve you and your organization's needs, you need to:

- Discover other people's *Unspoken Expectations* of you
- Determine the impact of other people's *Unspoken Expectations* on all of your goals
- Consider *Unspoken Expectations* when you're under time pressure to respond
- Integrate *Unspoken Expectations* into your goals

It's foolhardy to set goals until you assess your *Unspoken Expectations*. The difference can be dramatic. Review the following examples of goals set without considering *Unspoken Expectations*, and those that do.

Goals without *Unspoken Expectations*	Goals with *Unspoken Expectations*
Get my daily expense report done by five each day.	Return all phone calls by five and get the week's expense report done by five each Friday.
Meet my sales goals.	Be in the office by seven each morning, and meet my sales goals.
Keep the house spotlessly clean.	Play with my kids for at least an hour a day, and keep the house neat.
Maximize use of our equipment.	Never say no to XYZ clients when they need something, and maximize the use of our equipment in scheduling other jobs.

Think of it this way: in order to manage your priorities effectively, you have to know all of the factors that affect your success. The first step in avoiding the pitfalls associated with *Unspoken Expectations* is to recognize that they exist. Once you know what they are, you're in a good position to avoid potential traps and to use them to your advantage. The trick is to focus the light on them, to ferret them out, so that you can control the outcome. There are three ways that you can discover those *Unspoken Expectations* that affect you.

1. *Ask* others to tell you about any *Unspoken Expectations* they have for you. This may or may not be a good idea. Sometimes people may feel put on the spot or challenged by your questions. Sometimes they think you ought to know without asking. Yet in some circumstances, opening up the issue of *Unspoken Expectations* as a topic for discussion can be an effective way of discovering those that apply to you. For example, if you work with an *Optimist*, you might engage him in a discussion of *Unspoken Expectations* by saying, "Hey, I learned a neat concept called *Unspoken Expectations*. If you have a minute, I'd love to explain it to you and find out any that you have for me." On the other hand, if you're working with *Producers*, or if your organizational culture precludes open discussions, it might be best to rely on the third option below, observation.

2. *Tell* other people about any *Unspoken Expectations* that you have for them, thereby initiating conversation. Another effective way to tell people your *Unspoken Expectations* is to integrate it into the discussion while asking for their feedback, as discussed above. For example, after asking for their *Unspoken Expectations*, you might add, "Thanks for the information. Here's a couple that are important to me."

3. *Observe* success and try to copy it. How do you define success? If you're most concerned with job security, wouldn't it make sense to observe the people who seem to survive all of the reorganizations, downsizings, and acquisitions? Look at their behavior. How can you adapt it to your circumstances? On the other hand, if you're more concerned with getting ahead, doesn't it make sense for you to observe the people who keep getting promotions? Who in your organization seems to be on the fast track? What do they do that's different from what you do?

No matter which of the three approaches you use—or whether you employ all three in combination—you need to be extremely cautious. As you consider your *Unspoken Expectations*, look for patterns and resist predicting outcomes based on one single example. Be forewarned that generalizing is risky. One event cannot imply a pattern; in fact, it might be an aberration.

FAQ: *How can I tell what my* Unspoken Expectations *are when I'm brand-new in my job?*

A: Use the same approach whether you've been in the job for years or it's your first day: ask, tell, and observe. Keep in mind, when you start a new position, to give it ninety days before you make lasting judgments.

"It was my first week on the job," explains Noriko, "and I wanted to give a good impression, so I stayed late every day. I was in a department with only one other person, and he stayed until after seven every day, so I did too. On Thursday of that first week, my boss called me in and said that he'd noticed I was staying late. He wanted to know if I had a time-management problem in that I wasn't able to get my work done by five. I couldn't believe it. I'd been modeling on my peer's behavior without realizing that the guy was on probation for poor work and was staying late to try and save his job. My boss had been thinking, 'Oh, no! What did I do, hire another under-performer?' I learned then and there to be certain you know what the behavior you're observing represents before you copy it. It worked out all right. Once I told my boss why I'd been staying late, he started laughing at the irony. Here I'd been thinking the *Unspoken Expectation* was working long hours, when all along the actual *Unspoken Expectation* was getting your work done on time. Very different.

"In addition to sharing a good laugh about it, it opened up the lines of communication. My boss was intrigued by the concept of

Unspoken Expectations, and we ended up having a productive conversation about them."

Notice that Noriko was prepared to accept an irrational *Unspoken Expectation.* "There was no question that I could get the job done by five. But I was willing to stay later to create the perception of extra effort on my part if that's what was required to impress my boss."

Reality versus perception. In order to succeed, you need to know what the perception is, not the reality. Saying, "But it's not fair!" isn't going to help you. Noriko's experience isn't unique; time is an issue rife with *Unspoken Expectations.* Faye discovered this when Arthur, her boss, told her that she wasn't getting a promotion because she wasn't working hard enough.

"I did my work," Faye explained, "and I did it well. It didn't matter. Arthur likes it when he walks by your office at seven and you're there. If you're not, he thinks you're slacking off. It's all perception.

"I thought I was being judged by my output, but I was wrong. I was being judged by a combination of output and physical presence in the office." Note that the issue wasn't whether Faye had an *Unspoken Expectation* influencing her success. The issue was whether she was *aware* of it, and whether she assessed it accurately. In other words, don't leap to conclusions about *Unspoken Expectations.* Verify that you *know* what they are before you make decisions based on what you *think* they are.

"To me, being evaluated on hours worked, not output was patently unfair, so I assumed that once I pointed out the reality of the situation to Arthur—that I was a good worker—he'd change his mind. Boy, was I wrong.

"The first thing I did was to make a joke about it. I said, 'Try me! One hand tied behind my back, eyes closed, you name a project; I bet I'm on or ahead of schedule.' Arthur said, 'I believe you—but you're *not* putting in the hours.'"

Faye was right. This is a classic example of an *Unexpected Expectation* because despite the fact that her boss knew she was getting the work done, he still was irritated by her leaving at five. Furthermore, it's natural to try to get people to change their minds—Faye's joke, for instance, seems to be a reasonable effort to convince Arthur to rethink his impression of her. However, this approach rarely works. It rarely works because trying to change an *irrational* opinion is essentially impossible.

"Arthur knew I was getting things done; but that was irrelevant," Faye wisely recognized. "It didn't matter that I'm an efficient person; nor did it matter that he knew that I was an efficient person. What mattered was that every time he looked into my office after normal working hours and it was empty, it set his teeth on edge. He perceived me as lazy—and it was the perception that mattered, not the reality. The only reality that mattered was that every time he saw my office empty, he lost a little respect for me."

To Arthur, Faye's working hours represented more than merely a block of time in which work was accomplished. His perception was that Faye was not working hard enough, and therefore he concluded that she wasn't committed to the job or organization. He felt concern that she might be irresponsible, maybe even untrustworthy. Despite knowing—rationally—that Faye was productive, Arthur didn't feel comfortable giving her a promotion.

In other words, when considering *Unspoken Expectations*, understand that *perception is more important than reality*.

"So guess what I did?" Faye asked. "Surprise! I started working longer hours. I never liked it, don't get me wrong. But it worked. I got a promotion six months later, and Arthur specifically told me he was pleased to 'reward my new attitude.' As the years went by, I came to be very grateful to Arthur. Because he told me. I'm not a mind reader—how could I have known if he hadn't told me?"

Look at the situation from Faye's point of view. If you were Faye, wouldn't you want to know that that's how your boss perceived your working hours? Think about it: Arthur felt bugged by Faye's empty office *regardless of whether he told Faye about it or not*.

Arthur was smart. He told Faye of his perception (an *Unspoken Expectation*) that she would have no way of knowing had he not told her. By telling her, Arthur gave her a chance to fix it.

Hunt for Categories of *Unspoken Expectations*

You have powerful *Unspoken Expectations* in your personal life too. You know the old saw about the couple who got divorced because he left the cap off the tube of toothpaste? That's an example of an *Unspoken Expectation*. Yes, he left the cap off, and no, probably that's not why they divorced. Perhaps the incident was the last straw. No doubt it was a symptom, an example of ongoing problems and just happened to be the precipitating event.

From the specific example—the cap off the toothpaste—we can't know the category. We can't know *why* she was so bothered by the cap being left off the toothpaste. But we can speculate. Consider the list that follows. The cap being left off the toothpaste might represent an *Unspoken Expectation* regarding:

- *Neatness.* "It's messy, and you never clean up after yourself."
- *Territory.* "It's *my* toothpaste—you don't respect *my* possessions."
- *Maturity.* "I'm not your mother. Can't you put things away without my having to harp at you?"
- *Money.* "If the toothpaste dries out, we can't use it. It's a waste of money."

How can you tell which of these applies? *Ask.* Asking for clarification is one of three ways that you can assess your *Unspoken Expectations*.

Ask for the Truth—Carefully

If your spouse tells you that leaving the cap off the toothpaste drives him or her crazy, you shouldn't assume you know what the underlying issues are. Maybe the cap off the toothpaste is only a symptom of something else. Given that you have only one example, you need to be careful about generalizing. In order to deal with *Unspoken Expectations*, you need to first identify what is truly going on.

Probably the most efficient approach is simply to ask why. Not in a hostile way, but in a curious way. Don't argue, don't dismiss it as unimportant, and don't act disrespectful in any way. Don't be defensive. Instead, position your questions as part of your efforts to gather information.

Let's say that you are trying to find out what the cap off the toothpaste represents. You've asked why it's so bothersome and received the reply, "Because it's my toothpaste. Get your own if you want to leave the cap off." From this response, you conclude that the issue is one of *ownership*. Perhaps you'd been thinking that you shared the toothpaste, not knowing that your spouse wanted his or her own tube.

But that answer could signal other issues. For example, it could be *neatness*. Your spouse could be saying "my," referring to the bathroom which *she* (or *he*) cleans, as opposed to a hotel, where a housekeeper comes in to clean. Because you can't know what the true *Unspoken Expectation* is from only one example, it makes sense to follow up by asking about other examples as you try to uncover the truth. For instance, you might ask, "What else do I do that bugs you?" or "Does it irritate you when I read one of your books and then leave it lying around on the floor as well?" As you elicit additional examples, a pattern is likely to emerge.

Asking questions is a powerful technique to uncover the truth. The mere act of inquiry shows respect for the person or the people you're asking. It implies that you're interested in working together to find a solution.

Consider the assertive approach taken by W. F. Tom Burch, Jr. When he was senior vice president of a $600 million savings and loan institution, he knew that he needed to get people talking in order to find out employees' and customers' *Unspoken Expectations*.

"I was responsible for operations at fourteen branches. My responsibilities included overseeing a hundred and sixty people. Talk about communication being a big deal," he explained. "My success depended on other people meeting tough standards. For example, I demanded that every teller close out his or her window in twenty minutes. I knew—or thought I knew—that they hated the pressure and thought I was unreasonable. I would have bet money that my tough stance on this issue created a lot of anxiety. But that was all speculation. I needed to *know* the impact on employees and customers. And the only way for me to know was to get people talking.

"System-wide, we used surveys and customer satisfaction measures, but I wanted to delve deeper. Now I can give a name to what I was trying to discover—*Unspoken Expectations*—but at the time we senior managers simply referred to endeavors of this sort as trying to figure out 'what's really going on."

"Here's what I did. I got these big pins. Every employee had to wear one. Ugliest things you've ever seen—the graphic was a huge, ugly ear. The copy—it said, '*I can't hear what you're thinking.*'

"I set up a whole system of responses with tight deadlines, so that people—customers and employees alike—knew they'd receive immediate feedback. I believed that knowing someone would respond helped motivate people to risk making suggestions or getting gripes off their chest. The pins were my way of asking for the truth, and it worked. It got people talking. I was able to better understand by learning the truth.

"For example, that twenty-minute deadline that I thought made people anxious? I was wrong. Once they discovered that they could meet the standard, they realized they loved getting out of work on time. Over the years, I've seen time and again—asking for the truth works. And you need to be very careful about speculating."

Ask. But ask in such a way that people feel comfortable responding. Create an environment wherein they aren't intimidated. Consider assuring people that:

1. There'll be no reprisal.
2. Any *Unspoken Expectations* they discuss will be taken seriously.
3. A response is guaranteed within a specific period of time.

Note this approach isn't saying that you'll change what you're doing; nor does it imply that they'll get everything they want.

Rather, you're assuring them that their comments won't disappear into some vast abyss never to be addressed again.

Help people to tell you the truth, and you'll be astonished at what you hear. For instance, here are some examples of what people heard when they asked directly for feedback:

- My mom told me, "When you're coming for dinner, I hate it if you arrive late without calling. Even if there's no urgency, I fret." (*Follow-up comment:* "So I make a point of arriving on time or calling to let Mom know I'll be late.")
- My boss told me, "You give too much background. Get to the point!" (*Follow-up comment:* "I immediately tell my boss the conclusion—what would normally, to me, be the last thing I'd say. He then asks questions to get the amount of detail he wants. It's worked out great.")
- "In a Chamber of Commerce networking-breakfast speech, a judge before whom I frequently plead remarked, 'Lawyers who use the word *basically* in my courtroom lose my respect.' (*Follow-up comment:* "I no longer use the word *basically* in his courtroom.")
- One focus group member mentioned that he hated it that we used a pull-the-heartstrings photo in our fund-raising appeal letters. (*Follow-up comment:* "When the other focus group members said they were touched by it, and I pointed out that appeals that featured the photo worked better than those that didn't, the member admitted that his objection sprang from the fact that the photo touched him almost too much. We kept the photo.")

Think about how to phrase your request. Most people report good success when they say something like, "I learned about something we might find useful—a thing called *Unspoken Expectations*. Let me give you a couple of examples, because any *Unspoken Expectations* you have for me, I'd love to know about."

Tell the Truth—They Want to Know

Brendon announced that despite having maintained an un-comfortable silence for over twenty-five years, he was going to tell his employees about an *Unspoken Expectation* that affected them. "I'd never thought of *Unspoken Expectations* in just this way," he said. "As soon as I did, it made perfect sense. The secret is in talking about them. So I determined that I would. I'd never told any of them because I know it's irrational. So what? It's real. So I'll be embarrassed—but I'm resolved. After all, what do I have to lose? I own the business!

"Here's an example of what I mean. Ursula has worked for me for twenty-five years. I started the business, and she joined me that first year. I wouldn't be where I am without her. She is as im-portant to me as my right arm, maybe more important. But for twenty-five years she's done something that has driven me nuts. She's not the only one, of course. The worst part is, she's trained them in this way—to be like her. It's funny, actually, if you look at it that way."

What Ursula had done was strive to be thoughtful, according to *her* standards. What she'd never considered was her boss's standards. For example, whenever she had a doctor's appoint-ment she scheduled it—in her mind, courteously—for first thing in the morning, so as to be as unobtrusive as possible. What she didn't know—and what she had no way of knowing because her boss had never told her—was that he couldn't stand it if any em-ployee came in even one minute late. He explained that he'd never said a word because he felt stupid. "The truth is, if they leave an hour early, I don't care," he said.

Think about it from Ursula's point of view. Wouldn't you rather know?

Now consider how Brendon feels when it's Christmas bonus time. Say Ursula had a doctor's appointment the day before. He *knows* his resentment isn't reasonable. Still, with the best will in the world, how could he possibly keep yesterday's irritation from affecting his decision about how much to give Ursula as a bonus? It's doubtful that he can. Thus, it's better for *both* of them to know the truth—early in their association.

When telling people about your *Unexpected Expectations*, it's important that you avoid the following traps:

- Don't try to justify how you feel (given that irrational thoughts are unjustifiable).
- Don't act defensively (instead, acknowledge that you understand they may be surprised, disappointed, or simply not like the particular *Unspoken Expectation*).
- Don't explain *why* you feel as you do (it's not relevant).

Consider saying some version of "I want to tell you about this concept I've run into called *Unspoken Expectations* and give you a few examples. There are a couple I have that affect you, and I'd like to explain what they are. And, of course, any you have for me, I'd like to hear about them as well." Most people discover that others are very receptive of the truth.

However, don't forget to integrate personality:

- To an *Accommodator*, for example, you might start by saying something like, "You would be doing me a huge favor if . . ."
- To an *Optimist*, say, "Nifty new concept! We get to tell each other exactly what we think. Okay, maybe not exactly. Are you ready? Let me explain."
- For a *Producer*, this would work well: "Do you have any idea how productive we'll be if we use this idea of *Unspoken Expectations*? Let's be direct."
- For *Data-Collectors*, say, "The model of *Unspoken Expectations* will help us create a system of . . ."

Observe What Works for Others

Examining what has worked for others, or analyzing what has worked for you in the past, is a good way to get a feel for what is likely to work for you in the future.

For instance, whenever Jake, a human resource benefits planner, wins a new client, he routinely asks to see previous reports that have met the client's standards. As he explains it, "When I first started, one client told me she wanted really *professional* reports. I didn't think anything of it, because I know my reports are always professional. Well, guess what? She hated my reports.

"Turned out, she wanted documentation of *everything*. I'd never had a client as detail-oriented as she was. Knowing what I know now, I would have recognized two things. First, I would have recognized that she was a *Data-Collector*, so I would have automatically provided a lot of details. And second, I would have been aware that the word *professional* was a potential trap, an *Unspoken Expectation* waiting to get me. Think about everything the word *professional* could represent. It could mean 'paid,' or 'polished,' or 'appropriate,' or 'not amateurish.' What *she* meant was 'academic.' She expected footnotes, formal conventions, and a pedantic style. 'Academic' would never have entered my mind because I have a business—not an academic—orientation. I could have avoided the entire problem if only I'd asked her for samples."

FAQ: *I'm a single mom, so I have to go home on time. I do my work, and I do it well, but I have a colleague who's been given a promotion ahead of me. I think it's just that she stays later than I do. What can I do?*

A: Sounds like you're dealing with an *Unspoken Expectation*. Whenever you identify an *Unspoken Expectation*, follow the steps outlined in this chapter in a methodical manner. You'll either convince the people involved to change their minds, decide you can live with it, persuade them to your point of view, or decide you can't live with it, and quit.

Understanding the concept of *Unspoken Expectations* both releases you from guilt and helps you win acclaim. While there's no way Jake could have known what his client meant by the term *professional*, he knows so much about his business that a quick scan through the reports she liked—on any subject—would have given him an understanding of what she expected.

Learn from Jake's experience. Be realistic about what you can and can't know. And ask to see samples. Watch what others do.

Four Options for *Unspoken Expectations*

Understand that *Unspoken Expectations* need to be taken seriously and dealt with immediately. No matter what the specific circumstances, when confronting an *Unspoken Expectation*, you have four options available to you:

- Try to change their minds. Sometimes people respond well to this approach if your point of view is one they haven't considered, and if their *Unspoken Expectation* isn't entrenched.
- Decide you can live with it. Most of us adapt and live with *Unspoken Expectations* well. Be aware that doing so can lead to burn-out, the feeling that you can't stand living with the *Unspoken Expectation* one more second.
- Make a specific recommendation for improvement. This is the heart of the *End of the Rope Strategy* discussed in Chapter 8.
- Remove yourself from the situation. You're "outta there."

Acknowledging a Problem Is the First Step Toward Solving It

Hal worked for a toy company. "I run the computer help line. You know what I mean—if you're having a problem with your computer, you call me. I love it. It's a great job. I deal with everything from software installations to Internet search questions, from hardware issues to simple word-processing snafus. Ninety percent of the time I'm able to field the question then and there. The truth is that when it comes to basic business applications and computers, I know a lot.

"Also, most of the questions are pretty basic. I love to trouble-

shoot problems. It's great talking to people, and it's great helping them out. But about three months ago, my boss assigned me
the job of writing a procedure manual for all the frequently asked
questions and the basics of all the commonly used software packages. To me, this is a horror show. I hate to write. It's almost
painful for me. It's *so* slow. I'm not good at it, and I hate it."

Consider Hal's personality. He's obviously a mixture of personalities, but don't stop your thinking there. Ask yourself, what
kind of person loves a job that features these qualities:

- *The unknown.* (While Hal didn't know his callers' specific
  problems, he knew the categories of problems they'd be
  likely to call about. He noted, however, that he enjoyed the
  pressure associated with the unexpected.)
- *Predictability.* (He felt secure that his level of technical ex-
  pertise was sufficient ninety percent of the time.)
- *Helping people.* (Hal loved that he could solve their problems.)
- *Verbal.* (He hates to write but likes to talk.)

There are other clues too, of course, but review the above
four qualities. Based on the brief explanation Hal provided, and
the short analysis above, wouldn't you expect Hal's personality
to be comprised primarily of *Optimist* with a hint of *Accommodator* and a pinch of *Data-Collector* thrown into the mix?

"My boss was getting angry. He's mostly a *Producer*—very out-
spoken and direct and no-nonsense. He also has a fair amount of
Data-Collector in him. He's very technical in orientation. In other
words, he thinks that this assignment—designing the format and
writing the procedure manual—is a plum job. I'm sure it's never
even occurred to him that I don't feel the same way. Because *he*
thinks it's so interesting, he doesn't understand why *I'm* not making quicker progress.

"Finally, I realized that my job was in jeopardy. Not because I
wasn't doing a good job at what my boss and I both agreed was
my primary responsibility—manning the phone—but because
my boss was perceiving me as lazy.

"I knew I needed to back away from my emotions—the frustration and irritation at my boss. So I approached it as an *Unspoken Expectation* and went to Jane's system."

Hal is smart. Whenever there's a difference between your boss's perception of a situation, and the reality as you see it, you're in trouble. Going to the step-by-step system associated with *Unspoken Expectations* makes sense. The first step is:

- Try to change their minds

  "The first thing I tried to do was get him to change his mind. I asked if I could hire a consultant. I said, 'I've analyzed what I need to do to create a comprehensive procedure manual, and I've identified what skills are required.' Notice my language? As an *Optimist*, it's not natural for me to talk about analyzing things, but I did. It didn't work, though. He said no. As a result he gave me deadlines, and to tell you the truth, that was better for me."

- Live with it

  "I work well against a deadline—no surprise, given that I'm mostly an *Optimist*!—so I was able to live with it. I hated it, but you know what? I made it more fun for myself by finding some cool-looking clip art cartoon characters to use in the manual. My reward for finishing a section was selecting the next clip art character that I'd use. It worked. I got it done!

  "We're still using it too, although I now have an assistant who's responsible for keeping it up-to-date. Thank goodness!"

The beginning of Hal's success was acknowledging that there was a problem and then identifying exactly what the problem was. Once he acknowledged that his boss's expectations were at odds with his, he was able to use the *Unexpected Expectation* model to clarify what to do.

Problem-Solve Your Way to Success

Identifying *Unspoken Expectations* at work serves an important related purpose. In addition to protecting you during the goal-setting process, knowing your *Unspoken Expectations* also helps you solve problems wisely.

When we have a problem, most of us immediately focus on finding a solution. But there's a real risk inherent in this straightforward approach. The danger of jumping in to solve a problem is that you might not know what the real issue is. Just because you think you know doesn't mean you're right. In the examples that follow, you'll see how to investigate whether *Unspoken Expectations* are at work. If they are, you can decide whether the issue is a crisis, a symptom, or a straightforward problem.

Problems are sometimes camouflaged. Maybe you're convinced that you understand what you're dealing with, but you may be seeing only what's on the surface. One or more underlying issues may be hidden from your sight, like an iceberg. If you don't detect what's below the surface, your proposed solutions are likely to be superficial. If you don't properly address the actual problem, ultimately your solutions will be ineffective.

Great news, though! When you pinpoint what's really going on, your solutions are likely to work. Keep in mind that problems reveal themselves in many ways. What appears to be a straightforward problem may not be. As you work to set your goals and your organization's goals, you'll need to become adept at sorting through issues. All may not be as it appears at first glance. Use the *Unspoken Expectations* model as a tool to identify whether what seems to need attention falls into one or more of the following three categories:

- crisis (immediate action required)
- symptom (action may be required to address the symptom; certainly action will be required to solve the underlying problem)
- problem (whether the problem is straightforward or you become alerted to its existence via a symptom, action will be required)

FAQ: *I have a clear understanding of my job responsibilities, so I don't need to worry about* Unspoken Expectations. *All I have to do is look at my job description, right?*

A: Job descriptions identify broad areas of responsibility, and address the issue of how an employee will be judged in general terms. No matter how comprehensive your job description is, there are still important *Unspoken Expectations* that you must identify. Ferreting them out enables you to anticipate pitfalls that otherwise might short-circuit your career or personal relationships.

Get to the Truth: Is It a Crisis, a Symptom, or a Problem?

Do you feel as if you work in crisis mode most of the time? Do you run from putting out one fire only to dash to put out another fire—and then before you can catch your breath, you have to run to cope with another emergency? Unless your job is in emergency services, these events probably aren't crises, no matter how you feel. Usually, however, they are unexpected. Most often, no one has thought about why events that you and your colleagues are labeling a crisis occur, and so there's no system of response in place. Often someone in authority has an *Unspoken Expectation* that creates a crisis environment.

Justin put it this way. "I'm a manager in a small company. I report directly to the president. In our company salespeople always seem to call with an emergency request. One fellow called from his car on route to a meeting. He'd decided that he needed next quarter's projections in a pie chart format, not the data sheet he'd taken with him, so I had to scramble to find someone to create the chart and e-mail it to him before he got to the meeting. Another called from the lobby of a customer's building as he was getting into the elevator. He realized that he needed to have a contract faxed to him right away. From my point of view, as a manager, this was a real problem because everything stops when we get an emergency request. Yet these so-called emergencies were commonplace.

"After I'd been in the position six months or so, I complained. I mean, it was pretty clear what was happening. Somehow it had become okay for salespeople not to plan. I wanted to institute a policy that required advanced notice for most material. Planning . . . hello! I mean, not one thing, nothing, that a salesperson had requested couldn't have been prepared before they'd left. It was as if they intended to create crises. Come on, I thought, get it together.

"Whew. I was pulled up short when I heard the president's response. He said, 'I know it's tough on you, Justin, but our salespeople are the best! They're always thinking. If they come up with an idea at the last minute, I don't want you to think of it as a crisis. I want you to think of it as them being extra smart. And I want you to pull out the stops in getting each and every one of them what they need. I love to hear this sort of thing. It shows me they're on top of it.'

"Is this an *Unspoken Expectation* or what? The president was evaluating salespeople not on their sales, but on their emergency requests. I tried to point out to him that we could send them out into the world armed and ready to go if we knew in advance what they wanted. No go. After my second attempt to explain my point of view to him, I could see his eyes narrow. He was getting mad at me!

"Okay, once I realized what was going on, the definition of the problem changed. No longer was it my job to stop their last-minute requests. Instead, the problem was how to add time to the schedule for salespeoples' frequent requests. Thank goodness I was alert to the *Unspoken Expectation* and what it implied about the issue at hand.

"I would have hurt myself, and ultimately my company, had I not identified the true problem—my department's ability to field salespeoples' requests on an as-needed basis. If I'd tried to change the crisis atmosphere, I would have failed. And the salespeople wouldn't have had the material they needed to sell."

Justin is smart. At first, he was convinced that he'd identified an easy-to-change problem. By asking for feedback from his boss, he became aware of an *Unspoken Expectation*, which alerted him to the fact that there was no crisis. There was no problem. This was the culture of the company. It worked for them, and given that upper management didn't perceive any value in changing it, things weren't going to change.

Justin quickly adjusted his thinking. "I'd made a good-faith effort to change the president's view, and I was told that I was wrong. Fair enough. It's his company. He's the boss. My job is to alert him to issues I perceive to be important, and then to respond as I'm told to respond. It doesn't matter what I think reality is. What matters is what he thinks reality is."

In other words, Justin wisely used the *Unspoken Expectation* four-step model to address what he perceived as a problem.

- Try to change their minds

    Justin tried to persuade his boss to authorize a change in policy, but didn't succeed because his *Unspoken Expectation* was entrenched.
- Decide you can live with it

    Justin had no problem adapting his view to suit his company's culture and his boss's perceptions. Note that Justin solved his problem without going on to steps three or four.

Crisis Management Made Easy

Think about what you call a crisis. Your first responsibility in trying to sort out situations that feel like crises is to identify whether what you perceive as a crisis truly is one, or perhaps a *symptom* of some other issue, or a one-time event, a *problem*. *Crisis*, *symptom*, or *problem*, you deal with each differently. Thus you need to first analyze the circumstances. In fact, some situations might be a blend of all three. Keeping alert for *Unspoken Expectations* will help you identify the truth of the situations you face. Here's how to identify and address each.

- *Crisis:* After analyzing all aspects of the crisis, determine the best response and implement a system for automatically responding to future events of this type. Be alert for *Unspoken Expectations* that foster an environment in which creating and handling emergencies is rewarded.

- *Symptom:* Respond to the symptom if needed, then consider what it represents. Is it possible, for instance, that a symptom exists because of an untreated underlying issue? Perhaps there's an *Unspoken Expectation* at work that dictates that an underlying issue should be ignored. If that's the case, the symptom might linger; it might reappear; it might become the norm.

- *Problem:* Analyze what priorities apply, so you can speed up the decision-making process. The good news here is that a problem, by definition, has manageable parameters. *Unspoken Expectations* can alert you to unacceptable options and exciting opportunities.

For example, let's say you spill grape juice on a white carpet. You may well say, "Oh, oh! I've got a problem." But the truth is, this is a crisis. A crisis is time-sensitive—you don't have time to think, you simply must act. Before celebrating how well you handled the crisis, however, first consider whether in fact you have both a crisis *and* a symptom and whether there are any *Unspoken Expectations* at work.

Even if you succeed in getting the grape juice off the white carpet before it dries, you still have a problem—an untreated white carpet. It's just a matter of time before something else spills. When you deftly handle a time-critical situation, how tempting it is to say, "Whew! Dodged another bullet." But often this is not true. In other words, just because you've successfully handled a crisis, don't assume you've in any way affected an underlying issue. The difference is time. Without the time pressure, for example, you can investigate various treatment methods to determine what's best for your carpet. Thus a *crisis* can also be a *symptom* revealing an underlying *problem*. Evaluating any *Unspoken Expectations* related to the issue may help you sort through the options.

If your spouse has never liked the color or texture of the carpet, for example, his (or her) disinclination to help you clean it up may alert you to the fact that what is to you a crisis ("Oh, no! Grape juice!") is to him (or her) an opportunity ("Great! A major stain is a good excuse to replace the ugliest carpet I've ever seen!"). Without considering *Unspoken Expectations*, you might be dealing with only the tip of the iceberg and miss the weighty substance hidden from sight.

Symptoms are vulnerable to interpretation too, and considering *Unspoken Expectations* will help you figure out if the symptom is a warning sign or if it reveals additional complexity. For example, if your boss drops last quarter's overnight delivery bills on your desk and says, "Are you out of your mind? Fourteen thousand dollars in overnight delivery? Solve this problem," your first instinct is probably to grab the phone and start calling. Maybe you call all the competitors to get prices, then call your vendor and get ten percent off the bill. You feel pretty good. Fourteen hundred dollars—not bad for two hours' work. Except you didn't first ask *why* the bills were so high. Maybe, for example, your department handled an extra half million in sales. You're understaffed and up against tight deadlines. Who cares about $1,400 savings against revenue of half a million? You addressed a *symptom* of understaffing—not a problem. Maybe your two hours would have been better spent identifying a restructuring arrangement or locating a vendor to whom you can outsource part of the work.

Part of the complexity comes in recognizing that if you got ten percent off the bill that quickly, probably you were overpaying. In other words, symptoms are often serious unto themselves, and usually need to be dealt with. Don't delude yourself, however, that addressing a symptom necessarily impacts underlying issues. Furthermore, if you approach your boss with a report on the understaffing, and he says, "I told you to deal with the overnight delivery issue," you've probably identified an *Unspoken Expectation*. What do you do when you identify an *Unspoken Expectation*? Use the four-step process.

- Try to change their minds
    Perhaps you'll repeat your reasoning to your boss. If he resists your logic, most likely you'll move on to step two.

- Decide you can live with it

  If you keep meeting resistance, probably you'll decide you can live with it.

Rick, a survivor of a terrorist bombing overseas, says that about six months after the bomb went off, he found himself back in the States and about to start smoking.

"I hadn't smoked in seven years, and there I was, walking out of a convenience store with a pack of cigarettes in my hand. I couldn't even remember buying them. But with change in one hand and a pack of cigarettes of the brand I used to smoke in the other, well, I figured I'd bought them, all right. Within a couple of weeks I was back to smoking a pack a day.

"After a couple of months, I was talking to a pharmacist about getting a nicotine patch because I really didn't want to be smoking again. All of a sudden it dawned on me that maybe I wasn't recovering from the bombing as well as I'd thought. In addition to being injured myself—not badly—and absolutely terrified, I saw my coworker lose an arm. The whole thing was gruesome.

"I got some counseling, joined a support group, and guess what? Within three months I stopped smoking."

Rick was smart to look for *Unspoken Expectations* within himself, and to recognize the smoking for what it was: a symptom. Because the nicotine patch might have worked. And then what? What would Rick have done? Drink too much? Beat his dog? By addressing the underlying causes of the smoking, he was able to get rid of both the symptom and the problem.

"I was awfully tough on myself. That's an *Unspoken Expectation* I'm really glad I figured out—having unrealistically high standards for myself. No longer do I expect myself to be so strong, not to feel things deeply. It was liberating. Recognizing the *Unspoken Expectation* for what it was, I was able to stop beating myself up and to stop smoking. I won't say it was easy to stop," he explained, "but it wasn't as hard as when I'd stopped seven years earlier. Once I'd dealt with the grief and terror, the smoking became an irritant, something I had to deal with, and something I was motivated to deal with. No big deal."

Think of the intricacy involved in analyzing an issue seemingly this simple. In Rick's case, smoking was a symptom of unresolved issues as well as an indicator that he wasn't as tough as he'd perceived himself to be, an *Unspoken Expectation*. But that in no way implies that everyone who smokes has any underlying issues of which smoking is a symptom. People smoke for various reasons: peer pressure, habit, cultural reasons, preference, and so on. But smoking is clearly bad for you. In other words, symptoms are often bad and need to be dealt with, but doing so shouldn't lead you to ignore the even bigger problem that might be underlying the symptom.

Let's say that, after consideration, you're convinced that your situation is a crisis. Consider this: if you know in advance that an hour or two of a typical day is going to be spent handling something unexpected, why are you surprised when it happens?

You may never have thought of these so-called crises as predictable, but if you look at the structure—the skeleton, the underlying issues—of what you label a crisis, it's almost guaranteed that you can find ways to save yourself time and energy, and save your organization money. In other words, stop reinventing the wheel! Instead, identify the best response to the various sorts of crisis-like events that affect you, implement this best response, and strive to improve on it.

Remember that words are very powerful. Just because you perceive an event as a crisis doesn't make it one. Just because someone labels an event a crisis doesn't make it true. When you don't know the particulars of the event, ask yourself if you can't predict some parts of what's likely to happen. If you can, most likely you're not dealing with a crisis. Instead, it's probably a symptom of a problem—a lack of planning.

Consider what happens in a fire department, for example. Step by step, every action is prescribed. Specifically, when the bell goes off, the firefighter:

1. stands up and puts his feet in his pants—which are in the ready position
2. grabs the pole and slides down

3. goes directly to his locker where his coat is in the "arms in" position
4. puts on his hat

Notice that the firefighter has saved seconds by lining up his clothing in just that way. He then goes to the truck to his preassigned position, where his equipment has been placed in advance. And he's gone.

FAQ: *My last year's performance appraisal was excellent, so* Unspoken Expectations *won't apply to me, right?*

A: They still apply. My guess is that you have a fair amount of *Optimist* in your personality mix, and that you've adapted to *Unspoken Expectations* intuitively. Certainly, it can't do any harm to identify those *Unspoken Expectations* that apply to you. No matter how good your performance appraisal was, you'll probably want to make next year's even better.

Note all that he *doesn't* know. The firefighter doesn't know where he's going, nor does he know what he'll need to do when he gets there. But he knows enough about the kinds of calls he gets to make systemization possible. So do you.

Justin, the manager who discovered that the president of his company thought it was terrific that the outside sales staff created a crisis environment, says, "Once I acknowledged the *Unspoken Expectation* at work—that he liked the last-minute crisis feel of it all—I no longer tried to pretend that I could make the crises go away. Instead, I worked to create a system that would allow us to respond as efficiently as possible."

Justin learned from the experts in crisis management: firefighters. You can too. Firefighters have examined emergencies sufficiently to know how to respond most efficiently and effectively time after time. When considering how best to deal with anything you label a crisis, look for repeating occurrences. There are three steps to this process:

1. Examine events, looking for common factors.
2. Design the best response to situations that share these common factors.
3. Systemize the results (i.e., if x happens, we initiate y response).

Justin says, "I followed the three-step process. It was easy. First, we knew the common factors: salespeople on the road needing one or more of a dozen or so documents. Second, we designed the best response by getting the documents formatted as e-mail attachments. I set a procedure in place at the same time for keeping the data up-to-date. And third, systemization was natural. If a salesperson called, we e-mailed the document in question. Quick and easy. It worked. No more crises."

As you look for trends, it's handy to evaluate anything anyone calls a crisis for a period of time that's long enough to reflect the full work cycle. For some of you, that's a week. For others, it's a month. For still others, it's a quarter. Over whatever period of time you determine is appropriate, analyze events using the journalists' five W's: Who, What, When, Where, Why (and the How). Methodical and detailed, the five W's (and the How) are a useful tool in revealing patterns in content or timing.

Use the following questions based on the five W's (and the How) as you work to identify the problem:

- What do we label a crisis?
- Where do the problems occur?
- When do the problems occur?
- Who's involved in what we call a crisis?
- Why is it happening?
- How are we notified that there's a crisis?

For instance, maybe you're always under the gun in mid-month, not because of crises but because you have three reports due in two days. If you can arrange to defer one of the reports for a week, suddenly the flow of work is more balanced throughout the month. In other words, it wasn't a crisis—it was a scheduling problem. Had you not examined *when* the events you called a crisis occurred, you might never have realized a pattern existed. Once you did realize it, it was easy to fix by rescheduling one or more of the reports. Or, if it turns out to be an *Unspoken Expectation* (i.e., by the time the month's end data is compiled, it's already close to mid-month, and the executive committee needs all of the reports for its meeting on the sixteenth of each month), at least you know what you're dealing with and can plan for it.

The Twenty-Seven-Dollar Solution

Anytime you face what you believe is a crisis, it's important that you look for *Unspoken Expectations*. In Gillian's case, her careful analysis alerted her to three separate *Unspoken Expectations*. "Had I not forced myself to react cautiously, I might have undermined my career. To say nothing of the danger of not solving the problem. Luckily, I solved the problem well, and boosted my career."

Gillian, vice president of a large commercial printer, explained, "My boss, Nigel, owns the company. He and I get along very well. Nigel is an *Accommodator/Producer* combo, a sweet guy, very good at building relationships, but also very no-nonsense. He spends most of his time out of the office seeing customers, selling, networking, that sort of thing. He leaves the day-to-day operations to me.

"Nigel's a terrific deal maker, but he doesn't deal with conflict well. The *Producer* part of his persona leads him to think he can take care of any situation quickly and efficiently. He thinks he's delegating effectively, and he is. But he's also very close-mouthed. This was highlighted for me by his refusal to discuss a situation that I thought was a crisis. I took his refusal to discuss it with me to be one more example of his refusing to deal with conflict. I was wrong. Let me explain.

"First of all, as an *Accommodator/Data-Collector* I'm not good at handling conflict either, but I've had to develop the ability to handle negativity well. Partly, I've had to develop my abilities in this area because Nigel relies on me to take care of difficult situations.

"We have a joke about Nigel assigning me the duties that require dealing with conflict. He flips his index finger at me indicating, 'I'm not dealing with this situation, you are.' It's evolved as a kind of shorthand over the years. It all started, oh, maybe six years ago. I needed to consult with him about an angry customer. He heard me out, and when I suggested that he call the customer, he smiled a funny little smile—impish—and flipped his index finger at me, and said, 'I'm sure *you'll* handle it well.' So I did.

"That's been our pattern ever since. But I sure was caught off guard when Nigel flipped his finger at me last month. I'd asked him to sit down with me and figure out what to do about a very difficult situation. Two employees—account executives—had recently quit, taking some customers with them. Bad, bad news. Very serious. Their big complaint—both of them said the same thing—was that our shop wasn't big enough to handle their customers' needs, that we lacked adequate capacity to keep up with our explosive growth. The reps said that they'd worked like dogs to bring in business, and if we couldn't meet the demands, they'd take their accounts to a print shop that could. At first glance, this was a crisis. I had no time to think because two account reps already were gone and eleven others were upset and grumbling about a lack of organizational support. Organizational support translates into 'We need to increase capacity,' which meant we needed a new press.

"Unfortunately, the cost of a new press—at about a million dollars—is way beyond my authority. So naturally, I approached Nigel.

"It was, to put it kindly, not a satisfactory meeting. Nigel did his finger thing and said, 'I'm confident you can handle it.' I tried to get him to focus. He began to get irritated with me, and impatient, until he finally interrupted me and said, 'It's your job to make this place run smoothly, Gillian. Do it.'

"I assumed that this was just more of the same—Nigel not wanting to talk about something because it's a difficult situation. It was only later that I recognized the *Unspoken Expectations* at work. At this point I was simply focused on figuring out what to do. If we needed a new press, only Nigel could okay it. And he wasn't going to unless I could prove that it was needed. I remembered Jane saying your first step is to analyze what's going on, because it could be a crisis, or it could be a symptom of an underlying problem, or it could be both. All I knew was, I was struggling with the decision about whether to recommend that we buy a million-dollar printing press. Guess what? My analysis of why they quit saved us over a million dollars, and maybe my job.

"The first thing I did was go to the source—the account execs who had quit. I asked them what was going on. What they said on their way out the door was that they were sick and tired of explaining to their customers why their jobs were late.

"In order to understand the situation, you need to know a bit about how we work. The account executives represent their customers in every aspect of their relationship with the company. They sell. They're customer service. They advise on freelance designers and writers. They even collect money if necessary. Our clients are loyal to them, not the company, so from the company's point of view, if one of them leaves, it's a threat. Often it results in a significant loss in revenue—it's no surprise that their customers follow them, and it's no surprise that the company works hard to keep them.

"Few leave. We treat them well. The final straw for me was when Mo left. Here's what happened. Last month Mo got a call from a customer who wanted to know how his brochure looked. Mo put him on hold and walked back to the press room, where she discovered that her client's brochure had been bumped by one of the other account execs' clients' brochures, and her job had been rescheduled for the next day. She walked back to her desk, picked up the phone, and tried to explain to her client why the job had been bumped, and *why she hadn't known it in advance*.

"Mo was so mad after that call, I can't tell you. She was mad about the fact that the situation existed, but mostly she was mad about the fact that she hadn't known that it had been done. Well, she lit into the other account exec—the one who bumped her client. They almost came to blows. The truth is that she had absolutely no reason to get so mad. All the account execs bumped one another's customers all the time. It's a pretty standard policy in the industry. Good customers take precedence over less good customers. In fact, she'd bumped the other account exec's client's newsletter the day before. The point is that she just flipped. She finished yelling, and stormed into my office and quit.

"It's true that we had no rules about doing the bumping, but it was only in the last six months or year that it had been a problem. Because we've been growing like crazy, I assumed that there was a relationship between our growth and the account exec's frustration. After all, they both said that they quit over a lack of printing capacity.

"If I'd proceeded with my gut instinct, I would have recommended to Niles that we spend a million dollars that it turns out we didn't need to spend—and the problem *wouldn't have been affected in any way*. The underlying issue had nothing to do with capacity. It was only as I began thinking about it analytically that I realized that problems aren't always what they seem to be at first glance. One thought I'd had was that maybe we needed to hire someone to be in charge of scheduling. In other words, maybe it wasn't a capacity issue, maybe it was a scheduling issue. The truth is that the more I thought about it, the more confused I became. I didn't know what was going on.

"Using the *Unspoken Expectations* model, here's what I came up with:

- Try to change the account reps' minds about quitting. ("Too late—they had already walked out. In terms of the other reps, I tried to reassure them that we'd improve the systems, but it was no go.")
- Decide you can live with it. ("This is what we'd been doing. The end of the rope was in sight.")
- Make a specific recommendation for improvement. ("My boss made it clear to me that he expected me to do just this—and I wanted to.")
- Remove yourself from the situation. ("This is the point the account execs had reached, but I certainly wasn't there.")

"No, I was at the third step—*make a specific recommendation*. But I knew that in order to solve the problem effectively, I needed to know what the problem was.

"So I took a deep breath and considered the situation from our customers' point of view. That seemed like a good starting place, because we market ourselves as customer-oriented, and we truly want to be customer-oriented. I took a methodical approach to the analysis.

"As a mix of *Accommodator* and *Data-Collector*, I discounted my gut. Instinct told me to buy a new press, but I knew that maybe the instinct came from the *Accommodator* in me wanting to give the account execs what they were clamoring for. So I brought forth the *Data-Collector* part of my personality and resisted. I told them the truth. That until I'd carefully examined the situation, I was making no decision at all."

FAQ: *I work in a crisis environment. Utter chaos. There's no hope to manage priorities. We just work to keep up. Any ideas?*

A: Anytime you feel as if there's an emergency, look for underlying issues. Are you sure that it's a crisis? It might be a problem or a symptom masquerading as a crisis. Once you've confirmed that it is in fact a crisis, look for patterns and trends. By systematizing your response, you'll save time and reduce anxiety while improving quality.

Here's how Gillian assessed her situation:

- **What** do we label a crisis?

  "We call it a crisis when one of us has to tell a customer that their job is late. But it isn't the lateness that's the problem. It's that we don't receive advance warning; it's discovering that the job is late only when the customer calls in with an inquiry that's the issue. We're then in the awkward position of having to confess to our customers that we didn't know. This creates the perception to customers that they're unimportant to us. It is the frustration and embarrassment that's the problem—not that the job was late. Clearly, there are times when the jobs may be late. But the problems were unrelated to whether the jobs were late or not."

- **Where** do the problems occur?

  The problems occurred on site.

- **When** do the problems occur?

  There was no pattern as to when the problems occurred. "They were constant," Gillian said.

- **Who**'s involved in what we call a crisis?

  The crises involved everyone. No one account executive was more problematic than another. Several customers were especially demanding, but no one customer or category of customer was responsible. "It seemed to have nothing to do with customer expectations, which led me to conclude the problem was internal," Gillian added.

- **Why** is it happening?

  The problems were occurring because the account executives were being surprised that their customers were being bumped. Gillian explained, "The only issue seemed to be the surprise. Not the fact of the resequencing, but the fact that the resequencing occurred under a cloak of silence. In other words, it wasn't a capacity issue—it was a *communication* issue."

- **How** are we notified that there's a crisis?

  By the account execs saying so directly.

  "It became to clear to me that I needed to come up with a way for the account execs to communicate better. We needed some system of immediate notification. I played around with e-mail—you know, that one account exec had to e-mail the other before they could bump a customer. But it was too indirect. Instead I went completely low-tech."

Gillian bought an erasable white board and a step stool. Total cost? Twenty-seven dollars. "I mounted the white board high
enough so everyone in the open room could see it just by glanc-
ing up," she explained. "If you want to bump someone, you can,
easily, simply by climbing the step stool and writing on the white
board the name of the account exec whose client you're bumping, the client, the job, the press involved, and when the client
has been rescheduled.

"Isn't that great? If you want to argue, you can, right then and
there. You're going to be reasonable, though, because you know
you're going to be bumping them too. Assuming all the reps
agreed to use the system, here's the worst-case scenario. You're
out at lunch or something . . . you walk in and your phone rings
and it's a client wanting to know a job's status. You can look up
and if you don't see your client's name on the board, you know
you can tell your customer with confidence that their job is on
schedule."

Gillian confessed to some anxiety. "I really hesitated before
recommending the white board. I worried about what would happen if I was wrong. I mean, I figured I'd look pretty stupid hanging up a white board if it turns out that we needed a new press all
along. But then I realized that it was smart to proceed cautiously.
If I was wrong—heck, we could always buy a new press."

When Gillian approached her boss with her proposed solution, it was a low-risk endeavor on her part. "I told him, 'Let's try
the cheap alternative first and give it a month. If it's not working, we'll order the press.' " From her boss's point of view, she's
demonstrating:

- calm thinking under pressure
- clear decision-making (including having a backup plan)
- sensible concern for the bottom line (twenty-seven vs. a
  million dollars)
- helping him avoid having to deal with conflict

Note Gillian's time line. Remembering that it takes three weeks
for any new behavior to become a habit, she decided to wait a
month before evaluating her idea's effectiveness.

"The white board caught on quickly. It's been a year and it's still working. And no one else has quit," Gillian explained. "So my objective got met, but only because I correctly identified the problem for what it was—inadequate communication, not capacity.

"Nigel told me after the fact that we were being considered by a competitor as an acquisition. No way would he have approved the purchase of the press. And no way would he have allowed the problem to continue. He explained that he knew the presses were capable of handling our current workload. He said he hadn't known what the problem was, he just knew what it wasn't—it wasn't a capacity issue. And, he stressed, he knew it was my job, not his, to sort it out.

"There wasn't just one *Unspoken Expectation* at work in this situation—there were three of them. Thank goodness I took the time to methodically analyze the situation. Otherwise, I never would have recognized them for what they were.

"*Unspoken Expectation* 1. Nigel wanted me to handle the situation well, and because he believed that the current equipment was capable of handling our workload, he knew that my handling the situation well didn't involve buying a new press. Furthermore, he explained that he needed to know he could count on me to properly analyze situations without his holding my hand. He told me that if I couldn't handle this situation well, he wouldn't be able to trust me in the future to handle complex situations well.

"*Unspoken Expectation* 2. The reps wanted to know in advance of any schedule changes so they wouldn't look foolish to their customers.

"*Unspoken Expectation* 3. Nigel knew the company was being considered as an acquisition by a competitor, so he wasn't going to rock any boats. He was committed to showing sustained growth without new capital investment.

"I still can't believe how close I came to recommending that we spend a million dollars. Not only would my recommendation have been disapproved, Nigel would have lost some respect for me. Furthermore, even if it had been approved, it wouldn't have solved the problem, because Nigel was correct—we had adequate capacity. Thank goodness for thinking the situation through—and for identifying *Unspoken Expectations*."

Peel the Onion

There's an old saying, "Why bother to close the barn door after the horse escapes?" Have you ever thought about that? What does closing the barn door have to do with the *other* horses that may be in your barn? Just because you lose one horse—learn from that experience.

While *Accommodators* and *Data-Collectors* generally enjoy the analytical process, *Optimists* and *Producers* find the methodical system difficult or boring. If you're having a hard time, consider a team approach. Think of this process of analysis as peeling away the layers of an onion as you work to get to the essence, the truth of the situation.

First consider whether there is an *Unspoken Expectation* that may account for the situation. Look for clues that may reveal a crisis, a symptom, or a problem. If you determine it's a crisis, the second step is to systemize your response using the five W's (and the How).

Think about what we've covered thus far:

1. Set goals long-term and big-picture.
2. Use the CAN DO model to ensure you're navigating well.
3. Sequence your action steps using the *"In Order to . . ."* model.
4. Ensure you've evaluated your *Unspoken Expectations*, especially if you feel as if you're in a crisis atmosphere.

Then get ready to move forward in a productive manner!

There's no magic to this system, and no mystery about why it works. The beauty of identifying your *Unspoken Expectations* is that by integrating them into your goals, you give yourself the best opportunity to deal effectively with your day-to-day responsibilities, and ensure your success at achieving your long-term dreams.

Tips

- You need to discover how you're evaluated. *Unspoken Expectations*, defined as the truth by which you're judged, must be considered when setting goals. If your boss evaluates you by your department's revenue figures, it does you no good to talk about how late you work every day. Don't set goals in a vacuum. Instead, integrate the *Unspoken Expectations* that affect you and see your success rate soar!

- Managing crises well requires that you accurately assess the issue or issues at hand. Use the journalists five W's (Who, What, When, Where, and Why) plus How to analyze anything you label a crisis. Once you're certain that you know what you're dealing with, then work to systemize your crisis-management responses. You'll save time and provide a higher-quality response by not constantly reinventing the wheel.

✦

Evaluate Priorities—Time and Significance

My Life Is One Big Emergency! Now What?

If you're like most people, you have multiple goals, and they all seem central to your own or your organization's success. Having broken them up into baby steps using the *"In Order to . . ."* model, you're ready to go. Except that accomplishing each goal requires time, attention, and energy.

Many business people report that they work in environments so fast-paced and distracting that they rarely look at a to-do list, and never plan. Your boss, for example, calls from the other room instructing you to begin a new project, thus changing your priorities. Perhaps you are staring at your desk, wondering where to start, when your assistant calls in sick and your e-mail flag pops up. You ask yourself how can you possibly set or manage priorities in your chaotic, stressful world. The answer is by:

1. streamlining the priority-setting process
2. not overscheduling
3. being realistic about your capabilities

If you know that a couple of hours of unexpected events are going to occur each day and you schedule eight hours' worth of work, why are you surprised if it takes you ten hours to complete your assignments? If you want to work eight hours, and you know that a couple of hours' worth of something or other is likely to occur, schedule six hours' worth of work.

Some of you are thinking, "But I have to get it all done." That may well be true. Working longer and harder is a common *Unspoken Expectation* of our time. It's not simply that you're working longer hours than ever, you're also *expected* to do so. It doesn't make any sense to pretend it isn't so. Remember, the trick is to turn the light on to reveal your *Unspoken Expectations* so that you can sensibly deal with them. Don't pretend you can get eight hours' worth of work done in six hours. And if your organization expects you to work ten hours, don't pretend that they don't. Pretense begets a lack of self-confidence. Reality leads to self-assurance.

In this chapter you'll learn to use two tools that will help you analyze priorities quickly, and in a meaningful way. The 1 to 5 system will help you separate tasks into sensible groupings. The *Time Sensitive vs. Key* model allows you to rank your priorities by realistically determining their relative significance.

Sort Through in Broad Swipes First

The first step is to separate tasks into broad categories. The 1 to 5 system allows you to take any responsibility or task and put it in a logical category. Use the 1 to 5 system as a guideline and customize it. Adapt it to your own situation. The numbers 1 through 5 represent:

- 1 = Crisis
- 2 = Sooner
- 3 = Later
- 4 = Whenever
- 5 = Never

While many people feel as if they live in a Crisis environment, unless the situation is one involving life and death, probably the event isn't truly a Crisis. The number 1 (Crisis) speaks to the fact that they do, however, exist. In a Crisis, there's no time to think. You simply must act. In Chapter 6, tools to distinguish between a crisis, a problem, and a symptom of an underlying problem were discussed. Once you identify that a Crisis is, in fact, a Crisis, you act. By default, all other priorities fade in the background until the Crisis is controlled. Here are some events that most of us would deem to be a Crisis:

- The president of your most important account calls to tell you that he's thinking of canceling your contract and demands your immediate presence in a distant city to meet and discuss the problem.
- The governor announces a mandatory evacuation due to a hurricane.
- A customer falls to the floor, unconscious, in your office or store.
- The venture capital firm funding your Internet start-up suffers a major reversal and tells you that, with regret, they can't give you the additional four million dollars they'd promised.

2 (Sooner) implies that the task is both significant and time-sensitive. Perhaps there's a time limit about to expire, or there's a deadline looming. Maybe someone is at your desk waving their arms at you, trying to get your attention. Perhaps the phone is ringing. Or possibly there's a customer waiting in the reception area. There's time sensitivity implicit in calling a task a 2 (Sooner). Some examples of tasks most of us would put in the 2 (Sooner) category include:

- completing the analysis of this week's revenue figures
- finishing your report for the staff meeting that begins in ten minutes
- calming a raging customer
- keeping your promise to attend your five-year-old's school play this afternoon

3 (Later) makes a different statement. 3 (Later) doesn't imply a lack of significance. Rather, it suggests that a task can be completed in a less demanding atmosphere than a task assigned to category 2 (Sooner).

A 3 (Later) may be just as critical to your success as a 2 (Sooner). The difference lies in the timing. Usually, there's no deadline looming over you. "I want your budget submitted by next quarter," the chief financial officer might instruct you, for instance. Perhaps the deadline is flexible. "Get me a quick update on the computer project when you get a chance," your boss might say. Notice that both of these projects are essential to your business success, but there's nothing attention-getting about them. No one is running through the office. No one is shouting at you. There's no implication that a deadline is about to expire.

3 (Later) responsibilities are not immediate, but they might be just as significant as tasks you deem a 2 (Sooner). Although it's up to you to determine what's worthy of being placed on your schedule, most of us would put the following items in the 3 (Later) category:

- scheduling your annual physical (assuming you have no health problems that require immediate care)
- buying tickets to next week's concert
- drafting your staff's performance appraisals
- writing a proposal for a new business opportunity due in three months

4 (Whenever) refers to those things that it would be nice to do, if you get a chance. Many people, for example, keep a pending file. (Later in this chapter you'll learn alternatives to a pending file, approaches that many people report help them complete tasks that never seem pressing enough to get out of the pending status.) By definition, anything you place in a pending file is something that you expect will evolve into a 3 (Later). Eventually you plan on each task moving into the 2 (Sooner) category. If it doesn't evolve into a 2 (Sooner), most likely it will become a 5 (Never). Some people keep things in their 4 (When-

ever) category indefinitely, even forever. The following items are examples of what might be in a 4 (Whenever) category:

- learning macramé (if you're a busy professional who already does needlepoint)
- reading a book on mystical events in the third century B.C. that was reviewed in your local newspaper
- planning your family's summer vacation
- meeting with someone from the information technology (IT) department about the wisdom of linking your Web site to a "how-to" site related to one of thirty applications for your company's newest product
- investigating alternative vendors that have the potential of saving your company a small amount on its annual shipping costs

5 (Never) refers to those tasks that you deem to be unimportant, irrelevant, or for which you determine there's insufficient interest or commitment. In other words, if you decide that a task is not worth putting on the schedule, by default you're putting it in the 5 (Never) category. Most people underuse the 5 (Never) category. Instead of expecting that you'll get to things someday, it makes more sense to assess realistically how likely you are in fact to do something.

Do you hope that someday, some way, you'll get everything done? An attribute you likely share with most people reading this book is a good work ethic. Think about it: if you didn't care, you wouldn't be trying to discover ways to become more productive. Many people who have a good work ethic also have unrealistic expectations. Perhaps you are chided by an internal critic. This critic has a loud and nasty voice. It admonishes you to be more clever and focused, or to be less lazy. Perhaps you search for organizational tools or priority management systems that you hope will render the 5 (Never) category unnecessary.

Instead of feeling guilty and inadequate because you're not doing more, acknowledge that there's simply not enough time and energy available to do everything you'd like. If you want to have adequate time to do your favorite things as well as those tasks you deem critical, it's essential to place items in this grouping. Many of us find this difficult. We hold out hope that we'll find a way to fit more in, to get more done.

Maybe you feel as if everything is critical, and nothing can be deemed a 5 (Never). As you begin to work with the 1 to 5 system, you'll notice that, in general, there are two kinds of tasks that appropriately end up in the 5 (Never) category:

1. irrelevant or inconsequential items
2. items that are important but that, to you, aren't possible because of the cost (in time, money, or effort)

Moving items into the 5 (Never) category requires that you acknowledge your limits and your schedule's limits. In other words, you can do only so much and you only have so much time. One way to motivate yourself to move tasks into the 5 (Never) category is to consider the process to be a positive one, not a negative one. Think of it as creating an opportunity in which you'll be able to focus on those things that are most important to you, not that you're avoiding tasks. Moving items from your 4 (Whenever) category to your 5 (Never) category can be liberating, and doing so increases your likelihood of completing those activities that you most value.

It is critical to your success that you give yourself permission *not* to do things. Certainly, part of being an adult is doing things you don't want to do, but that are in your best interest to do (i.e., going to the dentist regularly and submitting a mandatory report in a timely manner even though you find it tedious to complete). Likewise, part of being an adult is selecting where your time and energy will be spent when there's not enough time to do everything (i.e., joining your family on the once-in-a-lifetime Alaska cruise and skipping the beach trip because you are allowed only two weeks' vacation, or deciding not to proceed with a joint venture despite its viability because you don't have adequate staff). Only you can set priorities, and it is naïve to think that managing priorities well means that you can avoid putting tasks in the 5 (Never) category. You can't. Be realistic.

Here are some examples of items that many people would place in the 5 (Never) category:

- reading a misdirected catalogue that is of no relevance to you or your work
- counseling an employee about his relationship with his mother
- accepting a promotion if it requires that you relocate your family, no matter how much you'd enjoy the challenge or how large the salary increase, because your wife would have to restart her law practice, your son would have to complete his senior year of high school at a new school, and your daughter wouldn't be able to enjoy her weekly outings with her grandmother; you realize that it's essential to you that you live close to your extended family
- developing a new product that promises little or no revenue potential, even though it's requested by a small percentage of your customers

1 (Crisis): Resist Someone Else's Definition

Jahal recalls the day the fire alarm went off in the middle of his presentation. "I was pitching new logo designs. The bell started and everyone looked at me. I realized in a flash that at that moment everyone considered me to be in charge. I was the authority figure. As an *Optimist*, I'm not usually in that role. It didn't matter that I was about half the age of most of the people in the room, nor that I was the lowest-ranking person there. All that mattered was that I was the one standing at front of the room talking. Luckily, I handled it well. I calmly asked people to please follow me, and I quickly left the building."

Sensibly evaluate a crisis by considering these questions. Might someone die if you don't respond? Is there the potential of injury? Will there be a loss of property? Only if there are dire consequences is an event a 1 (Crisis). This surprises some people who have adapted to working in a crisis culture, where everything seems as if it's an emergency.

There are various reasons why people call a non-emergency event a 1 (Crisis), including:

1. enjoying the feeling of heightened urgency
2. mistaking the rush of adrenaline for an actual crisis
3. feeling heroic by handling a crisis well
4. desiring other people's acclaim for handling a crisis well
5. believing that other people perceive a situation as a crisis, and substituting their judgment for your own

Ginger, a *Producer*, recalls that when she was a little girl, she was appointed a hall monitor. "This was a major deal. All the kids wanted to be a hall monitor. I was so proud. I loved the power. I held up my hands and kids had to stop. They had to obey my signals. It was very heady stuff to a *Producer*.

"I remember one day, a little girl tripped and fell. She didn't want to go to the nurse. I made her go with me to the girls' room so I could examine her knee. It was scraped but not bleeding. She insisted on going to class, and I remember feeling disappointed that she wasn't more badly hurt. It's not that I wanted her to suffer or anything. I just thought it would be cool to calmly handle the situation. I would have taken her to the nurse and then gone to tell her teacher. I could almost picture myself whispering to the teacher, and having all the other kids in class wonder what was up. I love a good crisis. Always have. I guess it's no accident that I went into police work, is it?"

Make the decision about whether an event is a Crisis based on rational judgment, not on how it feels. For all the events that *feel* like a crisis but aren't, use the analytical approach discussed in Chapter 6.

2 (Sooner): How Soon Is Sooner for You?

Evelyn, an account rep for a temp agency, explains, "If I get a call at seven-thirty in the morning from a client saying they need a receptionist for the day, how long do you figure I have to fill that position? An hour? A half hour? An hour and a half? Not much longer, that's for sure. Can you see me calling my client at four-thirty that afternoon and telling them, 'Great news! I found you a receptionist for today.' Not likely. For me, 2 (Sooner) is as long as my client will wait, and not one second longer."

Vinnie, a colleague of hers in the agency, had a different view. He defined 2 (Sooner) as encompassing a week or so. "Future business. New contracts. Submitting proposals. That's my job. So that's a 2 (Sooner) to me. Don't get me wrong. Evelyn is great at client care, at filling their orders, but to me, taking care of future clients is far more important. Generating proposals is the most significant thing I do."

Note that given their different jobs, neither Evelyn nor Vinnie is wrong. While satisfying current clients is central to maintaining their business, missing a commitment to submit a proposal sabotages winning new business. They're both right. Each definition of 2 (Sooner) reflects a different, but accurate, perspective.

How long is 2 (Sooner) to you, in your world? An hour? A day? There's no right or wrong. Rather, consider whether you have enough big-picture information to make a judgment about 2 (Sooner). If you don't know your company's future plans, for example, how can you make wise decisions about what's worthy of being a 2 (Sooner)? There's nothing wrong with asking for direction or clarification from your boss. (Remember to change your vocabulary and position your request based on your read of your boss's personality.)

Lenny, a financial analyst for a food-service company, faced this dilemma. "I have two reports due on the same day of each month. The distribution list is identical—all high-level managers. I have absolutely no way to rank their importance. I'm pretty systematic in my approach—no surprise, I'm a *Data-Collector*. I methodically work away on them both. No problem.

"Last month, without any warning or explanation, I start getting all this extra work. It's very unusual that there's unexpected work in my department. It's pretty predictable, given that we analyze past events and report trends. Now all of a sudden I'm getting a question or a request for a new analysis once or twice a day. Some of the questions took only a few minutes to answer, but some took much longer, an hour or even more.

"It seemed pretty clear to me that something was up. I didn't know what. It could have been anything—from my boss's work being audited to a reorganization of all departments in our division.

"So I asked. My boss is an *Optimist/Data-Collector* combo, so I phrased it with a little more pep than if I'd been speaking only to someone like myself—a hundred percent *Data-Collector*. I said, 'From where I sit, it seems as if something new is happening here. Is there anything I need to know? Do I do my work as usual and complete the two monthly reports, or do I let those reports slide and only work on the new questions?'

"Turns out the company was being reorganized, although I didn't learn that for about six months. What she said at the time was, 'The reports are very important, but if they have to be a day or two late, I can live with that. Do the spot work as I assign it.' And that was that. I was glad I asked. If I hadn't, I wouldn't have known what my 2 (Sooner) was. How could I have known? I wasn't privy to the company's plans."

Definitions of 2 (Sooner) are changing worldwide. Everyone seems to be expected to produce more in a shorter amount of time. John Casey, chief executive of the Marketing Institute in Dublin, blames technology, specifically e-mail. "Expectations have changed," he explained. "It used to be that you sent someone a letter, and nothing more could be done until they responded. Now you send them an e-mail, and you hear back in five minutes. Things are moving faster." For him, a 2 (Sooner) has evolved from a week or so (the average length of time it used to take a letter to be delivered and responded to), to less than a day.

Whatever your definition of a 2 (Sooner) versus a 3 (Later), you may be feeling extra tension too. If you're like most people, you're feeling more and more pressure to produce more and more output without any increase in resources. Before determining remedial actions, however, it makes sense to verify where your time is going. In order to do so, you need to know two things: how predictable is your future schedule, and how long do things take you to complete?

3 (Later): Schedule Wisely

The first step in allocating time by sensibly slotting tasks into your 3 (Later) category is to consider realistically your work flow. How predictable is your schedule? There's no magic formula, but the following questions will help you determine how much of your time is available for you to schedule in advance.

- What period of time (a day, a month, a quarter) reflects a typical range of work?
- Over the course of this typical range, how much of your time is taken up with events you couldn't possibly have anticipated?
- Over the course of this typical range, what percentage of meetings and appointments have to be canceled or re-scheduled due to changing priorities?

Notice that the questions build on one another. Your answer to the last question enables you to schedule sensibly without setting yourself up for disappointment and defeat.

Rae, for example, an intake supervisor in a busy hospital admissions office, explained, "We've been reorganized four times in the last seven years. The net result? I have double the work. Literally. When I started this job about ten years ago, there were two of us. Now there's only me.

"I work every minute. Every minute! Unexpected things are a big part of my job, of course. Expect the unexpected, that's what I say. Some hospital admissions are scheduled, but many are not. Some administrative work, meetings, performance appraisals, and training are scheduled—but as any supervisor knows, lots of personnel issues aren't scheduled. Things just come up.

"I'm an *Accommodator*, and one of the ways it shows is that I always try to help. Always. It doesn't matter that I have an enormous work load. I was feeling so out of control, the idea of separating tasks into 2 (Sooner) versus 3 (Later) was a joke. But then I took a deep breath and answered the three questions."

- What period of time (a day, a month, a quarter) reflects a typical range of work?

"A month is reasonable. Maybe even a week. No, a month is fair, because I run a monthly staff meeting and I'm responsible for generating monthly reports. There's one quarterly report, but that's the only deadline that is out of a weekly or monthly time frame, and as I think of it, I update the data month by month, so even my quarterly report is, in fact, a monthly responsibility."

- Over the course of this typical range, how much of your time is taken up with events you couldn't possibly have anticipated?

"It's funny. When I first started to think about this, I couldn't get a handle on it. It seemed all across the board unpredictable. But then I remembered what you're supposed to do when everything seems impossible—baby steps. So I considered yesterday. Then the day before. And then the day before that. I used my calendar to tickle my memory. Some days nothing happened. On most days, though, about two hours of unscheduled events came up. Twice during the month they took over half the day. I added up all the time and divided by the number of days to get a pure average. It came out to be three hours a day—roughly forty percent of my time. I was astonished. Shocked."

- Over the course of this typical range, what percentage of meetings and appointments have to be canceled or rescheduled due to changing priorities?

"I went back to my calendar and literally traced events. I could see that a meeting on the third of the month was rescheduled for the eighth, and again for the tenth. This rescheduling happened over and over. I calculated that nearly fifty percent of all scheduled events had to be rescheduled at least once.

"I knew that the answer to this last question was the key. If things have to be rescheduled half the time, that implies I'm scheduling twice as many things as appropriate. So I stopped. If another department supervisor asks to meet, instead of automatically slotting the meeting in next week, I'll slot it in for two weeks ahead—much more realistic a time."

FAQ: *My desk is piled high with important projects, the phone is ringing off the hook, two people with appointments are waiting to see me, and I can't figure out what to do first. I'm totally overwhelmed. Now what?*

A: After confirming that you know how long it takes you to accomplish various tasks (because how else can you sensibly schedule?), use the 1 to 5 system to separate tasks into realistic groupings. Then use the *Time Sensitive vs. Key* model to balance these two critical variables and reach intelligent priority-setting decisions.

In addition to making her schedule more realistic, Rae did something else that was smart. She told people what she was doing. "Many meetings had to be rescheduled because of *other* people's overscheduling," she explained. "By telling them what I had learned by researching my own schedule, I was able to ask, without appearing combative or confrontational, 'So, what do you think, is a week from Wednesday realistic, or should we slot it in the week after? I'm trying hard to *not* have to reschedule things.' Things still have to be rescheduled, but less frequently."

Rae reported two additional benefits as well. "I feel more in control, and others perceive me as more in control."

If you sometimes feel like a wood chip floating down the stream of life, being tossed one way, then another by currents completely out of your control, analyze your days, and use the information to schedule wisely. If you don't know how vulnerable your schedule is to change, how can you possibly predict when tasks will be completed?

Stop the Interruptions!

It's hard to keep to your schedule when you're being interrupted. In order to stop this, you have to know why the interruptions are occurring.

Many people report that they get interrupted all the time. There are four reasons why people get interrupted. Knowing why it's happening enables you to plan a sensible course of action to counteract the interruptions.

1. Social chitchat

Problem: People like talking to you, and you tend to be warm and welcoming. *Accommodators* especially are vulnerable. Since *Accommodators* avoid confrontation, they're most likely to allow these interruptions to continue, even if they wish it weren't happening.

Solution: You must control the amount of time you spend on unproductive chat. Politely saying no is key.

There's nothing wrong with admitting you're working while you're at work. It sounds silly, but many people are afraid to interrupt someone who's interrupting them without cause. Instead, follow the simple system for politely regrasping control of the situation introduced in Chapter 3. Remember that in our society it's perfectly polite to interrupt someone once you tell them what you're doing and why.

- Say, "Excuse me."
- Tell them what you're doing and why you're doing it. For instance, you could say, "If I may, let me interrupt you. I'd love to know more about your ski trip, but I have to finish getting ready for the staff meeting, which starts in ten minutes." (Note that you could add, "Let's have lunch," "Let's have a cup of coffee," if you choose.) There are many appropriate ways of beginning this statement. For example, you could say, "Let me jump in . . ." or "Let me break in . . ." or "I hate to interrupt, but I need to because. . . ."

Note that you won't offend them, and you shorten the duration of the interruption.

FAQ: *I know a lot about our telecommunications systems. I've worked here for years, longer than anyone else, and I'm technically oriented. Whenever there's a question about the systems, I'm the one who gets interrupted. How can I stop it?*

A: Why are they asking you? Isn't the information available elsewhere? For instance, does your company run orientation sessions or seminars for new employees, or is there a procedure manual? If you're being asked the same questions over and over, you need a way of systematizing the dissemination of the information. Perhaps you're an *Accommodator* and it's hard for you to say no to people who ask questions. First you must identify why you're being interrupted. Only then can you determine a sensible response.

---

2. Keeper of the knowledge

Problem: Asking you a question may be the easiest way for other people to get information they need. If you answer their questions, either because you enjoy being the person who knows things (*Producers* have a potential problem here, in that they believe that "knowledge is power"), or from habit, interruptions can become routine.

Solution: You must avoid answering repetitive questions. If you're getting the same question over and over again, there is obviously a need for the facts, tips, shortcuts, or whatever it is you're asked about. Disseminating the information without your being interrupted is guaranteed to increase your productivity.

Alicia, an executive assistant to an executive in a small chemical company, explained, "I've been with my boss for eighteen years, ever since he opened the business. I know the history of the company. I know the procedures. I have most answers on the tip of my tongue. In other words, I understand why someone would come to me. But meanwhile, I get interrupted all the time. As an *Accommodator*, I find it very hard to chase people away.

"Finally, my boss noticed that someone was in my office asking how to do a mail merge. He lost it. Whew, did he yell! He made it very clear that that was not an appropriate use of my time. It occurred to me that in the eighteen years since we started, we've grown. I mean, I know it sounds stupid, but it's true. It never really occurred to me before.

"So what I did—with my boss's permission—was write the answer to each question on an index card as I answered in person. I created a sign and hung it right beside my cubicle opening. The sign said, 'Question? Check here first before interrupting Alicia.'

"What my boss and I realized is that over time I created a skeleton of a procedure manual. And we needed one. Clearly, we needed one because people had questions. Reasonable questions. Their questions weren't the problem. Their questions interrupting me—that was the problem."

Mitchell provided technical support for one department within a large city's transportation department. He explained, "My situation was different. No way was I supposed to tell people how to use the spell checker in their word-processing program. I'm not the help line. My job is working with the engineers to be sure their survey calculations are right before they authorize digging."

Mitchell explained that it didn't matter what his job was supposed to be. What mattered is that he knew a lot about computers. "I'm an *Accommodator/Data-Collector* mix, so it's really hard for me to resist helping someone who says they need help about technical issues. It was when I was bitching to my boss about all the interruptions that we had an idea. I had it actually, but wouldn't have pursued it seriously without my boss's support. Which he enthusiastically provided.

"My idea was that I tell people they have to e-mail their questions. I promised I'd get back to them by e-mail within two hours. Do you know how long two hours is when your computer isn't working? A lifetime.

"What I did was make it more painful to wait for me than to look it up in the instruction manual themselves or call the help line. And I did it in such a way that I didn't have to argue with anyone. I understand their dilemma. Looking something up in a computer manual is a nightmare. Talking to techies if you're not one can also be a nightmare. I understand. It's like trying to look up a word in the dictionary when you don't know how to spell it. It's frustrating at best, hopeless at worst. But the bottom line is that my time needs to be spent helping my engineers—and nothing else. That's my priority."

Just because something gets your attention doesn't mean it's deserving of your attention. An important key to managing priorities is to focus on those activities that matter most to you and your organization, not on those that are raised with the loudest voice. Don't allow interruptions to become priorities simply because they insinuate themselves into your consciousness.

3. Decision-maker

Problem: You're the only person who can decide something, and in order for work to continue, someone must be able to interrupt you.

Solution: You must find a way to group the interruptions to minimize distractions.

John, general manager of an auto parts–manufacturing company, and a *Producer*, said, "Changes in *anything* have to be okayed by me. I've worked for this company for almost twenty-five years. And I have a real case of 'been there, done that.' A couple of months ago I hired a guy who is turning out to be one of the best employees I've ever hired.

"I mean, this kid—he's right out of college—this kid is completely gung-ho. Filled with enthusiasm and good ideas. He's got a lot of *Producer* in him, but he's also got a lot of *Optimist* and *Data-Collector* too. The problem was that he was driving me crazy. Interrupting me every other minute, it felt like. My *Producer* inclination was to rush him away. But I knew I shouldn't.

"I had to figure out a way to keep this young man's enthusiasm, keep the flow of good ideas, and make him go away. Sounds funny, but it's true. I had to be careful. After all, it was perfectly reasonable that he interrupt me. I was the only one who could approve or disapprove his ideas.

"What I did was tell him the truth. I told him that he had terrific ideas and great enthusiasm, but that the interruptions had to stop; that the frequency of his interruptions was hurting my own productivity. I handed him a pen and a notebook, and gave him the instruction to jot his ideas down—to never rely on memory.

"I told him to use as few words as possible, to aim for three to five words per idea. I explained that if I had questions or needed more information, I'd ask. I told him that, starting the next morning, he and I were going to hold a stand-up, two-minute meeting first thing in the morning and midafternoon. I wanted him to read me the idea with no embellishment. And I promised I'd immediately tell him what to do next. I'd say yes, no, get me the costs by next Wednesday, not now but revisit in six months. I told him that whatever I told him to do, do it.

FAQ: *I get interrupted all the time. What can I do? I'm not getting my "real" work done.*

A: Figure out *why* you're being interrupted. Only then can you design a plan of action. If it's not part of your job to be interrupted, there are three possible reasons: first, it's social; second, you're the "keeper of the knowledge"; or third, you're the only one who can decide, and thus must be interrupted. Once you know the underlying cause, respond accordingly, using the systems detailed in this chapter.

"Guess what? He loved it. He was completely flattered. If anything, he started generating more ideas. He told me later that he'd known I was irritated by the interruptions, but that he hadn't known what to do. By making it a planned activity, I didn't just manage my own time better, I also motivated a good employee to be even better."

4. It's your job

Problem: Interruptions form a core part of many jobs. If you're a receptionist, for example, greeting an arriving customer isn't an interruption, it's your job.

Solution: You must change your perspective so that what you now think of as an interruption you redefine as your chief priority.

Most of us have spoken to a customer service representative who acted as if they could really get some good work done if people like us would stop bothering them. If this speaks to you, it may be that you need to rethink your priorities, not eliminate interruptions. In order to solve a problem, you must know what the problem is. In this example, the problem isn't the interruption, it's the perception of interference.

For instance, Carla, a rabbi, explained, "I'm very scholarly, and I spend a lot of time studying esoteric details which I know are of interest to no one—or at least to very few people—but me. Last year I caught myself feeling impatient with a member of the congregation who called with a question. I was so involved in my research, for several moments I couldn't remember who he was and I had no memory of the situation he was asking about.

"Once I forced myself to concentrate, it all came back to me, of course, but I felt ashamed of myself. I immediately refocused my priorities. My primary job is to care for members of my congregation. Therefore, by definition, anytime any member contacts me, it's not an interruption—it's my job.

"As a direct response to that realization, I hired a calligrapher. I had her put a wonderful quote by Dr. Samuel Johnson, the eighteenth-century dictionary fellow, on parchment and hung it directly across from my desk at eye level. The saying reads, 'The true art of memory is the art of attention.' "

Carla's absorption in her research made what was a reasonable interruption feel unreasonable. However, sometimes reasonable interruptions irritate you not because you're focused on something else, but because it seems inconsequential or obvious. It's important to remember that what is routine to you as the provider of the service may not be routine to others. Taking extra time to explain processes in advance often shortens the time required to deliver the service and generally reduces or eliminates interruptions. The old adage is true: if you have time to do it over, you have the time to do it right. It applies to training as well. If you have the time to redo the work, you have the time to train someone how to do it properly in the first place. *Producers* have a lot of trouble here; their impatience tends to make them intolerant of novices and acolytes.

Phoebe, an intern in a major beer producer's public affairs department, hated to interrupt her boss but had to. She explained, "As a college student here to learn—and to help out—I have to ask a lot of questions. It became a real problem. I report to the deputy director of public affairs, and she resented it a lot when I interrupted her with a question. I didn't know what to do because I needed to be able to ask questions, and I knew that it was her job to teach me how the department works. I found myself apologizing all the time, and that seemed to irritate her even more.

"After I'd been here about a month, she said she had an idea. Before she gave me an assignment, she would explain to me step by step how to do it and how it fit into the big-picture activities of the department. I would take notes and ask questions then, and we'd see how that worked as a way of reducing interruptions. It was terrific! By reviewing the overall procedure, the steps of the process became clear to me.

"For example, a lot of business students use our corporation as a case study in their research. Instead of just telling me to send them an annual report, which is what she used to do, my boss explained to me that the students are terribly important to the corporation for several reasons. They may be future employees or investors. They certainly are future consumers of our products. By positioning ourselves as their allies when they're students, we're creating a reservoir of goodwill. She even explained some market research—that alcohol preferences don't change once they're set, so the more efficient way to build a loyal customer base is to win them early. In other words, the students contacting our department for help with their research were our ideal potential market segment.

"So we want to cheerfully answer their questions and provide

them with any data they need that's available to the public—
much of it is in the annual report. She encouraged me to become
familiar with the annual report, so I could discuss it with them
and refer them to specific sections. The more helpful I am, the
better. By spending fifteen minutes explaining the big picture to
me, she didn't just make my life easier and my duties more clear,
she also helped me feel more like a part of the department—and
she reduced the number of times I needed to interrupt her
in the future. By anticipating my questions, she got her own priority met—fewer interruptions."

What's your job? What do you do that's central to your and
your organization's success? Be sure an interruption *is* an interruption before you work to eliminate it.

Time Yourself Doing Things

Once you know how much time is available, the next step is to
identify how long routine tasks take. Many people have no idea
how long things take. If you say, for instance, that you have a
quick phone call to make, how long do you imagine that will take?
Does quick mean two minutes? Does quick mean ten minutes?
There's no right or wrong, but boy, are there differences. If you
don't know how long things take, how can you possibly schedule?

In Chapter 5, we discussed the value of timing yourself doing
things as a tool for setting realistic deadlines. In Chapter 8 we'll
see how timing yourself can be the key to getting additional resources. We're now seeing the significance of timing yourself doing things as an aid to proper scheduling.

Only when you have a realistic idea of how long things take can
you schedule wisely. Most people think tasks they enjoy take less
time than they actually do, and that tasks they dislike take longer
than they actually do. Here's how to quickly and efficiently time
yourself doing routine tasks.

1. Over whatever time period you deem appropriate (usually
   a week or a month), create a list for yourself of those tasks
   that occur over and over again. They may include phone
   calls, e-mail, meetings, conversations in the hallway with

coworkers, lunch with customers, analyzing last month's numbers, doing data entry, and so on.
2. Time yourself doing each task several times to ensure an accurate guesstimate of how long each takes.

Cheney, manager of programming for a cable TV channel, found a quick and easy way to use this information. Timing himself doing things enabled him to create a system that worked for his nonmethodical *Optimist/Producer* personality mix.

"I did some rough guesstimating, looking through my schedule to get some ideas about work flow, and determined that a 3 (Later) for me is a week. After taking a look at what I did for a week—it's not fair to say I actually analyzed it, but I did keep pretty close track for a week or so—it became clear that about two hours a day of my time was taken up with important work that I couldn't have predicted.

"So I got five manila files and wrote on them in huge letters, Monday, Tuesday, Wednesday, Thursday, and Friday. I put a sticky note on each with the number seven on it. That's how many hours' work I want to schedule, more or less, each day. Given that a nine-hour day is pretty normal in my world, I wanted to put about seven hours' worth of work on the schedule.

"So here's what I do. Let's say that when I get in on Monday morning, an e-mail from my boss wanting an update on a programming contact I'm pursuing is waiting for me. I know from experience that it's going to take me about an hour to call the guy and write a summary of the conversation in e-mail to my boss. So I glance at Monday's folder. No time. Tuesday's folder, same thing. No time. Wednesday, the sticky note reads 1.5, so I slash out that number and write .5 because there's now only a half hour left.

"I open up the folder and annotate a sheet of paper that's there—literally a sheet of scrap paper. I write, 'See e-mail,' and the date of the e-mail and enough of a reminder about the subject so I'll find it easily. Sometimes I print out the e-mail; it depends on my mood. I never rely on memory."

When Cheney comes into work on Wednesday, the first thing he does is flip through the folder. "I think of the folder as a to-do list," he said. "Flipping through the papers, reading my notes. I put things in order and spend the day working my way through the contents. Pretty much, I have a rule that I can't leave until the folder is empty. Using this approach has made my work load more manageable. Much more manageable. It's a quick and dirty approach to scheduling that works for me."

Note that Cheney found a way to combine 2 (Sooner) and 3 (Later). By scheduling a week or so in advance (his five manila folders), he's planning what he'll accomplish 3 (Later). As each day arrives, each task naturally evolves into a 2 (Sooner), as he works his way through his allotted workload.

4 (Whenever): Better Alternatives to a Pending File

Not everything fits nicely into 2 (Sooner) or 3 (Later). Many tasks have no time sensitivity, nor do they have obvious significance. Nonetheless, you want to pursue them. These are the tasks commonly assigned to the 4 (Whenever) category.

A common application of the 4 (Whenever) category is a pending file. Many people have one. Most report it's a failure. Lucy, a curator in a small art museum, sums it up this way. "Every time I look at it, I feel guilty. I never actually get back to it. It just keeps on growing, along with my sense of guilt."

Sedgewick, on the other hand, works beautifully with a pending file. "I use it all the time. When I'm waiting to hear from someone, and then I do, I know I'll find the document in my pending file. What's so hard about using it well?" Sedgewick, like most *Accommodators*, is methodical and organized. Of course they use a pending file well. For everyone else, a computerized organizer or a thirty-one plus twelve tickler file are alternatives.

Many people report success in using an on-line calendar, scheduler, or organizer. The primary advantage of using actual files is that they provide a physical location for papers, folders, books, and the like while they're not in use. It's one thing to receive a computer-generated reminder that you're still waiting to hear back from Ed about some research. It's another thing altogether to know where you put the customer letter that initiated the contact with Ed in the first place.

To use a tickler file system well, first set it up properly. Instead of one large pending file, label thirty-one hanging folders with the numbers one through thirty-one. No days of the week, no months, just the numbers. In back of them, place twelve additional hanging folders labeled January through December. You now have a never ending fail-proof follow-up system. First thing you do when you go into work on any day is pull out whatever's in that day's folder.

Let's say, for instance, you've been waiting to hear from Ed so you can respond to a customer's letter. You ask Ed your question on the third of the month, and you want to give him about a week to respond. Take the customer's letter and put it in the folder marked the tenth. First thing when you come into work on the tenth, you'll see the letter. "Oh, yeah," you say to yourself, "I haven't heard back from Ed." You decide to give him a day's grace period and slip the letter into the folder marked eleven. The next morning, you pull out everything in the folder marked eleven, and say, "Hmm, still no word from Ed. Guess I'd better call him."

Lucy found the system a lifesaver. "No more missed deadlines. It was amazing! Even deadlines far in advance got met in time. A good example is an association's call for papers. I wanted to speak at a conference in two years. This group always has a June deadline for submitting abstracts. The few months' notice they give coincides with our busiest time, so I never get to write a proposal.

"So last June I made a photocopy of this year's call for papers, added a margin note about the topic I was thinking about proposing, and slipped the paper in the folder labeled October. Four months later, on the first working day of October, I pulled out what was in October's folder, and there was the photocopy. 'Great!' I said to myself. 'Now's a good time to write the proposal, while the museum is a little slow.' "

Customize it for your world. Here are some examples of how other people have successfully used a tickler file:

- "Our budgets are due in April. I put notes about new capital requirements in April's folder. First working day of the month, I pull out my notes, create a manila file called budgets, and place it in the folder labeled 'eight.' On April 8, I pull out the file, and I'm ready to go. What a relief to no longer wonder where I'd put the year's worth of budget notes."

- "I use it for my personal bills. I know when I get paid, so I put bills into the folder on the day I want to pay them. No more memory required—which is terrific, because mine is terrible!"

- "We got a file cabinet on casters, so the entire department can use one tickler file. It rolls around from desk to desk depending on who's available. We're the accounts receivable department, so it's our job to collect overdue bills. We don't collect on assigned accounts. We share all the work as a team. Whoever is available takes the next call. It's a continuous flow. Very reliable. It supports us working together."

- "I added a folder labeled 'Next Semester.' This allows me to update my syllabus, for instance. Note that it doesn't specify winter, spring, or whenever. Simply 'next.' It works well."

FAQ: *I have a pending file that's five inches thick. Can you help me make it go away?*

A: Many people report that a thirty-one-day tickler file is a better alternative to a pending file. Instead of one big guilt-inducing folder, you have folders labeled for each day of the month. Many people add twelve additional folders for the twelve months. One college professor added a folder called "Next Semester" as well.

However you modify it, a tickler file is a great way to keep things in front of you without relying on memory. You can still let things pend, but eventually they come back to you. Take all of the items you've decided belong in the 4 (Whenever) category and place them in the appropriate place in your tickler file. Note that a tickler file is actually a way of tracking your 3 (Later) items. It's an example of planning. Further, when you pull out the day's contents, you've moved the process from 3 (Later) to 2 (Sooner). By using a tickler file and consulting it on a daily basis, you're keeping tasks in front of you. You're much more likely to complete them or to decide that they really belong in the 5 (Never) category.

"That's what happened to me," said Marge. You'll recall that earlier in this chapter, one of the items listed as being a 4 (Whenever) was learning macramé (if you're a busy professional who already does needlepoint). The busy professional was Marge. "I love needlepoint," she explained. "It's terrifically relaxing for me. Last year I began to see that macramé was making a comeback. I've always liked the style, so on impulse I bought an instruction book and some supplies. I put them in a big basket that I keep near my favorite chair in the living room. And I never once picked up the book. I was too busy to devote a block of time to learning it, and besides, I had several needlepoint projects under way that I wanted to finish. Well, the net result was that the book and supplies just sat there making me feel guilty, even a little deprived.

"I'd heard about a thirty-one-day tickler file years and years ago, but had never tried it myself. After attending Jane's seminar, I decided to give it a try. Once I set it up at work, it occurred to me that I could slip in a few personal items too. I mean, I wouldn't put bills in there or anything, but after booking a vacation to Orlando, I put in a brochure for Disney World, for example. It was fun! Once a month or so I'd come upon it. Boy, did it put a smile on my face. All I would do is to give it a glance and pop it back into a folder I randomly selected. It was motivational for me. I'd say to myself, '*That's* why I work so hard, so my family can have this terrific vacation we've planned.'

"Well, that's what I did with the macramé instruction book—I put it in a folder. I figured that seeing it would motivate me to jump in and begin. Unfortunately, it didn't work. After a few months I realized that it wasn't motivating me. It was irritating me. What it did was motivate me to move it out of my life and into the 5 (Never) category.

"It's not that I changed my mind. I finally recognized that there's simply no way my schedule was going to allow me to learn it—at least not in the foreseeable future. The tickler file allowed me to visualize priority setting. And I realized that despite the pleasure that learning macramé would give me, I needed to face the fact that it wasn't going to happen.

"What I did was give the material away. A woman I work with expressed an interest in learning to do it, so I gave her my book and supplies. It was a relief to be rid of the darn thing!"

A tickler file is a versatile tool. It helps you:

- track projects, even when deadlines are far in the future
- remember to follow up
- facilitate teamwork
- motivate yourself
- decide not to do something

5 (Never): Liberate Yourself by Saying No

There's not enough time to do everything that you want to do. You must make choices. 5 (Never) encourages you not to pretend that you'll eventually get to do things when the reality is that you won't.

Of course, as adults there are many times when we must do things that we don't want to do. Likewise, there are tasks that must be accomplished by a certain deadline, even if we'd rather not. The 5 (Never) category is not intended to help you procrastinate doing projects, tasks, responsibilities, or activities that are in your best interest to complete. (See Chapter 5 for suggestions on how to overcome procrastination.) Rather, the 5 (Never) category is intended to help you be realistic.

One way to move tasks into the 5 (Never) category is through delegation. We delegate responsibilities all the time, although you may not always think of what you do as delegation. Here are what some people give as examples of tasks they've put into their 5 (Never) category through delegation:

- " 'I'll cook dinner if you wash the dishes.' Most people say it once in a while. I made it official. When my roommate moved in, we agreed on that as our division of work. It's been great. I haven't washed a dish in three years of graduate school. And he hasn't cooked."
- " 'I'll take care of the inside-of-the-house things if you do the outside-of-the-house things.' This was natural. My husband and I never discussed it. But as I think of it, outside of the house tasks are absolutely a 5 (Never) for me."
- " 'I'll return your phone calls if you do my invoicing.' No one in our department had ever thought of it. But I knew that Patsy hated phone work. I don't. Our work loads are similar, so I made the offer. She grabbed it. It works for us."

Items in the 5 (Never) category also can include:

- Those things you don't want to do, and for which there's no good reason for you to do. For example, many people report that they sort their mail over a trash can. As you toss letters away unopened, what you're saying is, "No! Not me! I'm never going to read you!"
- Those things you do once and don't need to do again. You read a letter from your insurance company, for instance, note the change in policy date, and file it away.
- Those things you wish you could do, but decide you're not going to do because there simply isn't enough time. "When I was young," Jolene recalled, "my brother and I shared a love of photography. We had a darkroom set up in the basement, and I really enjoyed the work. I wish I had the time to set up a darkroom again. But I don't. Maybe someday, but not now. It was liberating to put it on hold. A real guilt reducer to deem it a 5 (Never)."

You need to make choices. Managing priorities concerns not only what you will do, but also what you won't do.

Tell Others Your Priorities—
Don't Make Them Guess

Some companies believe that the customer comes first, and act on it. Oliver, a founding partner in a structural engineering firm, explained, "I've been pulled out of meetings, I've been called on weekends, I've been tracked down at my son's soccer game, when a customer needs me. That's my job. It's not *part* of my job. It *is* my job.

"I had a new assistant, who was great, but she didn't understand the extent to which we provide service. About three years ago, a customer called with a little anxiety. He wasn't upset, but he needed reassurance before he went before a government committee for a review. I was ready to leave for a conference in Florida—I was ten minutes away from stepping into the limo—and I wanted those three days in Florida.

"Thankfully, I overheard her putting him off and was able to intervene. I spent over an hour helping him rehearse, and as a result I missed my flight. I got to Florida the next morning. No big deal. Before I left, I made a point of explaining to her how we define customer service. No one, including the boss—especially the boss—gets to go to a conference if a customer needs us. She'd been thinking the call was a 5 (Never). Now she knows it was a 2 (Sooner)."

Dawn has a different view. "I work for a $5 billion company. We take customer relationships seriously and try to offer good service. But realistically, in my division our revenue runs about a $150 million a year, with our average customer worth about $500 annually. It's simply not worth a lot of our time to coddle any one customer. We strive to offer excellent service to all of our customers, but I wouldn't pretend that it's individualized service. It's not."

When Dawn was asked what she would do if a customer called—not upset, but anxious—she said, "No way would I take the call. I'd resolve the customer issue later. Calls like that are clearly a 3 (Later) to me. And depending on the customer, it may be a 5 (Never)."

Oliver and his company had values that were clear and consistent: *the customer above all else.* So did Dawn: *the customer in context.* That Oliver and Dawn and their companies had different values doesn't mean one value was right and the other wrong. All that matters is that you know what the company's values are, and that you support them.

Balance Immediacy and Enduring Significance

If you're like most people, as you begin using the 1 to 5 system, you'll find that most tasks end up in the 2 (Sooner) category. The second tool, *Time Sensitivity vs. Key* (see the chart on page 240) allows you to sort through tasks when everything seems most critical.

Part of the value of this tool is this: even if you're wrong, your decisions are defensible. Because you're not simply responding to a squeaky wheel, whimsy, serendipity, or personal preference, you can explain the logic behind a decision. Even if you're mistaken, your priority setting reflects thought.

Time Sensitivity vs. Key is an amorphous tool, flexible and easy to customize. As the examples demonstrate, using this tool allows you to rank priorities quickly and effectively. You can even do it in your head.

As you review the chart, note that the vertical axis defines time. At the top, at its most pressing, there's an *emergency*. On the other end, there's no sense of immediacy at all. You'll get to it *whenever*. On the horizontal axis, notice the range of significance. Tasks fall somewhere between those that are most significant to you or your organization (*critical to your success*) and those that are utterly *irrelevant* to you in every way. Consider what the center of the vertical axis represents. There's no emergency, nor is there any reason to delay the activity. Now think about what the center of the horizontal axis represents. The task at hand is not critical to your success; neither is it irrelevant.

Let's say, for example, that your job doesn't include answering the phone, yet you're the sort of person who hates to stare at a ringing phone. Let's further assume that you don't have phone ID. Think about it: you have no way of knowing whether it's *critical to your success* or *irrelevant*.

Answering the phone clearly doesn't fall into the *whenever* category because eventually it will stop ringing and you might miss an important call. Let's say that you assume it isn't an emergency. Perhaps you place it slightly above the midpoint (where the axes cross).

It turns out that on the other end of the phone is a telemarketer for a product your company will never use. Most of us would conclude that speaking to him is therefore *irrelevant*. (See the chart on page 242, circled #1.) The behavior implied here is to *stop*. Stop doing things that are irrelevant to you simply because they got your attention. *Accommodators* often have trouble here. They are most likely to have trouble getting off the phone.

FAQ: *I have three important projects. They're all a number 1 using the 1 to 5 system. Now what?*

A: The *Time Sensitivity vs. Key* model allows you to make on-the-spot priority decisions. Consider *Time Sensitivity*. Are any of the three emergencies? Which has the tightest deadline? Now consider *Key*. Which of the three is most critical to your success? The model allows you to make shrewd decisions and to defend your decisions with confidence.

Carlos, a meteorologist, explained, "I was in my office when the phone rang. It was someone from a charity trying to get me to donate money. There was zero chance that I was going to give money to them. And I couldn't get off the phone. I was as assertive as I know how to be. I was as direct as I know how to be. And I still couldn't get off the phone. I know that I'm an *Accommodator*, so I know this is a weakness of mine. Luckily, my secretary is a *Producer*. She has no trouble with assertiveness.

"When she walked into my office, I covered up the mouthpiece, cast my eyes heavenward, and explained in a whisper the problem. She shook her head at me, took the phone, said, 'We're not interested,' and hung up the phone. Thank goodness she

Time Sensitivity vs. Key, Chart

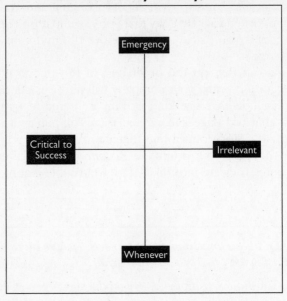

came into the office! If she hadn't, probably I'd still be on the phone. The truth is that I'm terrible at this. It's a weakness.

"What if my secretary isn't around? While acknowledging a weakness and compensating for it by having someone else take care of it works sometimes, it doesn't always work. Looking at the *Time Sensitivity vs. Key* model, it's easy to see how this phone call was utterly irrelevant to me. I decided I needed to develop the skills to take care of it myself. I decided to set a goal for myself to start using the polite technique to interrupt with the Rule of Affirmation First (RAF) (discussed in Chapter 4) principle of saying no."

Carlos was smart to recognize his weakness, and smarter still to develop a plan to compensate. "I may never be as direct as my secretary," he concluded, "but there's no reason I can't learn to say, 'Excuse me. Let me jump in here because I don't want to waste your time—or my own. We're not going to donate money, so I'm going to hang up. Bye.' That's polite. I know I can do that."

By using the *Time Sensitivity vs. Key* model, it's easy to see how important it is that you avoid doing things simply because they get your attention.

But what if it's the president of your company on the other end of the phone, insisting on seeing you right now? Most people would decide that's *critical to their success* (see the chart on page 242, circled #2) and would do it immediately.

Let's say you're not a plumber, you're not in construction, and you're not building a dream house. In other words, you have no idea why a catalogue called *Plumbers Weekly* has landed on your desk. In order to use the *Time Sensitivity vs. Key* model properly, consider each axis independently from the other, one at a time. First, ask yourself if there's a deadline associated with looking at the catalogue. Is it an emergency that you do so? No. Is your boss going to ask you to summarize what you learned by reading it? No, of course not. It's clearly a *whenever*. Second, ask yourself whether looking at the catalogue is significantly going to contribute to your success. Obviously, not. Looking at the catalogue is clearly *irrelevant*. (See the chart on page 242, circled #3.)

April, a flight attendant, says she has a terrible time with this very issue. "I'm a *Data-Collector*. It doesn't matter to me what kind of catalogues they are. I like them all. It's like window-shopping. I really enjoy it. I have stacks of catalogues at home. The problem is that there's no deadline, so I never feel like I need to get cracking. Now I'm knee deep with catalogues.

"I bought a big wicker basket to store them, so they don't look so sloppy. What I decided to do was consider it a hobby. I take a bunch with me on flights. Changing my perspective changed everything. It's great."

In order to avoid the situation, April needs to decide that looking through catalogues is a hobby and put it on her schedule. As long as she considers it a *whenever*, she knows that she need never get to it. Once she shifts its position on the time axis, moving it closer to the center point, and changes her view on its relevance, moving it closer to center on the horizontal axis (see

Time Sensitivity vs. Key, Chart with Examples

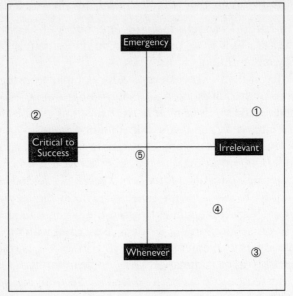

the chart, circled #4, above), she'll know more clearly what to do: slot it into her schedule.

Only April can decide how much she values looking through catalogues. She's the only one who gets a vote about how she spends her leisure time. Defining what gives you pleasure is key to managing priorities. Knowing your interests and passions, as well as knowing what you dislike, equips you to make wise judgments along the horizontal axis.

Tyson, manager of a sporting goods store, explains, "I love walking through the store, stopping randomly to chat with sales associates. It's important to me, and I think it's important to them. But there's never any time. So, I made a commitment to myself to spend a half hour on the floor without a specific agenda every Tuesday and Friday. I decided to take the time, to put it on my schedule.

"I was able to justify this decision by using the *Time Sensitivity vs. Key* model. At first I thought chatting with sales associates was a *whenever*. But then I realized that I could make the decision—think about that, *I* could make the decision, what a great feeling that was!—to move it up the axis. As I considered the value of my being accessible in an informal way to sales associates, I realized that this very accessibility contributed to my success. (See the chart on page 242, circled #5.) Now that it's part of my routine, I no longer have to think about doing it. I don't feel guilty, as if I'm sneaking away from my 'real' work."

The *Time Sensitivity vs. Key* model is a quick and efficient way to determine—and justify—priorities among competing projects. Which project has the tighter deadline? Which one is more critical to your success?

It Even Helps When It Doesn't Help!

One hopes it's rare, but occasionally people report that there's no way to sort through the priorities, that the *Time Sensitivity vs. Key* model didn't work because all tasks at issue share the same deadline, or because they all seem equally critical to you or your organization's success.

What do you do when nothing is working? Baby steps. If nothing works, if no tools help, and if you can't receive additional direction from your boss, break competing projects into smaller units and methodically work your way through them.

Adrienne said, "I'm an executive assistant in the general counsel's office of a major consumer products company. I'm a floater. That means that it's my job to help whoever needs help. This department, like most, has been told to keep its 'head count' steady. In other words, it doesn't matter that the work load has increased. What matters is that the body count doesn't increase.

"What that means to me is that everyone needs me. I might have eighteen projects from four different lawyers on my desk at any moment, and ten of them might have identical deadlines. The stress of making priority decisions was enormous. Every attorney thought his or her work was most important, and I certainly didn't have enough big-picture knowledge to sort through them in any logical way. Plus which, things seem to change all the time.

"I use the *Time Sensitivity vs. Key* model as much as I can, and it works most of the time, but when it doesn't work, I use baby steps. I work for a half hour on project A, then a half hour on project B, and so on. I'm oversimplifying a little, but not much. I make a point of doing at least a little work on every single project every day.

"That way, if at any point one of the lawyers comes to me and says, 'Where are you with my B project?' I'm further along than I was the last time they asked, and I have a non-defensive, sensible reason for having focused on the work in the sequence that I did."

Use the tools, make sure you have adequate knowledge to define *critical to success*, then proceed in a methodical manner, nibbling away at projects. For some of you, however, even this doesn't work. You feel as if you're at the end of your rope. Chapter 8 provides a working model to regain a sense of control.

Tips

- Overscheduling is one of the most common priority-setting problems. Sometimes people schedule too much because they have no idea how long tasks truly take them to complete. Think about what you call a quick phone call. Does it take two minutes or ten minutes? Time yourself doing things so you can make educated scheduling decisions.

- Instead of only relying on a pending file or an electronic reminder, consider use a thirty-one-day (plus twelve-month) tickler file. Never ending, always revolving, a tickler file is a fail-safe follow-up system. Instead of tasks pending indefinitely, you'll be reminded frequently of deadlines, whether actual or self-imposed. It's a great way to keep things from falling through the cracks.

✦

CHAPTER EIGHT

What to Do When You're at the End of Your Rope

Nothing Works. Now What?

What do you do when nothing works? You've:

- ✔ Set goals integrating *Unspoken Expectations* and confirmed that they're properly framed with the CAN DO model
- ✔ Broken your goals down into sequential baby steps using *"In Order to . . ."*
- ✔ Considered other people's personality types, repositioning your requests with approaches and vocabulary that target each
- ✔ Identified your strengths and are capitalizing on them
- ✔ Identified your weaknesses and have worked to find ways to avoid the pitfalls associated with them
- ✔ Used the journalist's five W's to analyze your situation, alert for underlying issues

In other words, you're doing everything right, but you still feel overwhelmed, out of control, and as if your priorities aren't being considered, let alone managed. It seems that no matter what you do, your situation continues to deteriorate. You know

that you have a good work ethic. You know that you're persistent.
You're putting in so much time on the job, you have no personal
life, and still you're barely keeping up. You're burning out. Your
temper is wearing thin, and your frustration level is growing.

Specifically, you've been trying to be part of the solution, not
the problem, and have been making rational, reasonable requests
to get more of what you need—a larger staff, more up-to-date
equipment, a better facility, whatever—and you've failed. No matter how compelling your arguments, the powers-that-be keep saying no. Instead of help, you keep getting more work. You feel as if
you're at the end of your rope.

If the above analysis describes you and your situation, you're
in good company. People with a good work ethic who modestly
try to do their best report a common result: they're assigned
more work. Have you ever noticed this? From a company's point
of view, this makes sense. Why *wouldn't* they assign more work
to those people who do it well and without complaint? Some
corporations openly foster a cutthroat attitude: if you can't cut
it, there are plenty of people who will. Even the most worker-
friendly and family-friendly organizations, however, expect you to
perform to your highest abilities all the time. That's business.

So now what? What do you do?

Getting the Resources You Need

In Chapter 6 we reviewed a methodical approach to dealing with *Unspoken Expectations*. The four steps we discussed
included:

- Try to change their minds (which rarely works, given that
  Unspoken Expectations are usually irrational)
- Live with it (which often leads to burn-out, the feeling that
  you can't stand it one more second and makes you think,
  "I'm at the end of my rope")
- Make a specific recommendation for improvement
- Remove yourself from the situation (you're "outta there")

At that time, the third step was referred to as the heart of the *End of the Rope* strategy. The *End of the Rope* strategy is a step-by-step approach to:

- acquire resources that you need
- win approval for resources that you want
- identify options you may have missed through other forms of analysis
- satisfy yourself that you've done everything possible to rectify a situation
- justify leaving an unacceptable situation

The *End of the Rope* strategy is focused and action-oriented. It will help you achieve your objectives. Here are some examples of how people have used the *End of the Rope* strategy. They've used it to:

- ✔ win approval for purchases large and small
- ✔ add to their staffs
- ✔ negotiate more time with their spouses
- ✔ increase their authority
- ✔ improve their decision-making
- ✔ persuade others to their points of view

The *End of the Rope* strategy is comprised of two principles:

1. Principle 1 helps you position your requests properly.
2. Principle 2 helps you prove to your organization the value of your requests.

Together they provide you with the ammunition you need to get your needs met.

In the discussion of Principle 1 below, you'll learn to use a four-point checklist. Considering all four points will help other people hear your message. The simple truth is that making your request properly will markedly increase your chances of winning approval. So too will proving the value of your request. Principle 2 provides a seven-step formula to assist you in calculating down time and seeing how that relates to productivity.

The formula is complex but straightforward. Don't feel intimidated. Go through the formula step by step. It's logical and it's organized for ease of use. You'll know some of the numbers needed to complete the calculation, and you'll be able to research others. Even if you don't know the answers, guesstimate. After working with the formula a few times, you'll begin to understand how it will help you prove your points. You'll be delighted with its potential impact. Yes! You too can win approval for your needs and wants!

By combining the two principles of the *End of the Rope* strategy, you'll be able to approach management with a well-framed request.

FAQ: *I've been begging for a new assistant in my department. They keep saying no. How can I get the help I need?*

A: By proving the assistant's value to the company. Central to the *End of the Rope* strategy is quantifying the consequences of *not* doing what you ask. Why do you need a new assistant? For instance, are you losing customers because your staff can't provide proper service? If so, assess how many customers have been lost and multiply that number by your average sales adjusted for overhead, productivity and the like (see the step-by-step *End of the Rope* strategy discussed in this chapter). Contrasting that figure to the cost of an assistant should win you speedy approval for the expenditure.

Principle 1. How Can I Get Them to Listen?

No matter how desperate you are for a particular resource, or how well you've proven your need, if the powers-that-be are turned off by your approach, your request may be turned down. It's absolutely essential that you state your request properly. If you don't frame your recommendation well, you risk alienating the very people who are in a position to approve your request. Certainly personality must be considered, but there's more. Here's a checklist so you can be sure that the request you make is likely to help, not hurt, you get the resources you want. Requests should include:

- ✔ no tone of complaint
- ✔ no emotion
- ✔ a statement of the problem that has been quantified through the use of numbers, statistics, or facts
- ✔ a specific recommendation

Principle 2: They're Listening . . . . How Can I Get Them to Agree?

Once you've positioned your message in such a way as to encourage people to consider your request with an open mind, you need to prove the value of your request. Think about it from your organization's point of view. It has limited resources. Budgets are only so large. Managers' time is finite. Determining where and how an organization:

- spends its money
- devotes personnel effort
- assigns manufacturing capacity
- chooses which new technology to embrace
- selects new ventures

are key decisions made by senior executives. High-level managers are generally experienced and savvy. If your request is sloppy in format or appearance, or if it features flawed logic, most likely it will not be approved. If, on the other hand, your request is carefully documented and articulately explained, and its value to the organization is proven, it's likely to be approved. The seven-step formula below provides a fail-safe approach to demonstrating your request's value to your organization.

Sometimes proving the magnitude of a problem is all it takes to win approval for your request. But often managers need additional information in order to justify doing what you want. The following seven-step formula offers a way to calculate a proposed resource's likely impact on productivity and thus help provide relevant ammunition to you as you submit your request. Take your time reading the formula. Think about each step. Consider whether you have access to the numbers required or whether you can research them. If you're not privy to the information, suggestions about guesstimating are made below.

1. Calculate your own and others' actual down time due to employee absence, a lack of technology, smoking breaks, broken equipment, or the like.

   - Time yourself and other people as they do things.
   - Maintain an activity log to track where the time is going.
   - Note how frequently various pieces of equipment are used and by whom, as well as how often they're out of commission, and add these numbers into the calculation.

2. Convert the total of time spent to dollars, based on the salaries of staff involved.

   - Use 2,080 to convert annual salaries into hourly wages (40 hours per week multiplied by 52 weeks per year equals 2,080 paid hours per year).

3. Add 25 to 30 percent to reflect the value of benefits paid to staff, assuming a typical benefit package; the easiest way to do this is to multiply the dollar value of the time by 1.25–1.30 (i.e., if benefits in your company equal 27 percent, take the total value of the time multiplied by 1.27). Check with staff in the human resources or finance departments to elicit the figure used in your company, or use 25 percent if you're guesstimating the value. Use a lower percentage if you work for a smaller company or a nonprofit organization, as they generally offer fewer benefits.

- Scan through your organization's benefit manual to ensure you don't forget any benefits as you tally the value of both financial and non-financial benefits.

4. Add in other relevant expenses such as consultant fees, travel expenses, and the like. This sum represents your total direct expenses. Examine past events to identify likely categories of expenses. Estimate costs conservatively to avoid inflating the value of a proposed resource.

5. Add an additional percentage for overhead based on your company's figures. The easiest way to do this is to multiply the total by 1 plus the percentage. In other words, if your organization calculates overhead at 17 percent, multiply the total times 1.17. If your organization calculates overhead at 19 percent, multiply the total times 1.19.

- If you're not able to research your organization's overhead figure, it's safe to guesstimate using 17 to 20 percent, a percentage range generally accepted as reasonable in most industries.

6. Multiply the total of steps one to five (i.e., the dollar value of direct nonworking labor costs plus benefits, plus direct expenses, plus overhead) by 72 percent (or whatever factor you deem appropriate) to derive the final value. Why 72 percent? That is a reasonable guesstimate of productivity when you lack a reason to use another figure.

How can you tell what percentage you should use? Let's start by defining the term *productivity*. According to the *American Heritage Dictionary*, *productivity* means "output per unit of labor." If you're a typist, your skill is measured as how many words you type per minute, but your productivity is measured as how many pages of properly formatted copy you generate per hour or per day. An accounts receivable clerk's productivity may be measured by the number of customer contacts he or she makes per hour.

Many companies have already calculated this figure. For example, most manufacturing companies use 60 percent, or as Rusty, vice president of an industrial belting company, put it, "Sixty percent if we're lucky." Grace, manager of a major bank's customer service department, uses 67 percent. "There's a lot of lost time that you never consider unless you focus in on it and actually measure it. I'd thought our productivity was much higher until I monitored it. Being able to prove the 67 percent figure through objective data enabled me to use it in reports and for budgeting purposes. I'm in a much stronger negotiating position now than before I measured productivity in our department."

FAQ: *I'm trying to calculate productivity in my department—what's reasonable?*

A: It's hard to accurately estimate the percent of time people actually work. For example, let's say that a member of your staff is staring into space, thinking. To a casual observer it may appear that he or she is engaged in unproductive work. But you know better. You know the value of that person's thinking to your department's bottom line. As a general rule, in an office environment you can feel confident using 72 percent (of total expenses) as a reasonable guesstimate of productivity. Many manufacturing companies consider 60 percent realistic. Whatever you decide, don't use 100 percent. It's not reasonable to expect people to be productive every moment. As people make personal phone calls, go to the rest room, chat with coworkers, and stare into space, you have to be very careful to have rational expectations about productivity.

Observing people as they work is always a safe place to start measuring productivity. However, doing so effectively requires that you know enough about the kind of work they're doing to make an accurate assessment. For example, a creative director planning a new marketing campaign may spend an hour doodling on a pad of paper. To this person, doodling fosters creativity, and no matter what you think of time spent doodling, you must count it as productive work. For senior managers, the measure of output is even more difficult to quantify. A high-level executive's productivity is generally tied to revenue increases, cost containment, new business initiatives, or other big-picture, long-term achievements. So what do you do?

Estimate productivity at 72 percent, unless you have a reason to believe that a different number is appropriate. People aren't productive every moment. We're not robots. We work with pauses and breaks. We're dependent on other people's cooperation. We perform creative work that comes in fits and starts, and that may require long periods of quiet thought. Equipment fails. Events and interruptions that we can't anticipate happen. We work in changing and unpredictable environments. However, many activities and occurrences do contribute to a lack of productivity. Use the checklist below to better understand the elements that diminish productivity. For example, people:

- ✔ stare into space
- ✔ chat with a coworker
- ✔ come back late from lunch
- ✔ go to the rest room
- ✔ wait for equipment to be available
- ✔ delay a job while equipment's being repaired
- ✔ wait for other people to complete something, so a project can proceed
- ✔ work at half speed because they have a cold
- ✔ make personal phone calls

If you're uncertain about your ability to accurately analyze productivity in your environment, or if you are unable to conduct the research, you can guesstimate productivity. You can feel comfortable using a percentage of between sixty percent (in manufacturing, where you know there's a lot of lost time for setup or clean-up, for instance) to seventy-five percent (in busy offices with highly motivated employees, such as a fast-growing entrepreneurial venture). The bottom line is that 72 percent is a reasonable guesstimate of productivity in most office environments.

7. Divide the total cost of a desired resource by the total cost of down time as tallied in step 6.

- Gather at least two or three price quotes for the resource you're requesting.
- Add in any taxes, shipping charges, maintenance contracts, or other fees to calculate the total cost.

Make Yourself Look Good with the *End of the Rope* Strategy

Using this strategy may help you get the resources you want or need. Even if you don't get them, the strategy conveys the impression that you're someone dedicated to finding high-quality solutions. Furthermore, it helps ensure that your boss knows the magnitude of a problem, a critical step in avoiding future problems. And you won't sound like a complainer.

"We're sinking!" "We need help!" "It's impossible!" None of these statements are likely to get you additional resources. Instead of winning management support, they'll probably be heard as whining. It doesn't matter if they're true. What matters is that you propose a solution, not merely complain about a problem.

Contrast, for instance, these two statements: "We can't keep up with the work load. Too many calls are coming in, and with the required follow-up, well, it's no surprise we're missing the quality standards" versus, "We're fielding eight calls an hour in our department, each one of which takes an average of seventeen minutes. When you add in the half hour it averages to do the follow-up research and the thirty-five minutes to draft the response, well, you can see clearly why we're missing the quality standards. If we added another person to the department, here's the impact that would have on meeting the quality standards. We either have to change the quality standards to reflect the reality, or we have to add staff."

Note that the latter example is documenting a proposed solution, whereas the former is simply complaining. Position yourself as a team player. Avoid saying "I." Instead talk about "we."

James Nield, a financial analyst at Ford Motor Company, says, "At Ford there is a strong fragmentation between the different areas of the company, such as manufacturing and finance. Finance is often seen as the enemy. Therefore, I try to use 'we,' 'us,' and 'our' so that everyone feels we're on the same team, and to reinforce the idea that I'm there to help them."

Furthermore, it's important that you go through the *End of the Rope* process because doing so provides managers senior to you with key information. If you don't tell the powers-that-be what's going on, how can they wisely make decisions about allocating *their* scarce resources? As you move up in management, you become increasingly responsible for allocating ever more scarce resources. So is your boss, and so is his or her boss.

Case Study 1:
Charlotte Wins a Budget Increase

Consider Charlotte's situation. A *Data-Collector/Accommodator* mix, Charlotte was responsible for her city's snow plowing. "I work for the maintenance department," she explained. "When I came to Jane's seminar, I was absolutely at the end of my rope. I'd been asking for an increase in my budget for years. No dice. And it was patently unfair. First, there's inflation. I mean, I know it hasn't been much lately, but it hasn't been zero. The real issue, though, was our city's growth. We're a booming suburb of Boston, growing a lot. New developments. New streets. Widened highways. There's a lot more pavement to plow now than there used to be. But my budget hadn't increased in seven years. Seven years. Every year I'd asked for an increase. I'd reasoned with them, I'd submitted the documentation, I'd followed the rules. Nothing.

"Year after year I'd been living with it. I'm not one to complain, so I've just done the best I could. A few years ago, we had a terrible winter. Twenty blizzards. Toward the end of the season everyone was feeling the strain. No one seemed able to catch up on sleep—as soon as you finished dealing with one blizzard, here came another storm. We were out of money, out of energy, and for many folks, out of good spirits. It was rough, lots of crabby people.

"During one of the last storms of that season, I was the only person who got into the office that day. I came in on snowshoes. As soon as I walked in, the phone started ringing. It was someone wanting to know why his street hadn't been plowed. As soon as I hung up the phone, another line started ringing. Same thing—why hasn't my street been plowed? All I did that day, all day, was answer the phone. I started keeping hatch marks on my desk calendar as the calls came in. It was pretty awful. I didn't know what to tell these people, and by the end of the day, I can tell you, I was pretty angry.

"I was doing my job properly. I had the sequence right—major artery, secondary, tertiary. No one was out sick, no equipment was down. Everything was leased that I had budgeted for. No one calling to complain cared that I was doing a good job. All they wanted to know was why *their* street hadn't been plowed. It was the single most difficult day I've ever spent at work. Over the next several days I analyzed my options.

"After I worked through the problem, using Jane's system, I realized it was all about money. I needed more money. I couldn't do any more than I was doing. Here's how I analyzed the situation. I asked myself if I'd:

✔ set goals integrating my *Unspoken Expectations* and confirmed that they're properly framed with the CAN DO model

"Yes, I had. I never lost sight of our department's major goal—ensuring that emergency equipment can get through. The problem was with the A in the CAN DO model. Keeping the streets plowed had become an unrealistic goal. It simply wasn't achievable given my budget. So in the last several years I'd been working to achieve an additional goal—to get a budget increase."

✔ broken my goals down into sequential baby steps using the *"In Order to . . ."* model

"Yes, I'd done it. I rehearsed my presentations. I documented the need. I worked through the process of creating baby steps."

✔ considered other people's personality types, positioning my requests with approaches and vocabulary targeting each

"My boss is a *Producer* and bored with details. Completely bored with details. Very impatient. When you try to talk to him about a problem, he gets irritated, as if *you're* somehow the problem, not the issue at hand. So over the years I've modified how I interact with him. I've had most success by being brief and direct. Typically, I use the imperative—I start sentences with verbs. I begin ninety percent of my sentences—both in person and in print—with a verb. Before I learned this approach, I way overexplained things, and apologized for bothering him, and so on—typical *Data-Collector/Accommodator* stuff. No more. I'm very direct and brief. It works well. We get along fine. But I still haven't got my budget increase."

✔ identified my strengths and am capitalizing on them, and identified my weaknesses and have worked to find ways to avoid the pitfalls associated with them

"The biggest weakness I identified here was my habit of overexplaining. My style of communication made my boss glaze over. But now that I've begun being more direct and concise and have been using the imperative, that weakness seems to be under control. I think I've taken good advantage of my strength in numbers and analysis. No one could ever accuse me of making emotional decisions. Every request is well documented."

✔ used the journalist's five W's to analyze my situation, and to be alert for underlying issues.

"After failing to persuade my boss to authorize an increase last year, I went through the five W's this way:

- *What* is the problem:

"My inability to convince management to increase my budget."

- *When* is it a problem:

"Primarily during winter seasons, when there are more storms, or worse storms, than expected. But last year was mild, and it was still a problem. So my new answer is that it's always a problem."

- *Who* is responsible:

"I am. There must be a way for me to be sufficiently persuasive to make my point. My boss shares responsibility as well, for not having enough confidence in my judgment to approve my recommendations. I don't care where they take the money from— I understand that other departments have critical needs too, but that's not my issue."

- *Where* does the problem occur:

"The lack of adequate snow plowing occurs all over town; no one area is worse off than another. If I focus on the budget issue, not the plowing issue, the problem starts at City Hall."

- *Why* is it occurring.

"There are several reasons, external and internal. The political atmosphere towards taxation, of course, faster-than-expected growth rates, and so on. Other departments' needs are deemed more pressing. Mild winters diminish the perceived need. There are lots of reasons. One issue that I forced myself to consider was the *Accommodator* part of my persona. Maybe by making it look easy, I was doing myself—and our snowplowing function—no favor. Maybe, I realized, that what I thought of as direct was, in fact, so indirect that management didn't understand the magnitude of the problem.

"What I did with that analysis was provide extra documentation, trying to compensate for this potential weakness of my personality with objective data. It didn't work, but I thought it was worth trying, and I still think my analysis was accurate."

Armed with this comprehensive analysis, Charlotte realized that she was, in fact, at the end of her rope. "That day on the phone, keeping hatch marks on the desk calendar, all alone, I was getting more frustrated by the minute. That was it—my line in the sand. I realized I couldn't pretend anymore that everything was fine. And I was determined to maintain my professionalism. I needed a plan.

"The way our division works, budgeting is a pretty formal process," Charlotte explained. "Each department head has to make a presentation. Next budget cycle, I went to my budget meeting, and instead of a fancy presentation, I handed everybody one sheet of paper. One sheet. At the top it read, '480 minutes divided by 240 angry calls = one call every 2 minutes.' At the bottom of the page I'd written my budget request.

"At the meeting, when it was my turn, I said, 'As you know, I've been requesting an increase in my budget each year for seven years, and I've been turned down each year. This year, before considering my request, I thought you needed to know that on such and such a day, when I was the only person able to make it into the office, I fielded a phone call from an angry taxpayer every two minutes during an eight-hour shift. Therefore please approve my request, which you see on the bottom of the page.'

"I got my increase. Not the whole thing, but more money than I'd gotten in the last seven years combined. It worked. It was a success."

Charlotte was smart. Her analysis gave her confidence, and she knew that in the worse case—if they disapproved her budget once again—her position was no worse. She'd been living with it, and she could continue to live with it. "But probably," she said, "I would have quit. I'd had it.

"My boss came up to me the day after the meeting and told me I'd done a good job. He said that selling *his* budget was going to be easier because I'd done a good job in demonstrating the magnitude of the problem in *my* department."

In other words, silence frequently leads to bad decisions.

People hesitate to report problems because they don't want to be the bearer of bad news. But the consequence is that decisions are made with inadequate information. The beauty of the *End of the Rope* strategy is that it allows you to show initiative, take action, and potentially get resources that you need—at low to no risk to yourself.

FAQ: *I don't have enough money in my budget to grant all my staff's requests, no matter how reasonable and well thought out. Why should I bother letting them request things? Doesn't it just set up frustration and anger?*

A: As a general statement, solvent companies make decisions about allocating resources based on their perception of the proposed resource's value to the company, not actual costs. My first question to you, therefore, is why can't you authorize reasonable and well-thought-out requests? Maybe there's an *Unspoken Expectation* at work in your world. Regardless, I recommend that you go through the *End of the Rope* process discussed in this chapter. Doing so will provide those who are senior to you with key information. Alerting them to unfulfilled needs will enable them to make educated decisions about allocating *their* scarce resources.

Case Study 2: Margot Gets Approval for Staff Training

Charlotte was able to persuade management to increase her department's budget by quantifying the magnitude of the problem. Often, you'll need to do more. In addition to documenting the problem, you'll also need to demonstrate the value of your specific requests to the organization.

When you're at the end of your rope, the last thing you want to do is get overwhelmed with minutia. You want a quick and effective solution. Follow along as Margot uses the seven-step formula to petition her supervisor for approval of her staff's training. The seven-step formula is the simplest and most reliable way to prove the value of a resource to your organization. It's also beneficial in confirming that your proposed solution will work.

Margot, an *Accommodator/Producer* mix, explained that she felt as if she were sinking. "I'm the supervisor of a tech-support department. All thirty-seven of my reps needed a one-week advanced training workshop, but I couldn't get it approved. The division is hot on holding steady with 'discretionary expenses.' Doesn't matter whether you need the training. It matters how someone else defines 'discretionary.' Frustrating, to say the least.

"I'd asked, and I'd argued, but nothing was working. Finally, I told my husband, 'That's it. I'm going to make one more stab at it, and if I can't get it approved, I'm going to quit.' I felt it was that important. Here's what I calculated, using the seven-step formula:

1. Calculate your own and others' actual down time, whether due to employee absence, a lack of technology, smoking breaks, broken equipment, and the like.

   - "For a month—a reasonable span of time to judge our flow of work—I noted all errors when work had to be redone, or when I had to be consulted. I tracked the time employees took to redo something plus the time I had to spend consulting with them about the error for those events where I believed that if they'd attended the advanced training, they wouldn't have needed to consult me and they wouldn't have made the error. Some errors are always going to happen, and some events are complex and require my participation—and would whether they'd taken the training or not. I used my best judgment in assessing the time factor.

     "It worked out to an average of a quarter of an hour a day per technician. Multiply that times 37 technicians and you get an astounding 9¼ man hours of wasted time a day times 30 days in the month equals 277.5 hours wasted time a month."

2. Convert that total to dollars based on the salaries of staff involved.

   • "Easy enough. As supervisor, I know everyone's salary. I added them up and did a pure average. All 37 technicians' salaries added together, divided by 37. Our average hourly salary is $30.29, so I multiplied that times the total wasted hours of 277.5, and got a total of $8,405.48."

3. Add 25 to 30 percent to reflect the value of benefits paid to staff, assuming a typical. benefit package. The easiest way to do this is to multiply the dollar value of the time by 1.25–1.30 (i.e., if benefits in your company equal 27 percent, take the total value of the time multiplied by 1.27).

   • "For budgeting we use 32 percent of gross salary, so that's what I used for this calculation. So I multiplied the total monthly salary of $8,405.48 times 1.32, and got $11,095.23."

4. Add in other relevant expenses such as consultant fees, travel expenses, and the like—this total represents your direct expenses.

   • "There were some travel expenses associated with errors. Some of our work is off-site, and if a rep had to return to an off-site location, for instance, that would lead to extra—and unnecessary—travel. I keep a spreadsheet and simply entered the data as the events occurred. I'm pretty organized—that's the *Accommodator* in me—so it was pretty easy to do. Over the month span that I analyzed, these direct expenses totaled $5,642.87."

5. Add an additional 17 to 20 percent for overhead, assuming these expenses fall in the typical 17 to 20 percent range. The easiest way to do this is to multiply the total by 1.17–1.20 (i.e., if your organization calculates overhead at 19 percent, use 1.19).

- "Corporate policy is that if a proposed initiative can't contribute at least 17 percent to overhead, forget it. Don't even bring up the idea. That tells me that headquarters considers overhead to be 17 percent. So that's what I used. The total salary plus benefits figure was $11,095.23. I added that to the total direct expenses of $5,642.87, and it equals $16,738.10. I multiplied $16,738.10 times 1.17 and got $19,583.58."

6. Multiply this sum by 72 percent (or whatever factor you deem appropriate) to derive the final value.

- "I used 67 percent. I wanted to be more, rather than less, conservative in my calculations. The total of $19,583.58 times 67 percent equaled $13,121. That's so much money. I just stared at the figure for a while, stunned at the total monthly cost to the company of our lack of training."

7. Divide the total cost of the desired resource by the total cost of down time as tallied in step 6.

- "I took the cost of the training, associated travel expenses, staff salaries, and benefits for those people taking training. I also added in staff overtime plus benefits to reflect the extra work everyone would have to do while the training was going on.
  "Here's what it totaled:

    ✔ training fees: 37 technicians times $2,250 each = $83,250
    ✔ travel expenses: it's local, so it's only lunch and mileage. I estimated high and called it $20 a day, or $100 for the week, so the total = $3,700
    ✔ staff salaries: 40 hours training times the average hourly salary of $30.29 = $1,211.60, plus 32 percent for benefits = $1,599.31, times 37 technicians = total salary and benefits for everyone while they're attending the training is $59,174.54

✔ I'd observed for years that when someone was at training, I spent as much on overtime as I did on their salary, so it was a reasonable guesstimate to add in another $59,174.54

● "I added these four numbers together: $83,250 plus $3,700 plus $59,174.54 plus $59,174.54, and it totaled $205,299.08. I divided that by the monthly cost to the company of $13,121 (from step 6 above) and learned that we would pay for the training in our improved productivity in about sixteen months. I'd hoped it would be paid for in under a year, but it wasn't. In writing up my request, I realized there were two other benefits to the company in paying for the training: employee and customer retention. If we don't enable the technicians to stay current in their field, they'll leave for a company that will. Also, our competitors would have an edge and might steal our customers if their technicians could provide more up-to-date work. I added these two benefits to my request when I wrote it up. I'm pleased to report that my methodical approach worked. I got it approved."

FAQ: *When I told my boss I wanted to attend an upcoming conference, she told me to run the numbers. As I'm an* Optimist *and hate detail work, I'm looking for a way to convince her simply to trust my judgment. Any ideas?*

A: Her request seems reasonable, so my suggestion would be that you develop the skills to quickly "run the numbers." As an *Optimist*, it's probable that you'll never like doing so, but proving the value of your ideas will help you get more of them approved. This is true whether the expense is relatively minor, such as attending a conference, or major, such as acquiring a competitor's firm. Additionally, acquiring a skill your boss obviously perceives as important is likely to win her respect.

Logic, not emotion, led to Margot's success. Note that you don't have to wait until you're at the end of your rope to use the *End of the Rope* strategy. Margot's analysis would have worked no matter when she undertook it. Because the *End of the Rope* strategy uses objective measures, it diffuses emotion while enhancing professionalism.

Margot reported, "Not only did I look like a hero to my staff, but also my boss was impressed by the initiative I showed."

Case Study 3: Ahmed Secures a New Computer

Ahmed, a graphic designer for a small company, used the *End of the Rope* strategy to get a new computer. "I realized that my situation fit the profile of when to use the *End of the Rope* strategy. I'd set a goal, confirmed it was properly framed, considered personality, nada. Nothing. Just because it wasn't a major issue didn't mean I wasn't plenty frustrated.

"I'd been asking for a faster computer with a full-size monitor for two years. And for two years my boss had said no. We don't have a formal budgeting process. There are only fifteen employees in the whole company. We just make our requests, and we get a yes or a no. I'm an *Optimist*, so doing research isn't exactly my favorite thing to do. But my boss is a *Data-Collector*, so research is what I needed to do.

"About a month ago, I was waiting for my computer to complete some task or other. It felt like I was waiting forever. Then I needed to see the layout full-size, which couldn't be done on my thirteen-inch monitor, so I had to wait again while it reconfigured and the text flowed.

"After a half day I went into my boss and made a joke about it. I asked him what I had to do to get a decent computer. His response sure got my attention. He told me that he didn't know why I complained, that I was doing great work.

"Think about it. Here's my boss telling me he's pleased with my work. I figured I'd better proceed with caution. For sure, I didn't want to argue with him. But I needed a new computer.

I knew I was doing a good job, but I also knew that I wasn't as productive as I could be. I realized that I was dealing with an *Unspoken Expectation*—that my boss wanted me to keep producing high-quality ads and brochures with no new technology.

"Once I recognized the situation for what it was, I knew what to do. I followed the *Unspoken Expectations* four-step model:

- Try to change their minds

"For two years I'd tried to change my boss's mind. Repeatedly. And I failed. But I'd simply asked. Maybe if I'd been more carefully prepared . . . It got me thinking. But I couldn't see an obvious answer."

- Live with it

"That's what I'd been doing. I'd been living with it. Unhappily, and with mounting frustration. I knew what the problem was—a lack of investment in technology. My issue was how to prove it."

- Make a specific recommendation for improvement

"Hmm, I said to myself. All I've done to this point is complain. Time to quantify. I realized that I could use the *End of the Rope* strategy. What's the worst that could happen? I'd be back to step two, living with it, or—worst case, step four—I'd decide I had to quit."

- Remove yourself from the situation (you're "outta there").

"So I decided to proceed with step three—the *End of the Rope* strategy. I went over the steps:

- ✔ no tone of complaint
- ✔ no emotion
- ✔ a statement of the problem that has been quantified through the use of numbers, statistics, or facts
- ✔ a specific recommendation

"What I did was go back to my seminar notes. Jane had given us some ways to calculate the value of down time. The seven-step formula was easy to understand. What I did was track my down time for a week. Every time I sat and waited for the computer to do something, I timed how long it took. While it zoomed, I timed it. While it reconfigured, I timed it. Because I had only a small monitor, in order to see an 11" × 17" spread, I had to print out the two pages and tape them together. While it printed and I taped the pages together, I timed it.

"At the end of the week I had a total of my down time associated with my old computer. I couldn't believe it—the total was three and a quarter hours. I'd known it was a lot, but not that much. Wow.

"From there I just followed the steps. After all, I know my own salary, so it was easy to convert the time I'd wasted into a dollar amount. I earn $49,500 a year. I didn't know the value of benefits, but I figured an exact accounting didn't matter. I did figure that I'd better be conservative, so I used the low estimate—25 percent. I used 17 percent to cover overhead items like insurance, rent, electricity, and so on, and then discounted the total by 72 percent. Me, an *Optimist*, doing an analysis! Can you imagine? But it was easy. Here's what the numbers looked like:

1. Calculate your own and others' actual down time.

   - "Three and a quarter hours a week."

2. Convert that total to dollars based on the salaries of staff involved.

   - "I took my salary of $49,500 and divided it by 2,080 (52 weeks times 40 hours a week). That equaled $23.80. That was my salary on an hourly basis. So I took the hourly salary of $23.80 and multiplied it by 3.25. The total was $77.35."

3. Add 25 to 30 percent to reflect the value of benefits paid to staff, assuming a typical benefit package; the easiest way to do this is to multiply the dollar value of the time by 1.25–1.30.

- "My hourly rate worked out to $77.35. I multiplied that by 1.25 to include my benefits. $77.35 times 1.25 equaled $96.69."

4. Add in other direct expenses such as consultant fees, travel expenses, and the like—this total represents direct expenses.

  - "It was just me involved, so no additional expenses applied here. "The total stayed $96.69."

5. Add an additional 17 to 20 percent for overhead, assuming these expenses fall in the typical 17 to 20 percent range.

  - "My salary plus benefits equaled $96.69. To add the 17 percent for overhead, I multiplied $96.69 times 1.17. It totaled $113.13."

6. Multiply this total by 72 percent (or whatever factor you deem appropriate) to derive the final value of the down time.

  - "When I multiplied $113.13 times 72 percent, it equaled $81.45 a week. This represented a realistic loss to my organization of my down time. The great thing here is that I wasn't just pulling a number out of a hat—it was logical."

7. Divide out the total cost of the desired resource by the factor representing down time.

  - "The computer setup I wanted costs just under $4,000. So I divided $4,000 by the weekly down time value of $81.45. It came out to about 49 weeks. In other words, we'd pay for the computer with my increased productivity in less than a year."

Notice that Ahmed wisely used conservative estimates when he didn't have actual figures in front of him. It's always better to understate value and overstate expenses. Doing so ensures that you'll look good, and that you aren't promising outcomes that will occur only if everything goes just right.

"I went in to my boss with the numbers neatly typed up. Guess what? I had a computer within the week."

No surprise. If an organization is solvent, decisions about acquiring resources are generally made not on cost but on the *perception of value*. Ensure that you get the resources you need, both large and small, by proving the value empirically.

Case Study 4: Glenna Refuses to Cross a Line

Clearly, there are issues worth quitting a job over—even a job you like. If you're asked to do something illegal, for example, the decision is easy. Likewise, there are clear reasons to leave personal relationships. For instance, if someone attacks you, most of us would decide that this isn't a relationship worth sustaining. Beyond the obvious, however, there are other factors that lead each of us to the end of our rope. It's personal. No one but you can set your standards. No one but you gets a vote.

Glenna quit her job because of a line she refused to cross. "I didn't even know that the line was there. But once I'd faced the situation, and had gone through the *End of the Rope* strategy, I knew I had no choice. So I quit. It was a good decision for me, although it was one of the hardest I've ever made."

Glenna explained that the nonprofit organization for which she worked was routinely short of money. "As director, one of my primary duties is fund-raising. A paradox of fund-raising is that if you seem desperate, no one wants to give you money.

"The treasurer—an unpaid volunteer, a board member—told me to redo the pro forma budget, lowering the telecommunications charges to such an extent that I objected. His motives were good: to make the expenses appear less onerous. Maybe it sounds like a small thing, but it's not. Forget that our total budget was over fifty million dollars, and the telecommunications expense should have topped a half a million. He wanted me to lower it by half.

"It made me uncomfortable. His point was that we could be optimistic that all of the promises of the Internet would come through, and costs would plummet. I understand that optimism doesn't equate to dishonesty, but to me it was patently unrealistic. No way were our telecommunications costs going down by half. I said no.

"I explained that as it was I who would be going before foundation boards and signing grant requests, I had to be comfortable with our numbers. As soon as I used the word "comfortable," I realized I was speaking from my own point of view—that was the *Accommodator* part of me talking. The treasurer was all *Producer*, so I knew he wouldn't care whether I was comfortable or not.

FAQ: *I'm at the end of my rope and am thinking of quitting. How can I tell if I should?*

A: Why do you feel as if you're at the end of your rope? While I have no way of telling you whether your particular circumstances merit quitting, clearly there are issues worth quitting over. If you're asked to do something illegal, immoral, or unethical, or if you so hate your work that you dread waking up in the morning, for instance, there may be no alternative but finding another job. Before quitting, however, consult the *End of the Rope* strategy detailed in this chapter.

"I tried again to persuade him, this time using language I thought would appeal to him. I said, 'Here's the bottom line—it will hurt us in the long run.' His response was, 'Do it anyway.' So although I thought I'd analyzed personalities well, it didn't work.

"I considered whether there was an *Unspoken Expectation* at work. If so, it translated to: make our organization look good no matter what. And that wasn't okay with me.

"Using the *Unspoken Expectations* response model:

- I'd tried to get him to change his mind.
- I'd considered living with it.

"And that's when I realized there was a line in the sand and I was looking at it. No. I wouldn't do it. I couldn't live with it.

"I decided to try to get them to change their minds one more time—saying no with the RAF principle—the Rule of Affirmation First. I went before the board and said, 'I know that every member of this board has only the best interests of the organization in mind when they make a recommendation. However, this isn't the way to do it. Let's put our heads together and see how we can get the bottom line looking decent without putting our long-term position in jeopardy.'

"No. They smiled, and they made a point of discussing it, but the reality was that they'd decided no before I opened my mouth. End of the rope.

- I decided to offer a specific recommendation.

    - ✔ no tone of complaint
    - ✔ no emotion
    - ✔ a statement of the problem that has been quantified through the use of numbers, statistics, or facts
    - ✔ a specific request

"So I reviewed my approach. I made sure that there was no tone of complaint. No problem, it's not my style to complain. I made a mental note to keep all emotion out of my presentation. This would be hard for me because I was hot, and because I cared so deeply both about the issue at hand and our organization. But I promised myself that I was going to be very matter-of-fact. Having that mind-set helped. Somehow, it let me separate myself from the issue, a good thing given how upset I was feeling. Okay, I told myself—no emotion.

"I had to organize a statement of the problem quantified through the use of numbers, statistics, or facts. How could I quantify a *potential* threat? I looked at all numbers related and started a list. I knew that the treasurer wanted me to reduce an expense item by 47 percent. That was a number. Grants and private donations have increased at least 10 percent every year for the last three years—another number. I started focusing on what we did—the help we provided to local environmental groups—and the numbers there were equally convincing. We had no need to fake anything. We were efficient and effective and growing in an appropriate manner. I put together a listing of the numbers with short comments about what the numbers implied. It was impressive.

"Finally, I had to make a specific recommendation. I worked it out carefully. I had no doubt in my mind. I passed out the one-page sheet with the data I'd gathered, and told the board, 'We don't need to do this; we don't need to shade the truth. We don't need to hope for the future of the Internet. What we have is sustained controlled growth. Please. Let me do my job.'

"It didn't work. So I faced the fact that probably I was 'outta there.' They said no. They were unsympathetic and unmoved. I told them I'd quit. They accepted my resignation. At first I was shocked. But almost as soon as I walked out of my office for the last time, I felt better. I felt relief. In hindsight, I learned something important about myself—that I have a line in the sand. Now I know where the line is, and it felt good not to cross it."

The Final Step Is the First Step

Where are the lines that you won't cross? How can you achieve success if you won't set priorities? How can you set priorities if you don't focus on what matters most to you?

Only when you know what causes you to reach the end of your rope will you be able to manage priorities well. No one but you can make these decisions.

The first step—and the final step—is to tell yourself the truth about what you value, and to use that information to set your priorities. Once your priorities are set, the techniques described in this book will equip you to handle life's challenges well. In the Conclusion, you'll find an exercise that enables you to put the techniques to work, to practice what you've learned, and to prove to yourself that you can manage priorities effectively and with confidence.

Tips

- When you've done everything you can think of to get the resources you need, and still you're turned down, you may feel as if you're at the end of your rope. Instead of feeling frustrated and helpless, use this chapter's seven-step formula to prove your request's bottom-line benefit to your organization.

- When calculating the value of resources to your organization, be sure you're realistic. People aren't productive all the time. If you're not going to conduct an objective analysis, use 72 percent as a reasonable guesstimate of productivity. Otherwise you risk overstating value.

✦

Make Your Dreams Come True!

Use the Techniques in This Book and Reach Your Peak Performance

Great news! You now know the techniques you need to achieve success. It's one thing to know the techniques, however, and another to actually use them. To ensure that you become more effective at managing your priorities, you need to practice putting the techniques to work. Are you ready? Let's start now!

By practicing putting the techniques to work, I guarantee that you'll become more adept at using them, which means that you'll begin the process of integrating them into your day-to-day life. From this integration springs success! You'll build confidence as the tools begin to work for you. By participating in the exercise below and completing the action plan that follows, you'll seize control of your time and energy. You'll take charge of your life. You'll live your life by *your* priorities, a grand thing! It's how dreams come true!

Fun and Helpful: An "In-Basket" Exercise!

"In-basket" exercises are fun! Take advantage of the opportunity to practice making priority decisions under time pressure with imperfect information. In other words, this exercise mimics the real world in an engaging manner. There are obvious differences between reality and any exercise, including this one. That said, you'll notice that the situations that follow are universal. They've happened to us all, or they might. At all supervisory levels, you need to be able to quickly determine priorities among competing and worthy contenders. The exercise invites you to do just that.

You'll be challenged to:

✔ guesstimate how long things take to accomplish
✔ integrate an *Unspoken Expectation* into your decisions
✔ use the 1-5 system and the *Time Sensitivity vs. Key* model to rank tasks in order of importance
✔ identify personalities and adapt your statements to suit

There are no right or wrong answers. After you complete the exercise, you'll be able to compare your decisions with the decisions other people have made. One of the important benefits of participating in an exercise such as this one is understanding that other people of goodwill and sincere effort make profoundly different decisions than you do, even when they have the same information. They make different decisions because they make different assumptions, and because their views about what's most important differ from your view.

In order to participate in the exercise, you'll need to make sensible assumptions for your own circumstances. For example, you won't be told, but you will need to consider, whether you have a cell phone or a secretary or assistant. What is your boss's personality type? What is your own personality type? Are the people who report to you located nearby, or are they off-site? Which assumptions you make don't matter. What does matter is that those you make are realistic and relevant.

In order to benefit fully from the exercise:

✔ Follow the directions carefully.
✔ Monitor the time as instructed, ideally by setting an egg

timer, your computer's alarm clock, or your watch so you can concentrate completely.

✔ Have scrap paper handy so you can easily work out various scenarios.

✔ Avoid reading the background information until you're ready to begin.

✔ Allow sufficient time to read the background information and instructions, and to complete the exercise. While the actual exercise requires that you time yourself for seven minutes, you should allow a total of about thirty minutes. (If you plan to read the debriefing section immediately upon completing the exercise, allow additional time for this as well.)

Set the Scene: Here's the Background Information

It's Monday. After a week's vacation, you return to your office. Your boss is leaving for a three-day conference. She left you a voice mail over the weekend to alert you to the fact that she has to leave earlier than she'd expected—not at noon as originally planned, but at nine-thirty in the morning. After learning of her schedule change, you decided to come in early. You'd planned to be in by eight because you wanted to get a jump on the day. However, because of an unexplained traffic delay, you don't get in until nine.

She also told you she wants to spend ten minutes discussing priorities with you before she leaves for the conference. She said that she's "looking forward to hearing from you what *you* think your priorities are."

You have twenty minutes before you meet with her.

Ready, Set, Go: Here Are Your Instructions

As you think about this exercise, consider the big picture. Specific and detailed instructions follow, but first, here are some things to think about as you get ready to begin:

- What sort of relationship do you have with your boss?
- Are you new in your job?
- Have you recently received a promotion?
- Do you like your job?

In reading the scenario above, did you recognize the *Unspoken Expectation*? Your boss wants to hear about what *you* think your priorities are. Doesn't it make sense, for example, if you're a *Data-Collector* or *Accommodator*, for you to spend some percentage of that twenty minutes getting your thoughts in order? You don't want to go into the meeting cold. On the other hand, if you're an *Optimist* or *Producer*, you know that you're going to do just fine right off the top of your head. You won't want to allocate any of your twenty minutes to preparation.

What about your boss's personality? Isn't that going to dictate how you phrase things? Keep in mind that you want to tell your boss the truth about your view of your priorities, not what you think she wants to hear. Presumably you were hired for your wisdom and experience. What you want to do is ensure that she hears your message in the way you intend it to be understood.

Remember that you're not on a hunt for the one and only answer to her question; nor are you on a hunt for the one and only item in the listing that should be selected as the highest-priority task to complete. There are too many variables and too much that's unknown for either hunt to be possible. There are lots of good answers! There are lots of *appropriate* answers—depending on your assumptions and judgments. The goal isn't that you come up with one best response; rather, that you choose your response with confidence, that you're able to use the tools in this book efficiently. Your job is to sort through the items that follow, making smart decisions based on assumptions that are appropriate for you. Ready?

There are two steps to completing this exercise:

1. Read the fifteen items in your "in-basket," making notes as you judge their relative priority ranking. (Once you begin reading the list of items in your "in-basket," begin to time yourself. Allow seven minutes. You should aim to complete the exercise in this time, but you must stop working after seven minutes whether you're finished or not.)

2. Complete the four bullet-point steps that follow:

   - Assess each of the following fifteen items as a 1 (Now), 2 (Sooner), 3 (Later), 4 (Whenever), or 5 (Never).

   - Among those items you determined to be a 1, use the *Time Sensitivity vs. Key* model (where on the *emergency* vs. *whenever* axis relative to the *critical* vs. *irrelevant* axis does each item fall?) to put them in priority sequence, i.e., which is your 1-1, which is your 1-2, which is your 1-3, and so on.

   - In other words, given that you have only twenty minutes before your meeting with your boss, what will you do with the time? (Note that, taken together, this and the previous steps require that you guesstimate how long things take.)

   - Be ready to answer your boss's question (an *Unspoken Expectation*). She wants to know "what *you* think your priorities are." Write a one sentence answer to her question.

Ready? Set your clock, gather your scrap paper, get your thoughts in order. Begin.

The contents of your "in-basket" include:

1. An e-mail, with "Urgent Question" in the subject line, is from Liza, a new team member. She explains that she can't submit her time sheet—and that it's overdue—until you clarify eight separate cost codes. She says that the team secretary said that you're the only person who can clarify the codes.

2. Your boss has left a stack of papers clipped together with a handwritten note on your desk chair. The note reads, "Am I missing any expenses? Have someone check the math on these expense sheets and submit asap. By the way, where's your expense report? Isn't it overdue?"

3. Billy, an employee in your department, left a color original on your desk with a note saying that he needs you to sign off on it by 10:00 A.M. so he can have it copied to show it to the marketing folks at the noon meeting.

4. Tanya, a supervisor, sent an e-mail request for an update on who is working on which project. She explained she needs to reassign work now that Julie has quit, so all assignments are on hold pending your report.

5. Suzanne, a new employee, sent you an e-mail last Wednesday. She asked for information about the company's vacation approval policy because she hopes to take tomorrow (Tuesday) as a vacation day.

6. A sticky note on your computer from Charlie, a supervisor in your department, says that he needs a copy of the technology plan before he leaves for a 10:00 A.M. meeting.

7. Your best friend left you a voice mail message at eight-thirty. Your friend's spouse had to cancel attending the company's annual outing—great seats at tonight's completely sold-out game—so you're being invited. The message says, *"Call me as soon as you get in! Where are you? I need to tell my boss right away whether you can attend, or someone else will grab the ticket."*

8. An e-mail from Khalid in the company travel department, dated a week ago, asks you to call him to arrange delivery of your boss's tickets for the conference. As the team secretary always arranges for ticket delivery, you're surprised you received the e-mail.

9. Ming-Lee, from the next office, left you a voice mail asking you to take her calls in the morning while she is at a client meeting. She asked you to call her by 9:00 A.M. to confirm and explained, *"It's an emergency! 'You-know-who' insisted that I call you."*

10. Daphne, who works for the boss's favorite vendor and is

one of your favorite contacts, left you a voice mail message three days ago asking you to call confirming that you received her FedEx.

11. Tom, a vice president, has left you a voice mail instructing you to return the labor lawyer's phone call asap, and expressing disappointment that it hadn't been done earlier.

12. Your boss left a note on your chair wanting an update on the logo design project before she leaves. In order to brief her, you need status reports from Sharon in marketing and Robbie at the outside design studio.

13. Your doctor's receptionist called; you need to schedule an appointment to redo last week's blood test.

14. Your boss left a voice mail date-stamped at two A.M. that you need to call Hugh, the human resource manager, as soon as you get in, to schedule a meeting for the two of you to discuss coordinating staff schedules at the mandatory sexual harassment training. She tells you to try to schedule it at 11:30 A.M. Friday. Also, as she wants the entire team on board without delay, you're to be certain that Tanya, Tom, and Sharon are able to attend a briefing she'll deliver immediately following the meeting with Hugh.

15. Frank, from AV, left a voice mail four days ago to confirm that your boss still needs the small boardroom for 10:00 A.M. today, and that she'll still need two slide projectors and an overhead projector. He asked you to call and confirm immediately because Charlie, a vice president, would like the room if your boss isn't going to use it, but doesn't want to force her to relocate.

Let's Compare Notes—What Did You Decide?

Time's up! Did you finish all of the steps of the exercise? What did you determine was the very first thing you were going to do? Remember, there's no right or wrong answer. The exercise isn't intended to achieve consensus. As long as your decisions were based on logical assumptions, they're likely to be good decisions.

Here's how Hollis, a toy buyer for a department store, decided:

"First of all, I'm an *Optimist*, so I knew I'd do fine talking to my boss. I didn't need to prepare. I went quickly through the fifteen items, and identified four that were clearly in the 1 (Now) category. There were several I would have liked to add to the list, but because they could be a 2 (Sooner), I decided I'd better leave them out of the 1 (Now) grouping. The four items that made the cut were:

   7. Pat and the tickets to the game
   8. the missing conference tickets
 12. logo design update
 13. my blood test

"I used the *Time Sensitivity vs. Key* model to sort through these four, and Pat came up first. Those tickets were going to disappear unless I acted. Emergency! I allocated two minutes for the phone call. Pat's my friend, so I knew I could get off the phone quickly."

When asked whether the fact that the tickets were personal, not work-related, affected his thinking in making the decision, Hollis replied, "Not at all. Or rather, yes, but not in the way you may think. Of course, I don't spend a lot of work time on personal matters. I'm very good about it, but I'm not a robot. I believe that I am a better employee because I have a full, well-rounded life. And we're only talking about a two-minute phone call. Besides which, it'll be a great game!"

Notice that Hollis felt confident in both the decision itself and in his ability to defend his decision. He continued, "Next were the calls to Sharon and Robbie for the logo update. I thought about calling Sharon's voice mail—it's quicker to just leave a message—but I decided not to risk going straight into the system. Because of the tight deadline, I actually needed to speak to her. Regardless of whether I got her or her voice mail, I figured I'd take two to three minutes for the call. Same with Robbie. So I've used as much as eight minutes—two minutes for Pat and three each for Sharon and Robbie. Next, I went after the conference tickets. I was certain that they'd been delivered, since the e-mail was a week old, but just in case, I figured I'd better check it out. Two minutes to call the team secretary, and if necessary, another three to follow up with Khalid. Thirteen minutes total gone at the most."

What about that three-minute call to Khalid? Does that sound realistic to you? Have you ever called your travel agent? Are you typically put on hold? Will Khalid have to research the tickets, or does his computer system allow him instant access to the history of the delivery? When asked to confirm that he thought three minutes was realistic, Hollis said, "Yes. I have an excellent travel agent. If he needed to research anything, he'd tell me directly and call me back. Three minutes—absolutely, I think it's realistic."

Fair enough. Only you can know whether it's realistic or not—as long as you evaluate how long things take with rational judgment, and not allow optimism or wishful thinking to influence your verdict.

"Five minutes for the call to my doctor. I'm in good shape with two minutes to spare," Hollis concluded.

Except that he forgot one thing. Did you notice that he—as did you—spent seven minutes planning? You just spent seven minutes reviewing the fifteen items and determining priorities. No matter how long planning takes, the time you spend on the activity must be scheduled. In this case, the seven minutes allocated to prioritize must be deducted from the twenty minutes available to you before you go see your boss.

Planning is more than simply a valuable activity, it's critical. How can you determine priorities if you don't take time to read the fifteen items and assess their relative significance? Don't forget, however, that planning must always be integrated into your schedule. Hollis decided, "I'd blow off finding the conference tickets because I can't believe that neither my boss nor the team secretary would have allowed them to fall between the cracks. So I'd save the five minutes I'd allocated to the team secretary and Khalid . . . and it'll work."

What did Hollis answer his boss when she asked, "What do *you* think your priorities are"? "I told her, 'Go to the conference and don't worry. Everything's under control. I'm back in the saddle.' I assumed that she was a *Producer*. My assumption was based on her direct instructions and the sense of 'do it now' that I got from her instructions. If she pushed me, I'd list the items she'd contacted me about—the sexual harassment training, the logo design update, and her expense report."

Hollis reported that the tools were extremely useful. "I was able to see, to envision, how critical it was that I call Pat and my doctor by using the *Time Sensitivity vs. Key* model. They were far up on the emergency axis."

Did You Think Big Picture?

How about you? Did you find the tools useful? Nasreen, an accountant, reported that she found them valuable. "They were excellent in helping me analyze alternatives. My problem was that I wanted to refine my thinking more and more. You won't be surprised if I tell you that I'm primarily a *Data-Collector*," she explained, "and I confess that I didn't get through all four steps of the exercise. I was still sorting through the 1 (Now)'s I'd identified. The *Time Sensitivity vs. Key* tool was so helpful, I found myself getting more and more involved in details. I lost sight of the big picture. The truth is that when the seven minutes expired, I was utterly unprepared to talk to my boss.

"Also, I was doing a good job of focusing on the priority decisions, but I found being under such tight time pressure very agitating. It made me aware of how disturbing I find time pressure in real life too."

This is an important lesson. If you, like Nasreen, didn't complete all four of the steps, it may be that you're focusing too much on the details. Nasreen focused so intently on minutia, she lost sight of the overall purpose of the exercise. She needed to be able to confidently answer her boss's question, "What do *you* think your priorities are"? Nasreen didn't assign proper weight to the fact that this question was presented as an *Unspoken Expectation*, and thus must be taken seriously. Nasreen succeeded, however, in making some decisions.

"Typically, I freeze. When there's time pressure, imminent deadlines, a critical memo requiring attention, anything of that nature, I freeze. Using the 1 to 5 system became a safety net for me. It helped me to unfreeze because it gave me something to think about. Likewise, the *Time Sensitivity vs. Key* model was very useful. Here's how I approached the exercise:

✔ First, I decided to find those missing tickets, and the first thing I'd do would be to walk down to the team secretary's desk and ask her one-on-one if she knew if our boss had them (six minutes). If she didn't, I'd delegate to her the duty to call Khalid immediately and find them. While I was there with the team secretary, I'd ask her to call Frank in A/V, explain that the boss's schedule has changed, and cancel the conference room (one additional minute).

✔ Second, I'd call Ming-Lee, knowing I'd get her voice mail, and leave her a brief message explaining why I wasn't able to fill in as she'd asked (two minutes).

✔ Third, I'd call Sharon (two minutes) and Robbie (three minutes) about the logo design update. I assigned more time to the call to Robbie than Sharon because Sharon was internal, and I would expect her to be more understanding of the time sensitivity of my request.

✔ Fourth, I'd place a call to the labor lawyer's secretary asking to schedule a time for us to talk later today (three minutes).

✔ Fifth, I'd e-mail Tom that I was out last week on vacation and expected to talk to the labor lawyer today (three minutes).

"And that was my twenty minutes! But of course, I forgot to include the time allocated to planning—seven minutes! When I took another look at my decisions, I realized that the call to the labor lawyer and the e-mail to Tom could wait, so right there is a six-minute gain. In trying to find the extra minute I needed, I realized that if I called directly into the voice mail system without dialing Ming-Lee's desk—our voice mail system connects in only a few seconds—I'd make my message briefer, and there, I did it!"

When asked to take an additional minute to think about what she'd say to her boss, Nasreen consulted the *Time Sensitivity vs. Key* model she'd drawn on a piece of scrap paper, and replied, "I'd tell her that my top two priorities while she was away were to discuss the situation with the labor lawyer and to ensure that the sexual-harassment training was on track. My boss is an *Optimist*, so I assigned this personality to my boss for the exercise, and I realized that I needed to be more upbeat in discussing these two serious issues with her. Otherwise, she'd just turn off.

"So, here's what I'd say: 'While you're gone, I'll take care of the labor lawyer thing—I'll keep you posted if there's anything you need to know—and I'll organize the meeting with Hugh. How about if we do the briefing with Tanya, Tom, and Sharon over lunch? Do you think you'll be in the mood for pizza?' "

What would *you* say to your boss? There are lots of good answers, depending on your organization's values, your boss's personality, and the assumptions you made. It's only if you didn't reach that step (and you're not an *Optimist*) that you might want to consider whether you, like Nasreen, spent too much time on minutia and lost sight of the big picture.

Consider the Role of Luck

Success comes from hard work, not good fortune. Be careful about attributing your success to serendipity. To attribute success to happenstance is to diminish the effort required to achieve it. People become successful because they have the requisite talent and skill, and because they do what's necessary to achieve success. If you do the work, be sure and take credit for doing it. Otherwise, you risk diminishing your confidence and others' confidence in you. Notice how what you do impacts what you get. Observe the connections between your actions and your success. Doing so builds up your self-esteem.

This is not to say that luck is irrelevant; nor can anyone guarantee that hard work leads automatically to success. You've heard the old adage about opportunity knocking on the door—but just because opportunity knocks doesn't mean that you'll be successful. You still have to listen for the knock, recognize the sound for what it is, and have the courage to open the door.

This admonition is important for you to think about because if you're like most people, you're going to find that the methodical approach outlined in this book works, sometimes surprisingly quickly. One consequence of your speedy success may be that you find yourself hearing things like, "Wow! You got the job? Boy, did you get lucky!" That's what happened to Tina, who found a way to achieve her dream.

Step by Step, Live Your Dream

"I wanted to see the world. I always did. I even thought about joining the navy. You know that ad . . . see the world? That's what I wanted to do," explains Tina, "see the world. But I'm not the military type. I'm a hairdresser.

"When I took Jane's seminar, I lived in rural Maine, and all I did was dream of getting away. I love Maine, and will probably settle back home someday. But I felt like I was just shriveling up. I didn't have the money to travel, and I was already in my early thirties. But I wasn't married, I had no ties, and as my friend Katie said, 'You want to go? Go now, before you own furniture.'

"At the seminar, I learned what to do. I used the CAN DO model to identify why I was stuck. Here's what I came up with:

Concrete

- "My dream was just that—a dream. It wasn't concrete at all. I knew what I wanted—I wanted to be a person who had been around the world. It was the next step that left me confused. The *how to* was a blank to me."

"I knew that if you can't complete the C—Concrete, you can't go any further. Given that I didn't know what to do, I was unsure how to proceed. Then I remembered, if you have a question and don't know the answer, go to the library. So I did. I drove to Portland, a big city. The librarian I talked to was wonderful. I said that I wanted to know about job opportunities for a hairdresser that would involve travel, that I wanted to go around the world. She found all sorts of Internet postings for me. Things like spas and resorts in exotic, far-away places like Tahiti and Cape Town and

Phuket. But I didn't want to move somewhere, I wanted to travel. We kept looking.

"She found the perfect job opportunity for me! Hairdresser for one of the major cruise lines. She printed out the posting and gave it to me."

Attainable/Realistic

- "Why not? I'm licensed. I'm good. I confided my dream to the owner of the salon where I worked, and she agreed to give me a leave of absence and be a reference for me. I thought she would because it wasn't like I was moving to another salon or anything. There was no risk of competition. But I was very grateful."

Narrow

- "I focused in a very specific way—on this one job. Although I confess that in the back of my mind I knew that I could always apply to other cruise lines if this job didn't come through."

Deadline

- "This made me pause, I can tell you that, because the job posting listed a deadline only a week away. But I decided that a week would have to be enough time for me to organize a response."

Objective Form of Measurement

- "Easy. If I got the job, I'd have reached my goal."

Tina's methodical approach put her in a good position to move forward quickly. "I used the *"In Order to . . ."* model to identify the next steps. It was pretty straightforward, but given that I'd never done anything like this before, I figured I'd better be safe than sorry. I created a list. Here's how it looked. In order to get the job I had to:

1. apply for the job by
2. faxing the application, which meant I had to
3. gather all the materials to be faxed, which required me to
4. decide what to fax, so I
5. reread the ad, and made sure to include all pieces, including a résumé, a copy of my license, reference letters, and a cover letter, so I had to
6. ask my boss to write a letter
7. ask two favorite clients to write letters
8. draft a résumé and show it to the librarian
9. call the librarian to confirm she was working on the day I wanted to show her the résumé
10. drive to Portland to show the librarian my résumé and also
11. show it to the résumé expert who works for the quick-print place nearby, then
12. revise it using the comments from the librarian and the expert, and also by considering comments from any books the librarian might show me, then
13. have the résumé professionally produced by the quick-print place, also
14. photocopy my license and
15. draft a cover letter and
16. ask Katie, my friend, to proof it
17. ask Katie to review all of the components, and finally
18. fax it off to the number in the ad

"It was so do-able! And I did it. I enjoyed checking off the items as I did them. It took me an extra day because one of my clients took a little extra time to write me a reference. I called her up to remind her, and ended up driving over to her house to get it. I faxed it on a Wednesday, and the company called me within twelve hours to ask me to come in for an interview. They paid for me to come to New York to meet them. New York! That was on the Monday of the next week.

"It was great. I met three people in the morning, and they

asked me to come back at the end of the day. And they made me an offer that week, which I accepted. I cannot tell you how excited I was. I was given a six-month contract starting in a month. Two times around the world on two different ships. I was flying high!

"And then it happened. I went over to my family's house. And my least-loved cousin said, 'You got a job with the first company you interviewed with? You sure got lucky!' It was as if someone stuck a pin in a balloon. Thankfully, Jane had talked about it being common to hear that it's luck—not that you did something that led to an accomplishment—or it really would have made me feel awful. I just smiled and nodded, and took my cousin off my postcard list."

When you use the tools described in this book, you are going to be more successful. If someone tells you you're lucky, remember that it wasn't luck. It was your effort applied in a methodical manner. You didn't get lucky, you succeeded. These are very different statements.

Thomas Jefferson once said: "The harder I work, the luckier I get." That makes sense. Remember that when people say something like, "Wow! You got lucky!" they may not mean any ill-will. They are likely to have no idea what went into your accomplishment. Tell them if you choose. But remember, you don't have to argue with them; nor do you need to persuade them that it was your effort that did the trick, not luck. You'll know the truth. Furthermore, the more you use the tools, the more successful you'll become. Soon it will be apparent and inarguable that it is your effort, not your luck, that's responsible for your success.

Legend has it that George Bernard Shaw's mother became so weary of hearing from acquaintances how their sons and daughters were good writers too, and how they were going to be writing a play or a book or a poem just as soon as they had the time, that she created a needlepoint sampler to hang in her living room. It read, "Everyone can write as well as George does . . . but George does."

If you do the work, you get the credit. Take it. Smile. Feel proud of yourself. The future is limitless, and your small successes will lead to greater successes. Go ahead and dream! Fulfillment awaits!

Do It Because It Works

Albert Einstein once remarked that he thought that a good definition of insanity was to repeat the same behavior and expect a different outcome. Think about that.

The statement holds true if you replace the word *insanity* with *stupidity*. It is stupid to repeat a behavior and expect a different outcome. Learn from your mistakes and approach the issue differently the next time around. Be persistent, but don't be foolhardy.

Which brings me to Emily, one of my cats. An absolutely beautiful little cat, she is, let us say, not the brightest star in the sky. One day Emily and I were in my den, where there's a glass top to the coffee table. Emily was across the room when she noticed my purse with its long strap on the table. She did what kitties do in this situation: she got low to the floor, wiggled her bottom, and ran as fast as she could to attack the strap—up through the glass top. Emily hit her head so hard, she wobbled. Guess what Emily did?

If you guessed that she did again, you're right. Except that it's even worse than that. She didn't just do it again, she went back farther, and she ran faster to get to the strap, trying to go up through the glass. Poor Emily nearly knocked her little self out! I put her on top of the table and let her reach the strap, of course, but not before I said, "Oh, my God! Emily's stupid!"

The next time you're about to try something that you've tried before, and you're about to try it in exactly the same way as failed before, remember Emily. Don't be stupid. All you get when you repeat a behavior that didn't work last time is what Emily got—a headache. Stop banging your head against the glass-top table.

Apply the twenty-one-day rule—it takes about three weeks for any new behavior to become a habit. Pick and choose among the various tools discussed in this book, and select those that have value for you. Create an action plan for yourself to help encourage yourself to use the tools. Write notes to yourself in your calendar or diary to remind you to use them. Add electronic reminders on your organizer. Send yourself e-mails. Leave yourself voice mail messages. Put sticky notes up on your computer monitor.

Commit to trying the new ideas for a month or so, and then take another look. Are they working for you? If not, stop using them. If, on the other hand, they are working—good news: they'll quickly become second nature to you, and you'll apply them automatically for the rest of your life, enjoying ongoing and increasing success in every aspect of your life.

What are your dreams? Do you want more money? More intimacy? More fun? Do you want a more challenging job? Or do you want more success at your current job? Whether your dreams are small or large, you can reach them. The tools you've learned in this book will help you get there. The rewards are rich. You'll live the life you want according to your priorities. You'll live the life of your dreams!

ACKNOWLEDGMENTS

✦

In the more than fifteen years I've been speaking on this and related topics, thousands of people have generously shared their frustrations and their dreams with me. Their successes form the foundation of this book.*

Thanks to Elinor Basso, Ellen Edwards, Denise Marcil, and Susan A. Schwartz, wise professionals who provided keen critical insight; and to Sandy Bagelaar, Jo-Ann Maude, Linda Raimo, and Katie Scheding for their loving friendship. Special thanks to David E. Cleland who, for nearly twenty years, has given me courage.

This book is dedicated to my mother, Ruth Chessman, who taught me to revere language and the truth.

*Many names and some identifying details have been changed to protect confidentiality.